The Guide to Careers & Training in the Performing Arts.

The Guide to Careers & Training in the Performing Arts.

by

Sarah Duncan

The Cheverell Press

The Guide to Careers & Training in the Performing Arts is
a Cheverell Press Book
Published by The Cheverell Press
Manor Studios
Manningford Abbots
Pewsey
Wilts, SN9 6HS

Copyright © Sarah Duncan 1993
First Published 1993

A CIP catalogue record for this book is available from the
British Library.
ISBN: 1-872390-25-0

Without Limiting the rights under copyright reserved above no part of this publication may be reporoduced, stored in, introduced into a retrieval system, or transmitted in any form or by any means (electronic, mechanical, photocopying, recording or otherwise), without the prior written permission of both the copyright owner and the above publisher of this book.

Printed and bound in Great Britain by
Redwood Books, Kennet House, Kennet Way, Trowbridge
Wilts, BA14 8RN
Cover by Dave Vivian at Avatar
Typeset by Christian at First Hand Publications

ALL RIGHTS RESERVED

Acknowledgements

This book would not have been possible to produce without the time and help given most generously by many people working in the television, film and theatre professions. Particular thanks must go to Robbie and Sue Stamp, Nikki Espinosa, Peter Layton of the Drama Studio London, Maggie Sampson of ft2, Inge Blackman, Christopher and Sarah Terry, Michael Gaunt of the Guildford School of Acting, Janice Cairns of Mountview Theatre School, Simon Curtis, Gary Desmond, Marilla Elliott, Alison Riva, Jeremy Whitton, Robin Wright, John Craney, Jackie Vance, Kimathi Spence, Simon Starling, Ailesh Heneberry, Livia Russell, Ian Campbell, Andy Prior, Graham Johnston, Jane Cowan and especially Christian de Larrinaga.

Sarah Duncan, 1993

Disclaimer:
The author states that the information contained in this book was checked as rigorously as possible before going to press. Neither the author nor the publisher can take responsibility for any changes which may have occured since, nor for any other variance of fact from that recorded here in good faith. The author and The Cheverell Press have used their best efforts in collecting and preparing material for inclusion in The Guide to Careers and Training in the Performing Arts. It does not assume, and hereby disclaims, any liability to any party for any loss or damage caused by errors or omissions in The Guide to Careers and Training in the Performing Arts, whether such errors or omissions result from negligence, accident or any other cause.

Contents

Section I

Performers 15
Actors 17
Types of courses 20
Three Year Degree Courses, Acting, Full Time 29
Three Year Courses, Acting, Full time 35
Two Year Courses, Acting, Full-time 46
One Year Post Graduate / Mature Student Course, Acting, Full Time 53
One Year Foundation Courses, Acting, Full Time 67
One Year Courses, Acting, Full Time 70
Company Courses, Acting, Full Time 72
Part Time Courses 76
Two Year Courses, Acting, Part Time 76
One Year Courses, Acting, Part Time 81
Weekend/Evening Courses, Acting 85
Classes 87
Courses Longer than Four Weeks 91
Four Week Courses, Acting 92
Two Week Courses, Acting 97
One Week Courses, Acting 100
Stage School (up to 16) 103

Musical Theatre Courses 106
Three Year Courses, Musical Theatre, Full Time 108
Two Year Course, Musical Theatre, Full Time 117
One Year Courses, Musical Theatre, Full Time 119

Short Courses 123
Four Week Courses, Musical Theatre 123
Weekend Course, Musical Theatre 124

Dancers 125
Dance Schools (up to 16) 126
Dance Degrees 130
Three Year Courses, Dance, Full Time 135
Two Year Courses, Dance, Full Time 145
One Year Courses, Dance, Full Time 146
Short Courses 151
Other Performers and Skills 153
Alexander Technique 153
Clowning and Physical Theatre 153
Mime 155
Radio 155
Voice 156

Presenter and Announcers 159
The Performers World..................................161

Section II

General Courses 163
Degree Courses 165
DRAMA 166
BA Combined Studies
(Drama not available as a single subject) 191
Combined Studies Index Drama + ... 202
FILM STUDIES 213
BA Combined Studies
(where Film can not be studied as a single subject) 224
Combined Studies Index - Film + ... 230

Post-Graduate Diplomas 234
Media/Communication Studies 238
BA Combined Studies
(Media not available as a single subject) 260
Combined Studies Index Media/Communications + ... 262
Post-Graduate Studies 268
Photography 269
Post-Graduate Courses 275

BTEC Courses 277
General Information 277
BTEC Performing Arts Courses 279
BTEC Design 289
BTEC Courses in Media/Communications 296
BTEC National Courses in Media 298
BTEC Photography Courses 303
Film & Television Courses and Training Schemes 309
Two Year Courses/Schemes 310
Short Courses 317

Section III

Production & Administration 321
Getting into the Film and Television Industries 323

Production & Administration 329
Production 330
Producer 330
Directors 333
Director Courses 337
Three Year Courses, Directors, Full Time 337
Two Year Courses, Directors, Full Time 339

One Year Courses, Directing, Full Time 341
Directing Courses, Part Time 345
The Production Team 347
Stage Management Courses 357
Three Year Courses, Stage Management, Full Time 357
Two Year Courses, Stage Management, Full Time 360
One Year Courses, Stage Management, Full Time 369
Short/Part Time Courses 373
Managerial 375
Arts Administrator 375
Arts Administration Courses 376
Casting Director 378
Writers 380
Writing Courses 382
Administration/Management 384
Technical 387
Sound crew 394
Post Production 399

Crafts and Trades 405
Carpenters, Scenic Painters, Uphosterers, Armoury, Metal Workshop, Scene Shifters, Electricians, Props.

Design 412
Two Year Courses, Design, Full Time 419
 One Year Courses, Design, Full Time 421
Graphic Design 424
Costume and Wardrobe 425
Three Year Courses, Wardrobe Design, Full Time 428
Two Year Course, Wardrobe Design, Full Time 430
One Year Courses, Wardrobe Design, Full Time 430
BTEC Fashion and Clothing 433
Make Up 438
Make-Up Courses...440
BTEC Beauty Therapy 442

Section IV

General Information

Types of course 447
N/SVQ's 447
City and Guilds 448
BTEC 449
Degrees 450
Diplomas 450
Trainee schemes 450

Accredited Courses 452
Accredited Courses - Film and Television 452
BKSTS Accredited Courses 452
BECTU Accredited Courses 454
Accredited Courses - Dance and Drama 455
CDET Accredited courses 455
NCDT Accredited Courses 457
Grants 460
Grant Authorities Policies: Discretionary Grants 460
Bibliography 469

Addresses 471
Degree Colleges & Universities 471
Drama and Dance Schools 485
BTEC Colleges 503
Film and Television Courses and Training Schemes 549
Regional Arts Boards 553
Make Up Course Addresses 551

Index 557

Section I

Performers

Actors

For the actor there is an almost bewildering range of courses to choose from. You should be guided by two features: your purse and future employment status. Acting degrees and BTEC Performing Arts courses (listed in the central section) are state supported and many grant authorities award grants to students with places on NCDT accredited courses (there is a list of grant authority policies towards the end of the book). Outside these courses you will almost certainly have to fund yourself, and this will certainly involve tuition fees of several thousand pounds a year if not more, let alone maintenance. The other important point is to consider future employment prospects as an actor. These will be greater if you attend a course at an established school for two reasons. The first is that agents and casting directors simply do not go en masse to graduation shows unless they know the school - and that means Central, Guildhall, RADA, Drama Centre, Bristol Old Vic and RSAMD (if based in Scotland) for sure, probably Guildford, Mountview, Webber, LAMDA, East 15, Arts Ed and possibly Drama Studio, Rose Bruford, Birmingham, Welsh College. This is not to say that a graduate from, say, Central will be more successful than a graduate from a school not included in the above list, but they will definitely find it easier to get auditions and interviews at the beginning of their career. The second reason for choosing one of the above schools is the quality of intake. If a school can choose 24 students from 2000+ applicants then it is likely that the 24 will be 'better' than the majority who are turned down. Better in this context means more attractive, more dynamic, and possibly more talented. As acting is a group activity (especially at drama school), an average group with a few 'good' students in it will raise the level of all the members of the group. Conversely, in an average group, a few 'bad' students may bring the overall year standard down. You can not know the level of your fellow students before you start but be warned; the recession is hitting hard and there are drama schools which receive few applicants and which will accept almost anybody who can pay the fees. Do not waste your grant or your money on training that will not give you a good start.

Auditions
To audition at most schools you will need audition pieces, usually one from Shakespeare play and one from a 'modern' author - modern can mean anything from 19th century onwards so check that post 1950 has not been requested. Some schools ask for a third speech. Speeches should contrast in mood; comic/tragic, intense/casual and so on. Choose pieces that are within your age range and above all read the play. Get help with your speeches if you can; even an hour with a decent coach is worthwhile. My book "How to become a Working Actor" has lots of advice on audition and interview technique which is as valid for the drama school applicant as the professional actor.

Most auditions now include some sort of workshop. This is to see how you work within a group. You may be the most brilliant actor in the world, but no drama school will take you on if they think you are going to be difficult to work with or if you contribute nothing to the group. This is not a time for pushing yourself forward or shrinking back. If you are not sure on how a workshop may work try one of the short courses

listed towards the end of this section - there is even one on how to get into drama school, with a money back guarantee!.
Finally remember that drama schools are looking for someone they can work with. You are more likely to be taken on if you are brave and try, even if you make mistakes. Exciting actors are ones who take risks, and risks mean failing sometimes. Drama schools are designed to be places where actors can have a go, where the mistakes don't matter. They need students who are prepared to try.

Types of courses

Courses which have CDET at the end of their entry are accredited by the Council for Dance Education and Training, those with NCDT are accredited by the National Council for Drama Training. Students with places on NCDT or CDET accredited courses are more likely to receive local authority grants. A full list of NCDT and CDET accredited courses is at the back of the book.

Acting degrees

Grants for drama courses are discretionary rather than mandatory and most education authorities have been making cut backs in the number of grants offered to students at drama schools. It was recently estimated that some 40% of those who are offered a place at drama school can not take them up because of lack of grants. Understandably this has caused concern within the profession, because the long term effect will be that a higher proportion of students (the future professional actors) will be judged solely on their ability to pay rather than their ability to act.

The drop in income and the threat of lowered entry standards has prompted most of the major schools to act. What were simply three year acting diploma courses have become degree courses - which generally have mandatory grant status. Usually the changes in the course are minimal; for example, entry to a degree course normally requires at least two A level passes, but the drama schools can waive this requirement if they feel the student has degree level potential. At some schools they run two courses side by side; the degree course is exactly the same as the diploma course, but requires a long essay or dissertation in the final year.

Some people feel that acting is unsuitable as a degree course, and that acting training should have nothing to do with the academic world, but they are in the minority. Most of the "top" drama schools have started to offer degrees this year or plan to do so in the near future (for example RADA and Guildford). It is worth noting that the first years of these courses are likely to be under subscribed until word gets around; for example, Central had places available on its new degree course starting in September well into the summer.

These schools are able to obtain degree validation because they are well established and have excellent reputations. The exception is the newly founded Arden School of Theatre which opened in September 1993 with degree status, but it does have established and reputable "parents", the Manchester Royal Exchange Theatre Company and South Manchester College among them.

A few drama or theatre arts degree courses have always had a strong vocational element. While not claiming to be an acting training it is possible to move straight into the profession from these courses which include those at the Dartington College of Arts, De Montfort University (formerly Leicester Polytechnic) and Bretton Hall (the University of Leeds). The drama degrees offered by Glasgow University and Queen Mary and Westfield, University of London has the technical acting element taught at the Royal Scottish Academy of Music and Drama and the Central School of Drama respectively, but neither of these would claim to be vocational acting courses. The course at the Manchester Metropolitan University (formerly Manchester

Polytechnic) is NCDT accredited and considered to be a full training.

Three Year Courses, Acting, Full-time

The three year acting course has always been the standard training for actors. The format for most courses is: basics in the first year, more performance based work in the second, with the final year being entirely performance led. Most of these courses are well established and will provide a thorough training. Some have already gained degree status and are in the section above, some will be gaining degree validation in the near future. Those with degree status are eligible for mandatory grants, otherwise expect to pay around £2000 per term. Most entrants are 18+, and schools generally prefer the student who has taken at least a year off rather than the school leaver.

Two Year Course, Acting, Full Time

The two year course is usually aimed at the slightly older student, say 20 +, perhaps post-graduates or more mature students who feel that they need more than a one year course but also feel that they do not have the time to spare three years. Cynics might say that the two year course is for those who can afford two years of fees, but can't manage three. Generally speaking these courses are not in the same league as the three year courses (there are exceptions). The schools are usually recently founded, and may be under-funded. They may attract fewer applicants so that whereas for one of the major three year courses the chances of getting in are close to 80 to 1, here it is frequently closer to 5 to 1, if not less. While this does not necessarily mean lower standards of acceptance, and hence lower standards on the course, it is certainly true that for most students this is not their first or even second choice of course (an obvious exception here is Bristol Old Vic).

One Year Post-Grad/Mature Student Course, Acting, Full Time

Less than ten years ago twelve of these courses did not exist, and some of the schools now offering a one year course claimed that there was no special dispensation in being a bit older; an actor needed three years of training and that was that. It would be cynical to suggest that post-graduate courses are flourishing because if you are already running a three or two year course, tacking on a post-grad course is relatively simple and post-graduates and mature students as a group find it easier to raise the money for a course.

On the other hand as there are now many graduates from one year courses happily making a living from acting despite having had only one year of training the insistence on three years has begun to wear a little thin (defenders of three year training would perhaps say that being a good actor and making a living from acting were not necessarily the same).

Most courses comprise: first term, class work only, second term, class work, some in-house performance; third term, public performances and audition evening(s). This is the format for all courses unless otherwise mentioned. Obviously most areas are not dealt with as thoroughly as on a three year course. Voice training in particular suffers, and there are fewer chances for a starring role when it comes to the final performances. It is of course possible to make up any deficiencies with voice and other technical classes after graduating.

On the plus side post-graduate and mature students tend to be more committed and are looking to get as much as possible out of the course in the relatively short time available to them.

Many students on one year courses within conventional drama schools comment how fed up they get with the lack of urgency their teenage counterparts feel, perhaps best expressed by the post grad who complained of being fed up with "non-stop giggling in the locker rooms". Only the Drama Studio offers nothing but post graduate/mature student courses.

Entry policies vary. Some courses are strictly for degree holders only (and in the case of Bristol Old Vic the degree should be in either English or Drama), but most are simply 21+. Few have an upper age limit although some schools express doubts about the feasibility of training the over 30's, in terms of stamina, fitness and openness. On the other hand it is worth noting that the over 50's can often easily find work in repertory theatre once they have finished training, because by this age most actors have either moved on to something else, or are too famous/grand to be asked or for financial reasons can not accept poorly paid rep work.

Many students, especially post-graduates from drama or theatre studies courses, feel that their priority is the professional polish, contacts and final showcase that a drama school will give. If this is true for you then choose your school carefully for some are better at this than others.

One Year Foundation Course, Acting, Full Time

These are intended for those who are thinking of a three year course and aim to provide basic training. Those who have attended a foundation course usually do better in auditions for further training, so these could be seen as a worthwhile investment to enable a student to get a place on one of the more sought after courses. On the other hand the BTEC National Diploma covers the same ground, often with better facilities and is usually free.

One Year Course, Acting, Full Time
The courses at the Richmond Drama School, St. Catherine's Drama School and the Actors Institute are considered (by them) to be of equally suitable for the school leaver and the mature student or post-graduate alike. This is debatable.

Company Courses
Company courses are becoming more popular as they seem to combine the best of both world; a training for the stage and the opportunity for near continuous public performance at a professional level. Most courses follow the format of mornings given to class work and afternoons to rehearsal. Performances are usually given as a short repertory or touring season at the end of each term. Many of the companies are flexible about the length of time actors stay with them, although most expect beginners to stay for three years, post-graduates for one. Intake may be restricted and dependent on the existing cast make-up. None of the companies have the status as training organisations within the profession of the major schools, with the possible exception of the Arts Ed company course.

Part Time Courses
Going to a drama school is an expensive business. Even if you get a grant which covers the fees there are living expenses to pay, and perhaps for older students families and/or mortgages to support. Without a grant the whole idea may seem prohibitively expensive. But some people are determined to act, and their need has led to the formation of a different type of training, the part time course which aims to offer a full training.

No one should suppose that taking on a part time course is an easy option to drama school Attendance is demanded at least three out of every five weekday evenings (and maybe more), and usually every weekend. In this way the courses can offer over 25 hours of training per week, which - as the part time schools point out - can be compared with the 10-4 day at a few drama schools. Most schools however regularly demand fifty or sixty hour weeks from their students, and can offer greater facilities.

The part-time hours may be taken after completing a full days work - the stamina and dedication required to complete these courses is enormous, and should not be underestimated. Most students have found it impossible to combine this type of course with any demanding work.

Consider the other financial options - taking both a day and an evening job for example and saving enough for a more conventional drama school, may be a better option for you in the long term than spending two years physically and emotionally exhausted and so not getting what you really want from the course. On the positive side, completing a course like this is a statement of determination, stamina, and hard work which are among the most important qualities you will need in the acting profession. In the last three years the number of colleges offering these sort of courses has doubled, and looks set to double again so there is obviously a demand.

Not all courses consider that their training is equivalent to that given by a more conventional drama school. Some deliberately take a different approach, while others aim to provide a basic foundation. Most of these are less demanding than the courses offered by the Academy and the Poor School and offer a viable alternative to full time foundation or short courses without the time or financial commitment. The courses offered by Questors, the Actors Institute and the City Lit have good reputations; Central, the Drama Centre and Mountview are major drama schools which have an evening/weekend acting programme; and finally the premise behind the Armstrong Academy's Saturday programme is one which many professional actors would agree with.

Short Courses

Look on a short course as a taster of what being at a "proper" drama school will be like. Most drama schools run them and although attendance does not guarantee a place on a full time course most will consider an application either without needing an audition, or will waive the audition fee. Obviously they will be able to assess your abilities more accurately over a course lasting several weeks rather than in a audition, so if you feel that shining at audition time is a total impossibility a short course could provide a way round it.

Many of the courses have a theme, the most popular being Shakespeare, and will often involve trips to a theatre. Some are primarily meant to be educational or entertaining while others concentrate more on acting development. A few lead to a performance.

Stage Schools

Most towns have their own 'stage school' which teaches dance, acting and/or voice training on a part time basis. These have not been listed here. The schools included are full-time stage schools, offering a complete training in the performing arts as well as an academic education. Schools which concentrate on ballet training rather than performing arts are listed under the Dancers section. Some of them offer boarding education as well as day, and are run on a par with independent schools, with the performing side continuing after the normal school day. Some continue to 18 and offer A levels, with a few going on to study academic subjects at university. Most schools run employment agencies offering pupils the chance to work professionally as child actors, models and dancers. After leaving most pupils will go on to further training, although a few may manage to break into the profession.

Three Year Degree Courses, Acting, Full Time

Arden School of Theatre
A new school set up in association with the renowned Royal Exchange Theatre Company of Manchester and using the facilities of South Manchester College. The course follows the usual format, and draws on the resources of the Royal Exchange for master classes, performances and contacts. A welcome addition to training facilities outside London. The first intake was in September 1993.

Auditions
"Applicants are expected to present a performance piece no longer than 10 minutes in total. This may take the form of two contrasting speeches from any play; or a performance devised by the applicant using elements of movement and music but a strong feature of which must be some form of text."
Audition fee: £15 Fees: c. £4000 (mandatory grants)

Central School of Speech and Drama
Central must be the most dynamic drama school at the moment; it has always been one of the best. Voice is strong here - until recently it was one of the few places that offered training for voice teachers. Musical theatre is a developing strand and students can now take a

musical theatre option into the second year. Other options are Radio/TV and Shakespeare. A school with good opportunities for strong personalities. 18-25+

Auditions

The audition starts with two speeches, a Shakespeare chosen from a list they provide and a modern of your choice, plus a brief interview, some aural tests, and perhaps a little work under direction. By lunch time applicants are divided into yes, no and maybes. Maybes do another Shakespeare piece, again from the list and are either on to the recall or rejected. The recall is a day long workshop with about 12 others covering movement, voice, improvisation and the speeches again. Some may be recalled again. About 1200 seen for 30 places.
Audition fee: £25 Fees: c. £3500 (Mandatory grants)
NCDT

Drama Centre

Without doubt the Drama Centre is one of the most important drama schools. It is also quite different from the rest in its approach. Where other drama schools aim for you to learn how to act largely through experience, working with directors on productions etc., the Drama Centre teaches a method of interpretation based on the work of Stanislavski, Laban and Joan Littlewood's Theatre Workshop. Character study and movement lie at the heart of the teaching. The first two years are entirely class based, with performance only coming into the last year. Texts studied are likely to be from classical theatre, and often from Europe. Subjects like television and radio are not studied; however Drama Centre students are snapped up by television companies on graduation with startling rapidity. The place for those who want to be able to think for themselves as actors. 18-27.

Auditions

Take place in front of the Entrance Committee, a large panel consisting of staff and current students. Two speeches are required, a classical piece chosen from a selection provided by the school and a modern one of your choice. There may also be some improvisation.
Audition fee: £18 Fees: c£5000 (Mandatory grants) NCDT

Guildhall School of Music and Drama

The drama department is a relatively small part of the school as a whole and benefits from excellent facilities and a marvellous location within the Barbican Centre. Classical theatre takes precedence in the training and here links with the Royal Shakespeare Company (on the same site) are prominent. All the teaching staff are working professionals. They are actively developing links with drama schools abroad, especially Hungary, the USA and the former Soviet Union. Perhaps the most popular school at the moment it only auditions the first 700 who apply each year. 18 -30+

Auditions

Preliminary auditions start with a short movement and improvisation session. Three speeches are required, at least one to be Shakespeare (or Jacobean) and one to be comic. None are to last more than three minutes. Recalls take two days, covering more improvisation, and detailed work on the audition speeches, voice and singing.
Audition fees: £25   Fees: c£3500 (mandatory grants) NCDT

The Manchester Metropolitan University

This is one of the original acting courses which had both degree status and accreditation by the NCDT. The School of Theatre is based in former television studios, and also houses the department of Film and Television so the facilities for television production are good, and there are always would be television directors looking for cast. The university used to Manchester Polytechnic and the school has access to their extensive facilities such as students bars and sports societies and equipment. The first year is entirely Stanislavski based, with no performance beyond a workshop production of a Chekhov play. The second year looks at Brecht, Shakespeare and devised work. The devised pieces are usually taken to outside venues. Acting for television is also introduced. The final year is entirely performance led, generally taking place in the school's own theatre and attracting audiences from the local television and theatre companies such as Granada and the Manchester Royal Exchange. Final productions are also held in London, usually at the Royal Court and the Drill Hall. Dance is movement based, concentrating on Laban and the Alexander technique. This is not a place to come to for musical theatre, but has a good reputation for producing strong contemporary actors (e.g. Julie Walters, Bernard Hill, David Threlfall) who can think for themselves.

Auditions

Three speeches are needed, one Shakespeare and in verse, one modern and a third which contrasts the other two (this third speech is used in border line cases or when the auditioners feel that the first two choices do not show off the performer). The recall audition consists of a day-

long workshop with classes in movement, improvisation, voice and speech, acting and an interview.
Audition fee: NONE Fees: Mandatory grants NCDT

Rose Bruford
The college is split between two sites. The main base is in a mansion with its own park land and lake in Sidcup on the edges of London, while at the Greenwich site they have workshops, performance, rehearsal and classroom space. Rose Bruford was for a long time the only college to offer an acting training that was also a degree course. It is now no longer unique in that aspect, but carries on offering flexible courses aimed at the needs of today's actors. The actors' course has four options that may be chosen for the second year: Classical and Modern Stage (Text based), Educative Theatre (TIE), Popular Theatre Forms (such as variety) and The Actor Musician (for potential actor/musical directors - the only course of its kind). 18+, no upper age limit.

Auditions
They try to make the audition as enjoyable as possible, and start with a group session of voice, movement and improvisation with some 30 applicants finishing with two speeches, one Shakespeare, one classical. From these 6 - 8 are chosen to complete the day with two short essays and another workshop.
Audition fee: £25   (£5 for the unemployed and those on income support) Fees: c£3000 (mandatory grants) NCDT

Welsh College of Music and Drama
Like Guildhall and RSAMD the drama department is a part of a larger organisation and generally facilities are

good. The degree course runs concurrently with the three year diploma course and is virtually the same, there being an extra academic element of about four hours a week on the degree. Musical theatre and singing are very strong here, with several joint productions with the music department, and there are strong links with the Sherman Theatre. Welsh speakers receive additional options in Welsh throughout the course and there is a showcase for Welsh language employers - a growing area, where actors find themselves (for once) in demand. There is a week of productions in a London fringe theatre for finals, plus an audition show.

Auditions

Two speeches, one classical verse, and one modern prose, not more than six minutes together, are performed in front of two separate panels. You can opt to choose your six minutes differently, perhaps using a selection of small excerpts, or to show other performance skills. You will still need to learn the speeches for the workshop. An unaccompanied song is also required. A selection is made of who is to continue - and unusually they are prepared to discuss why you haven't made it to the next stage. A workshop follows and includes voice, movement, improvisation and re-working the speeches.

Audition fee: £ 15   Fees c£3000 (Mandatory grants) NCDT

Three Year Courses, Acting, Full time

Academy of Live and Recorded Arts
Of the "new" drama schools, ALRA is probably the largest and most established. It was founded to fill the gap in training students for work in television. Now almost all schools cover television, but at ALRA television work is an integral part of the course, to be taught with the same emphasis as, say, voice. Final productions are held in the college which some see as being too far away from the West End to attract the large professional audience graduates hope for. A wacky prospectus designed by one of the founders perhaps gives a glimpse of the school's philosophy.

Auditions
No audition speeches required. Instead applicants take part in a day long series of classes - voice, movement, improvisation and an interview. At the recall applicants will probably work on scenes from a play, and perhaps perform a piece of poetry, or work in the television studio. 18+.
Audition fee: £29.37 Fees: c£7000 per annum Scholarships: 1 or 2 per year NCDT

Arts Educational
The Arts Educational Schools are well established and have a good reputation. The three year drama course is Stanislavski based and extremely demanding with long

hours and hard work expected of the students. Standards and the level of dedication required are high; it is not a course for slackers. The course moved location within the last few years and can now enjoy the facilities of the rest of the Arts Ed. This course is not as well known as it deserves to be.

Audition
A full day's workshop consisting of classes in movement, voice and improvisation. Two short contrasting speeches needed (preferably one classical, one modern) and probably an interview.
Audition fee: £25 Fees: c.£ 6000 per annum   NCDT.

Birmingham School of Speech and Drama
The school is run on traditional lines with a strong emphasis on voice. It is very friendly and relaxed, with enthusiastic students and staff. Their theatre is run as a proper theatre which has built up a loyal local audience. Final performances are also held at a West End theatre. Television facilities are limited but the school has built good links with Central TV. The school provides a thorough and traditional training away from the pressures of London.

Auditions
The audition day starts with two speeches, one Shakespeare, one modern, neither lasting more than two minutes. On the basis of this, candidates are rejected, given the chance of a second audition or go on to the afternoon audition. The afternoon session requires performance of a song and a lyrical poem, as well as taking part in sight reading, Improvisation and Movement.
Audition fee: £22 Fees: c£6000 per annum NCDT

Bristol Old Vic

Well established and respected, the course at Bristol Old Vic is known as being a strongly text based course with an emphasis on the classics, especially Shakespeare. Direct links with the Bristol Old Vic Repertory company in Bristol have always existed, and now are being fostered with BBC Radio Bristol and Bristol-based HTV, so that contact with directors are made throughout the course. Strengths include Voice work and the help given to students in preparation of leaving e.g. audition practise, CV preparation, meetings/auditions with directors. Final shows in Bristol and London.

Auditions

Students between 18-30 are eligible (though the average age is mid 20's). Preliminary auditions held in Bristol and London for approx. 15 minutes consist of two speeches, one classical verse(preferably Shakespeare) and one modern prose, to last no more than 4 minutes between them, plus a simple unaccompanied song. Applicants are chosen in groups of about 30 to come on a week end workshop at the school. This is arranged as classes with the main members of staff, and is likely to include a voice class, acting class, movement class etc.
Audition fee: £20 + £20 for the weekend School. Fees c£6000 per annum. NCDT.

East 15

East 15 is based on the methods of Joan Littlewood who pioneered ensemble work in this country. Understanding character is at the heart of this approach and involves much research and staying in character for days, even weeks. They are helped by the school's secondary site at Sheriff Hutton Hall in Yorkshire, a beautiful Jacobean mansion, where, for example, Miss Julie can be rehearsed (and performed) in an authentic servants hall beside a real 19th century kitchen range. Classical texts are almost exclusively studied, until the last year when modern plays may be performed. The approach is not to everyone's liking, but it makes for exciting, dynamic actors. Deliberately not NCDT accredited as founder/principal Margaret Walker is a critic of the criteria they use to judge schools. 18+

Auditions
Workshop based, in groups of up to ten. Three speeches required, one modern and two classical. Make sure you know the whole play and are prepared to talk about them. Also a song, bring sheet music. Expect lots of improvisation.
Audition fee: £20 Fees: c£6000 per annum

Guildford School of Acting

GSA is a friendly and enthusiastic place to study, lacking the hard edge and competitive spirit of some of the London schools. The course has two options, Acting and Musical Theatre (discussed later) which are not confirmed until after completion of the first year. Both groups do the first year together and then separate in emphasis. The teaching methods of Stanislavski, his student Michael Chekhov and Michel St Denis are included in the course, although the school would shy away from describing itself as a "Method" school. Links have been established with both the University of Surrey and Bulmershe College, Reading University - they use the latter's equipment for television courses and provide actors to enact case histories for the Social Work/Health/Education courses. They are continually improving facilities and are trying to obtain degree status for the course. Final productions are put on in Guildford and London.

Auditions
Applications are limited to 700 each year. Each audition takes a day and consists of classes in movement and Improvisation, and two speeches of not more than two minutes each, one from Shakespeare and one modern. Also a song is required, which will be accompanied so sheet music is required. As a policy they try not to recall. 18+, no formal maximum, but most students are in their early 20's.

Audition fee: £30   Fees: c£5500 per annum   NCDT
Several scholarships

Italia Conti

Italia Conti has been established as a stage school since the beginning of the century, but the 16+ courses are more recent developments, of which the drama course for the 18+ age group is the most recent of all. Many of the students have previously been to stage school. There are good facilities for radio and television which are used from the beginning. Like many stage schools, but few drama schools, the school has its own theatrical agency to help with the business of getting work on graduation. Minimum age 18, no official maximum. Most students are in their late teens/early 20's.

Auditions
Three short and contrasting pieces are required, one of which must be classical. There may be some sight-reading, and maybe asked to improvise.

Audition fee: £20   Fees c£5500 per annum

London Academy of Music and Dramatic Art

The longest established drama school of all, LAMDA is well known for its examinations in subjects such as Spoken English, taken by over 40,000 school children and students each year. Given the developments at other leading drama schools LAMDA, like Webber Douglas, seems content to stay as it is. This may well be no bad thing; LAMDA graduates have the reputation of being good, workmanlike actors. Training aims for students to be well rounded actors, able to turn their hands at anything. The third year is strongly aimed at getting work in British theatre and most overseas students leave after the second. 18-26 only

Auditions
Two contrasting pieces required, one Shakespeare, one modern (20th century), of three minutes maximum each. This initial audition is fairly brisk, but the recall audition is more relaxed with improvisation and singing added (no need to prepare a song).
Audition fee: £20   Fees   NCDT   Several awards for current students, no full/half fee scholarships

London and International Theatre School

LISA is by far the smallest school offering a 3 year course and the most idiosyncratic. Facilities (and permanent staff) are few, being hired as required. There are lots of performances in unusual places - a Greek play in a replica amphitheatre, street theatre in a department store, poetry reading in local libraries. Technically the third year of this course is called the "career launching" course, and is an extra year on top of the two year course. Four terms per year, with three weeks holiday in be-

tween. Realistically, LISA is not in the same league as the other drama school in this group. 18+.
Auditions
Based on interviews with the principal. Two speeches (not Shakespeare) and an unaccompanied song are required.
Audition fee: £20   Fees c£2500 per annum

Mountview

Mountview is a professional, forward looking school, constantly adding to facilities and fine-tuning the courses it offers. Compared to a school like the Bristol Old Vic it has a large intake, which can lead to some students feeling they have been left on the sidelines. The course starts with a Foundation year giving the basics in voice, Acting, Movement and Music and Singing which all three year students do. From then on students divide into a musical theatre group (discussed in that section) and an acting group. Both courses continue with the basics but there is a greater emphasis on textual based work on the acting option. Mountview was one of the first schools to introduce touring as a way of gaining experience. Tours usually operate in Europe and the USA, with acting workshops and lectures incorporated into the schedule. The school energetically promotes its final year students. No official age constraints.
Auditions
A day long workshop consisting of four work sessions e.g. voice, movement. Two acting pieces are needed, one from a modern play and another of your choice, either modern or classical, but neither piece may be longer than two minutes. Two songs of contrasting style are also need, and one must be from a musical. The pieces are

accompanied so bring sheet music for the pianist. About 50 places are offered.
Audition fee: £25   Fees: c£6500 per annum   NCDT. Several scholarships available.

Queen Margaret College

The college is a multi-discipline further education college with the advantages of a larger establishment such as a students union, bar, cafeteria, squash and tennis courts, swimming pool and fully equipped television and radio studios, two theatres and the social life that goes with 1500 students. The first year is common to both the acting and the stage management students (although it is not possible to change between the courses). Most students expect their first jobs to come from Scottish companies, and the choice of outside directors reflects this, as well as not having a show case in London. 18+, and they actively encourage mature students to apply.

Auditions

One pre-selected speech and one of your choice, which is more of a weeding out process. Recalls are more extensive and contain work on singing, movement, improvisation and voice.

Audition fee: NONE   Fees: vary from under £1000 to near £5000 (for international students) per annum

Royal Academy Dramatic Art

The most famous of all the drama schools, RADA is thriving and developing. The elitist image it once had has been thoroughly dispelled and now students are more likely to come from the North of England or the USA than the Home Counties (auditioning in Manchester has helped here). Teaching is Stanislavski based, and concentrates on the fundamentals of acting: voice, movement and physical skills, particularly the Alexander technique. Television is not a priority. Final shows are well attended by the profession. Definitely one to go for, particularly if it succeeds in getting degree status. 18+, most students in their mid 20's.

Auditions

Two contrasting speeches required, one from an Elizabethan or Jacobean playwright (e.g. Shakespeare) and one from any other author, to last not longer than 3 minutes each. Only one may be a direct address to the audience. A list of speeches to avoid is sent to applicants. Recalls last a day and consist of classes and working with directors. Some may be asked to come back again.

Audition fee: £20 Fees: c£5000 per annum NCDT Several scholarships, some for American students only.

Royal Scottish Academy of Music and Drama

RSAMD is said to be the best equipped drama school in Europe, and the facilities are extraordinary, with two theatres of a standard comparable to any repertory company theatre, a television studio, sound broadcast studio, and numerous rehearsal rooms (often with their own video equipment). Voice and movement are emphasised, and there is a lot of mask work and mime - the school has strong links with the Ecole Jacques Lecoq in Paris. Glasgow attracts many internationally known visitors and the school tries to arrange master classes whenever possible. The school rents a hall for the entire three weeks of the Edinburgh Fringe Festival for student productions - a useful source of experience. The school also runs the practical side of the University of Glasgow's

BA Dramatic Studies; this is not however seen as a course of actor training.
Auditions
Two contrasting pieces are required, and a first selection is made from that. If only a few are chosen to go through to the next stage they are asked to come back another time. Then, in the afternoon there is improvisation, sight reading, aural tests, and an interview. Final decisions are made in July so they can choose a group as a whole.
Audition fee: £30   Fees: c£1000 (Mandatory grants for Scottish Students) NCDT

Webber Douglas

Originally established at the beginning of the century as an opera school Webber Douglas has long had a reputation of producing consistently professional actors. However it seems a little complacent of its past reputation and has perhaps been left behind by schools such as Central and Guildhall. Voice and singing are taken very seriously, although musical theatre is not studied. Facilities are limited and crammed into a very small space. The school has a reputation for being quite tough and is not recommended for those who want a gentle ride through drama school. The 3 year course lasts for 8 terms and there are two intakes, one in September and one in April. 18+.

Auditions
Two contrasting speeches, one Shakespeare and the other modern (mid 19th century onwards), and one of them should be comedy. Some movement should be included in one piece. Neither piece should exceed 3 minutes. You should be prepared to sing, unaccompanied, a short excerpt from a song. Applicants are seen by

a panel of directors, not members of staff. There may be one or more recalls.

Audition fee: £18.80 Fees: c£6500 per annum (final year c£4500) 2 scholarships for existing students. NCDT.

Welsh College of Music and Drama

Like Guildhall and RSAMD the drama department is a part of a larger organisation and facilities are good. The degree course runs concurrently with the three year diploma course and is virtually the same, there being an extra academic element of about four hours a week on the degree. Musical theatre and singing are very strong here, with several joint productions with the music department. There are strong links with the Sherman Theatre in Cardiff. Welsh speakers receive additional options in Welsh throughout the course and there is a showcase for Welsh language employers - a growing area, where actors find themselves in demand. There is a week of productions in a London fringe theatre for finals, plus an audition show.

Auditions

Two speeches, one classical verse, and one modern prose, not more than six minutes together, are performed in front of two separate panels. If you wish you can opt to choose your six minutes differently, perhaps using a selection of small excerpts, or to show other performance skills. You will still need to learn the speeches for the workshop. An unaccompanied song is also required. A selection is then made of who is to continue - unusually, they are prepared to discuss with those they turn down why they didn't make it to the next stage. A workshop follows and includes voice, movement, improvisation and re-working the speeches.

Audition fee: £15 Fees c1000 per annum. NCDT

Two Year Courses, Acting, Full-time

Academy of Live and Recorded Arts
Of the "new" drama schools, ALRA is probably the largest and most established. It was founded to fill the gap in training students for work in television. Now almost all schools cover television, but at ALRA television work is an integral part of the course, to be taught with the same emphasis as, say, voice. The course covers the same ground as their three year course, but in slightly less depth. Final productions are held in the college which some students see as being too far away from the West End to attract the large professional audience graduates hope for. Wacky prospectus designed by one of the founders gives a glimpse of the school's philosophy. 20+

Auditions
No audition speeches required. Instead applicants take part in a day long series of classes - voice, movement, improvisation and an interview. At the recall applicants will probably work on scenes from a play, and perhaps perform a piece of poetry, or work in the television studio.
Audition fee: £29.37 Fees: c£7000 per annum

Bristol Old Vic
Well established and respected, the course at Bristol Old Vic is known as being a strongly text based course with

an emphasis on the classics, especially Shakespeare. Direct links with the Bristol Old Vic Repertory company in Bristol have always existed, and now are being fostered with BBC Radio Bristol and Bristol-based HTV, so that contact with directors are made throughout the course. Strengths include voice-work and the help given to students in preparation of leaving e.g. audition practise, CV preparation, meetings/auditions with directors. This course is comparable in intake to most other schools one year post-graduate courses. Final shows in Bristol and London.

Auditions

Students between 18-30 are eligible (though the average age is mid 20's). Preliminary auditions held in Bristol and London for approx. 15 minutes consist of two speeches, one classical verse(preferably Shakespeare) and one modern prose, to last no more than 4 minutes between them, plus a simple unaccompanied song. Applicants are chosen in groups of about 30 to come on a week end workshop at the school. This is arranged as classes with the main members of staff, so would be likely to include a voice class, acting class, movement class etc. After this 12 are selected for the course.

Audition fee: £20 + £20 for the weekend School.   Fees c£6000 per annum. NCDT.

London Academy of Performing Arts

LAPA has improved its facilities by moving premises within the last two years to give it more space and its own performance area. Television and radio studios are hired when necessary. Students are accepted on this course at 18+ and are assumed to have already completed a foundation course, such as the BTEC in Perform-

ing Arts. All the basic techniques are covered. Final productions take place at the nearby Lyric Theatre, Hammersmith with an extra New York venue available for an American Students Showcase.
Auditions
Two speeches required, one modern, one classical. A recall is held which features group improvisation.
Audition fee: £25 Fees: c£5000 per annum.

London and International School of Acting
LISA is by far the smallest school and probably the most idiosyncratic. Facilities (and permanent staff) are few, being hired as required. There are lots of performances in unusual places - a Greek play in a replica amphitheatre, street theatre in a department store, poetry reading in local libraries. They consider the third year of the three year course to be the "career launching" course, and is an extra year on top of the two year course. Four terms per year, with three weeks holiday in between. 18+.
Auditions
Based on interviews with the principal. Two speeches (not Shakespeare) and an unaccompanied song are required.
Audition fee: £20 Fees c£2500 per annum

London Institute of Performing Arts
The aim is for it to be a 16+ two year course which structures itself around the students. This means that if, say, a majority of students want more dance then the course puts on more dance classes. This works well in a large school such as the London Studio Centre where the flexible time table with over 400 classes on offer per week is at the heart of the course, but logically seem impossible

in a small school. What happens to those who do not want more dance? They also offer an A level, again, to be chosen by a majority decision. Perhaps this inherent uncertainty is why the course for 1993 has been postponed.
Audition fee: £25 Fees: c£4000 per annum

London Theatre School
The aim of the course is to provide a traditional training, i.e. one that concentrates on language and the classical theatre. They have developed a relationship with the International Globe Centre at the Bear Gardens, and performances are held at the reconstruction of the Cockpit Theatre (originally built by a member of Shakespeare's company). The school has a caring approach; this is not somewhere that aims to break students down and then build them up to the school's format. Acting is taught mainly through experience, using rehearsals of scenes and plays for actors to work out their own personal style, and also to gain experience by working with many different directors. The school has moved premises frequently in the past; let's hope that this is its last move.
Auditions
Two speeches are required, one Shakespeare and one modern (20th century), neither longer than three minutes. Applicants may also have to sight read, sing unaccompanied, and take part in an acting exercise.
Audition fee: £15 Fees: c£4000 per annum

Oxford School of Drama
The school was founded to offer summer courses. These still run, but they have added a one year and two year course and moved to the studios, a converted farmhouse

and buildings on the Bleinheim Palace Estate some 10 miles from Oxford. The school is small and offers individual attention. Facilities on site are limited but the school benefits from a close association with St Catherine's College, Oxford and The Old Fire Station Studio Theatre in Oxford. Students can attend lectures and seminars given by the Professor of Contemporary Theatre (currently Alan Ayckbourn). Productions take place at a variety of venues in Oxford and London, and further afield such as Paris. There is a clear structure of work development with analysis, interpretation and imagination playing a major part. A good course for the creative and imaginative student. 17+.

Auditions
Two contrasting speeches required, one Shakespeare, one modern.
Audition fee: £15 Fees: c£4500

School of the Science of Acting

The course is run in association with GITIS (The Moscow Institute of Theatre Arts) and follows its tradition of teaching inherited from the methods developed by Stanislavski. The principal claims that English translations of Stanislavski's books are "mis-translated, mis-edited and even mis-invented" and secondly, that the transcripts of Stanislavski's rehearsals show that they had not been based on his system as described in his book. The principal has evolved his own method which is now called the Science of Acting. Put simply, acting is a technique that can be taught, and this method teaches it (alongside other staples of drama school training such as dance, speech, improvisation and so on). All courses start the day with Hatha Yoga and finish with medita-

tion. The school is unique in offering a money back guarantee.
Auditions
Applicants must present a Shakespeare speech, a fable, a piece of modern poetry or prose, a song or a dance, with none of the pieces exceeding two minutes.
Audition fee: £20 Fees: c£5000 per annum

Webber Douglas

Originally established at the beginning of the century as an opera school Webber Douglas has long had a reputation of producing consistently professional actors. However it seems a little complacent of its past reputation and has perhaps been left behind by schools such as Central and Guildhall. Voice and singing are taken very seriously, although musical theatre is not studied. Facilities are limited and crammed into a very small space. The school has a reputation for being quite tough and is not recommended for those who want a gentle ride through drama school. The two year course follows the same syllabus as the three year course: the foundation year is the same for both but there is one term less for final productions. 20+

Auditions
Two contrasting speeches, one Shakespeare and the other modern (mid 19th century onwards). Some movement should be included in one piece and they recommend that one is comedy. Neither piece should exceed 3 minutes. You should be prepared to sing, unaccompanied, a short excerpt from a song. Applicants are seen by a panel of directors, not members of staff. There may be one or more recalls.

Audition fee: £18.80   Fees: c£6500 per annum   2 scholarships for existing students.   NCDT.

One Year Post Graduate / Mature Student Course, Acting, Full Time

Academy of Live and Recorded Arts

Of the "new" drama schools, ALRA is probably the largest and most established. It was founded to fill the gap in training students for work in television. Now almost all schools cover television, but at ALRA television work is an integral part of the course, to be taught with the same emphasis as say, voice. Final productions are held in the college which some see as being too far away from the West End to attract the large professional audience graduates hope for. The one year course runs over four terms, which enables an extra term to be devoted to public performance. Most students are graduates, but mature students are welcome.

Auditions

No audition speeches required. Instead applicants take part in a day long series of classes - voice, movement, improvisation and an interview. At the recall applicants will probably work on scenes from a play, and perhaps perform a piece of poetry, or work in the television studio.

Audition fee: £29.37 Fees: c£8000 for course

Advanced Residential Theatre and Television Skillcentre International

ARTTS is the only school where students are expected to live on site, about 17 miles south of York. Accommodation is in residential units continuing dining and sitting rooms, kitchen and utility room and single study/bedrooms. There are three advanced courses available in Acting, Directing and Production/Operations although each contains element of each other as the aim is to produce actors who can also direct or operate a sound boom, directors who can stage manage etc. Facilities are comprehensive and include television and recording studios and a 200 seat theatre. Audiences are almost entirely limited to locals except when productions are staged in York. There are no London based showcase productions. There are two intakes per year. Students are required to present a final written presentation. 21+

Auditions
All applicants are treated in the same way, regardless of which course/option they are applying for. Candidates are selected first on the basis of their application form, and then by interview.
Audition fee: None   Fees c£6500 + £2000 for accommodation

Arts Educational
See under Company Courses.

Birmingham School of Music and Drama
The school is run on traditional lines with a strong emphasis on voice. It is very friendly and relaxed, with enthusiastic students and staff. Their theatre is run as a

proper theatre which has built up a loyal local audience. Final performances are also held at a West End theatre. Television facilities are limited but the school has built good links with Central TV. The school provides a thorough and traditional training. Students can choose to emphasise either working in professional theatre or training to teach speech and drama.

Auditions

The audition day starts with two speeches, one Shakespeare, one modern, neither lasting more than two minutes. On the basis of this, candidates are rejected or given the chance of a second audition or go on to the afternoon audition. The afternoon session requires performance of a song and a lyrical poem, as well as taking part in sight reading, Improvisation and Movement. 350 audition for 30 places.

Audition fee: £22 Fees: c£6000 for course

Bristol Old Vic

Well established and respected, the course at Bristol Old Vic is known as being a strongly text based course with an emphasis on the classics, especially Shakespeare. Direct links with the Bristol Old Vic Repertory company in Bristol have always existed, and now are being fostered together with BBC Radio Bristol and Bristol-based HTV, so that contact with directors are made throughout the course. Strengths include voice work and the help given to students in preparation of leaving e.g. audition practise, CV preparation, meetings/auditions with directors. Final shows in Bristol and London. Open only to graduates with Drama and/or English degrees or mature students with previous professional experience.

Auditions
Preliminary auditions held in Bristol and London for approx. 15 minutes consist of two speeches, one classical verse (preferably Shakespeare) and one modern prose, to last no more than 4 minutes between them, plus a simple unaccompanied song. Applicants are chosen in groups of about 30 to come on a week end workshop at the school. This is arranged as classes with the main members of staff, so would be likely to include a voice class, acting class, movement class etc. After this 12 are selected for the course.
Audition fee: £20 + £20 for the weekend School.   Fees c£6000 for course

Central School of Speech and Drama
Central must be the most dynamic drama school at the moment; it has always been one of the best. Voice is strong here - until recently it was one of the few places that offered training for voice teachers. This course starts in autumn 1993, and is likely to become one of the leaders in the field. A school with great opportunities for strong personalities. 21+.

Auditions
The audition starts with two speeches, a Shakespeare chosen from a list they provide and a modern of your choice, plus a brief interview, some aural tests, and perhaps a little work under direction. By lunch time applicants are divided into yes, no and maybes. 'Maybes' do another Shakespeare piece, again from the list and are either on to the recall or rejected. The recall is a day long workshop with about 12 others covering movement, voice, improvisation and the speeches again. Some may be recalled again.
Audition fee: £25   Fees: c£3500 for course

Drama Studio London

The Drama Studio London was one of the first schools to offer a one year programme for post-graduate and mature students, and it is one of the most established, respected and professionally accepted of the one year training courses. The school only runs post-grad courses which has the advantage for students of knowing that they are the focus of the staff's attention, and not seen as an adjunct to a three year course. It is based in a large Victorian house in Ealing, a pleasant suburb of London. The largest of the rehearsal rooms doubles as a studio theatre, and there are radio and television facilities. There is particular emphasis on the 'work' programme which concentrates on the business of getting work and self-marketing. Graduation productions are held either at the school or an outside venue. After graduation there is a West End Showcase production which students may be invited to perform in; some years most are invited, others as few as half. Although the course is for one year starting in September, students may choose (and some may be required) to take an 8 week preparatory course during the summer holidays in order to gain the basic skills necessary for the course. 21+ (the oldest student so far was 72!).

Auditions

Applicants start by working as a group taking workshop classes. Those selected for the second stage continue in the afternoon with individual work on audition speeches. Two tutors take the group and must reach a unanimous decision; if they are split the applicant is asked to come back another day and re-audition with another pair.

Audition fee: £30   Fees: c£7500 for course (c£9000 including preparatory term)   NCDT

East 15

East 15 is based on the methods of Joan Littlewood who pioneered ensemble work in this country. Understanding character is at the heart of this approach and involves much research and staying in character for days, even weeks. Texts studied include Shakespeare or the Jacobeans, Restoration playwrights, Ibsen, Chekhov or Strindberg. The idea is to fit the entire three year syllabus into the one year course and students are expected to spend much or their time outside school hours in set research, such as living out the work and background situation of the characters in the plays during the holidays. The approach is not to everyone's liking, but it makes for exciting, dynamic actors. Deliberately not NCDT accredited as founder and principal Margaret Walker is a critic of the criteria they use to judge schools. 21+, for mature students who have already spent a year or more at a college or university and for professional actors wishing to extend their range.

Auditions

Workshop based, in groups of up to ten. Three speeches required, one modern and two classical. Make sure you know the whole play and are prepared to talk about them. Also a song, bring sheet music. Expect lots of improvisation.

Audition fee: £20 Fees: c£6000 for course

Guildford School of Acting

The School is a friendly and enthusiastic place to study perhaps lacking the hard edge and competitive spirit of some of the London schools. The course aims to provide the same syllabus as the three year course, and is primarily class and not performance based, there being only two public productions. The teaching methods of Stanislavski, his student Michael Chekhov and more recently Michel St Denis are included in the course, although the school would shy away from describing itself as a "Method" school. Links have been established with both the University of Surrey and Bulmershe College, Reading University - they use the latter's equipment for television courses and provide actors to enact case histories for the Social Work/Health/Education courses. They are continually improving facilities. Final productions are put on in Guildford and London.

Auditions

Applicants limited to 700 each year. Each audition takes a day and consists of classes in movement and Improvisation, and two speeches of not more than two minutes each, one from Shakespeare and one modern. Also a song is required, which will be accompanied so sheet music is required. As a policy they try not to recall. Students are usually graduates, but non graduates with experience in the theatre may be considered.

Audition fee: £30 Fees: c£5500 for course NCDT

Hertfordshire Theatre School

The school has been recently founded and this course aims to teach both acting and musical theatre equally. Course work is performance based and aims to cover a variety of styles, movements, playwrights and so on. The basics of acting technique, voice and movement are studied in specific classes. All acting is based on the principles of Stanislavski. Parts of the course can be tailored according to the demands of individual students. Productions take place in a local theatre and the final production showcase is in London. Hitchin itself is

a pleasant rural town with cheap accommodation while having easy access to London. For graduates or those with previous experience.
Auditions
Two speeches, one from a comedy and one from a tragedy, neither longer than three minutes each, and a song which may be unaccompanied, or with a backing tape or with piano accompaniment (bring sheet music). There is also a movement and dance class
Audition fee: £25 Fees £5000 per course or £3500 with the Sponsorship Bursary (presumably applicable for those who are unable to get a LEA grant).

London Academy of Music and Dramatic Art
The longest established drama school of all, LAMDA is well known for its examinations in subjects such as Spoken English, taken by over 40,000 school children and students each year. Where other leading schools are forging ahead LAMDA, like Webber Douglas, seems content to stay as it is. This may well be no bad thing; LAMDA graduates have the reputation of being good, workmanlike actors. Training aims for students to be well rounded actors, able to turn their hands at anything. This course was originally for overseas students only but is now open to every one. Visits and theatre going are part of the course and include a trip to the RSC at Stratford upon Avon. The emphasis is on learning and development rather than demonstrating results. The course is open to those who have previous acting experience.
Auditions
Two contrasting pieces required, one Shakespeare, and the second either restoration or 18th century English

playwright or a piece by Shaw, Wilde, Nichols, Pinter, Albee or Tennessee Williams, of three minutes maximum each. Applicants may be asked to improvise or sing unaccompanied (no need to prepare a song).
Audition fee: £20   Fees: c£7000 for course   NCDT

London and International School of Acting
LISA is by far the smallest school and probably the most idiosyncratic. Facilities (and permanent staff) are few, being hired as required. There are lots of performances in unusual places - a Greek play in a replica amphitheatre, street theatre in a department store, poetry reading in local libraries. Four terms per year, with three weeks holiday in between. For graduates or mature students.
Auditions
Based on interviews with the principal. Two speeches (not Shakespeare) and an unaccompanied song are required.
Audition fee: £20 Fees c£2500 for course

London Academy of Performing Arts
The Academy has improved its facilities by moving premises within the last two years giving it more space and its own performance area. Television and radio studios are hired when necessary. The course aims to build a sound overall base technique. Both classical and modern texts are studied, looking at each in the context of its period. These scenes are performed to the faculty every five to six weeks. Final productions take place at the nearby Lyric Theatre, Hammersmith with an extra New York venue available for an American Students Showcase. Students should be 21+ and either graduates or with considerable performance experience.

Auditions
Two speeches required, one modern, one classical. A recall is held which features group improvisation.
Audition fee: £25 Fees: c£7000 for course

London Theatre School
The aim of the course is to provide a traditional training, i.e. one that concentrates on language and the classical theatre. They have developed a relationship with the International Globe Centre at the Bear Gardens, and performances are held at the reconstruction of the Cockpit Theatre (originally built by a member of Shakespeare's company). The school has a caring approach; this is not somewhere that aims to break students down and then build them up to the school's format. Acting is taught mainly through experience, using rehearsals of scenes and plays for actors to work out their own personal style, and also to gain experience by working with many different directors. This course aims to cover the same ground as the two year course, with the last term for performance. The school has moved premises frequently in the past; let's hope that this is its last move. 21+.

Auditions
Two speeches are required, one Shakespeare and one modern (20th century), neither longer than three minutes. Applicants may also have to sight read, sing unaccompanied, and take part in an acting exercise.
Audition fee: £15   Fees: c£4000 for course

Mountview Theatre School
Mountview is a professional, forward looking school, constantly adding to facilities and fine-tuning the courses it offers. Compared to a school like the Bristol Old Vic it

has a large intake, which can lead to some students feeling they have been left on the sidelines. The first term gives a foundation in the basics of voice, Acting, Movement and Music and Singing. From then on students divide into a musical theatre group and an acting group. Both courses continue with the same basics but the acting option emphasises textual work, where the musical theatre option concentrates on voice, singing and dance. The final productions are usually held in central London theatre and the school energetically promotes its graduating students.

Auditions
A day long workshop consisting of four work sessions e.g. voice, movement. Two acting pieces are needed, one from a modern play and another of your choice, either modern or classical, but neither piece may be longer than two minutes. Two songs of contrasting style are also need, and one must be from a musical. The pieces are accompanied so bring sheet music for the pianist. About 50 places are offered.
Audition fee: £25 Fees: c£8500 for course NCDT

Oxford School of Drama

The school was founded to offer summer courses. These still run, but they have added a one year and two year course and moved to the studios, a converted farmhouse and buildings on the Bleinheim Palace Estate some 10 miles from Oxford. The school is small and offers individual attention. Facilities on site are limited but the school benefits from a close association with St Catherine's College, Oxford and The Old Fire Station Studio Theatre in Oxford. Students can attend lectures and seminars given by the Professor of Contemporary Theatre (cur-

rently Alan Ayckbourn). Productions take place at a variety of venues in Oxford and London, and further afield such as Paris. Unlike many other schools there is a clear structure of work development with analysis, interpretation and imagination playing a major part. This course is an edited version of the two year course and is particularly suited to the creative and imaginative student. 20+.
Auditions
Two contrasting speeches required, one Shakespeare, one modern.
Audition fee: £15 Fees: c£4500 for course

School of the Science of Acting
The course is run in association with GITIS (The Moscow Institute of Theatre Arts) and follows its tradition of teaching inherited from the methods developed by Stanislavski. The principal claims that English translations of Stanislavski's books are "mis-translated, mis-edited and even mis-invented" and secondly, the transcripts of Stanislavski's rehearsals show that they had not been based on his system as described in his book. The principal evolved his own method which is now called the Science of Acting. Put simply, acting is a technique that can be taught, and this method teaches it (alongside other staples of drama school training such as dance, speech, improvisation and so on). All courses start the day with Hatha Yoga and finish with meditation.
Auditions
Applicants must present a Shakespeare speech, a fable, a piece of modern poetry or prose, a song or a dance, with none of the pieces exceeding two minutes.
Audition fee: £20 Fees: c£6500 for course

Webber Douglas

Originally established at the beginning of the century as an opera school Webber Douglas has long had a reputation of producing consistently professional actors. However it seems a little complacent of its past reputation and has perhaps been left behind by schools such as Central and Guildhall. Voice and singing are taken very seriously, although musical theatre is not studied. Facilities are limited and crammed into a very small space. The school has a reputation for being quite tough and is not recommended for those who want a gentle ride through drama school. The course concentrates on classes and tutorials to lay a basic foundation in acting skills - they recommend that each student should have a clear idea of which acting skills they need to develop so that they can establish a clear order of priorities. Performances take place during the last term, the final production being the only fully staged play. 21+, graduates only.

Auditions

Two contrasting speeches, one Shakespeare and the other modern (mid 19th century onwards), of which one should be comedy. Some movement should be included in one piece. Neither piece should exceed three minutes. You should be prepared to sing, unaccompanied, a short excerpt from a song. Applicants are seen by a panel of directors, not members of staff. There may be one or more recalls.

Audition fee: £18.80   Fees: c£7000 for course   NCDT.

Welsh College of Music and Drama

Like Guildhall and RSAMD the drama department is a part of a larger organisation and facilities are good. Musical theatre and singing are very strong here, with several joint productions with the music department. There are strong links with the Sherman Theatre. Welsh speakers receive additional options in Welsh throughout the course and there is a showcase for Welsh language employers - a growing area, where actors find themselves in demand. There is a week of productions in a London fringe theatre for finals, plus an audition show. Applicants should either have a degree or previous relevant experience.

Auditions

Two speeches, one classical verse, and one modern prose, not more than six minutes together, are performed in front of two separate panels. If you wish, you can opt to choose your six minutes differently, perhaps using a selection of small excerpts, or to show other performance skills. You will still need to learn the speeches for the workshop. An unaccompanied song is also required. A selection is made of who is to continue and, unusually, they are prepared to discuss why you haven't made it to the next stage. A workshop follows and includes voice, movement, improvisation and re-working the speeches. Audition fee: £15 Fees c£2000 for course NCDT

One Year Foundation Courses, Acting, Full Time

The Academy
The Academy was the first school to offer a complete part time training. The school has its own theatre (which operates as a fringe venue for other, outside productions), and plenty of rehearsal/classroom space. This is a foundation course concentrating on the elements of "straight" drama, such as voice, speech, movement etc. Many students are aiming to continue onto full time training and the school provides coaching for drama school auditions, with good results. The course runs during the day, but ends fairly early. 23 hours per week. Entry requirements: No formal qualifications or previous experience required. 16+.
Auditions
One speech lasting not more than two minutes, plus a workshop lasting about three hours.
Audition fee: £20 Fees: c£2000 for course.

Advanced Residential Theatre and Television Skillcentre International
ARTTS is the only school where students are expected to live on site, about 17 miles south of York. Accommodation is in residential units continuing dining and sitting rooms, kitchen and utility room and single study/bed-

rooms. The foundation course is a multi media course covering acting, directing and production operations. The first two terms concentrate on acting and production techniques, theatre in the first term and television, film and radio in the second. The last term concentrates on the practical application of these techniques in performance contexts.

Entrance requirements: 16+

Audition

All applicants are treated in the same way, regardless of which course/option they are applying for. Candidates are selected first on the basis of their application form, and then by interview.

Audition fee: None Fees c£5000 + c£1500 for accommodation

Blair Theatre School

The Blair Theatre School is a new school, with limited facilities. The Foundation course covers the basics as well as classes such as audition technique, and the History of theatre. Students take the LAMDA exams for Bronze, silver and gold medals in acting. 16+. The Performing Arts course covers the same ground, but it also includes taking an "A" level in Theatre Studies. For this course students need to have at least two GCSE's grade C or above including English Literature or Language. 16+

Audition

Two speeches, one Shakespeare and one modern, neither longer than 3 minutes each, plus an unaccompanied song.

Auditions Fee: £15 Fees: c£2000 for Foundation course, c£3000 Performing Arts course

Italia Conti

As a stage school Italia Conti has been established since the beginning of the century, but the 16+ courses are more recent developments. Many of the students have previously been to stage school. There are good facilities for radio and television. This course covers all the basics of acting and is aimed at those who wish to specialise in drama (presumably having been on a dance based course before). LAMDA exams may be taken. Like many stage schools, but few drama schools, the school has its own theatrical agency to help with the business of getting work. 16+

Auditions
Three short and contrasting pieces are required, one of which must be classical. There may be some sight reading, and maybe asked to improvise.
Audition fee: £20   Fees c£5500 for course

London Theatre School

This course aims to be a preparation for drama training. Introduction to voice, movement, improvisation and theatre games and work on text. Stage management and stage craft will be introduced. The school follows a traditional approach to teaching classical theatre.

Auditions
Two speeches are required, one Shakespeare and one modern (20th century), neither longer than three minutes. Applicants may also have to sight read, sing unaccompanied, and take part in an acting exercise.
Audition fee: £15   Fees: c£4000 for course

One Year Courses, Acting, Full Time

The Actors Institute
The Actors Institute has been running for nearly 15 years and was originally started as a place where actors and others could explore and enhance their creativity. This developed into the Mastery, a weekend course that aims to put people - not just actors - in touch with their inner creativity. The Mastery still runs, but there are several other courses on offer, from one year and shorter foundation acting courses, evening classes and day long workshops. The full time course is intended for anyone, whether they are a school leaver or a post graduate. Apart from covering the basics there is a strength in self marketing and presentation - the Institute has been running courses in these areas for years. There is also the advantage of having access to additional evening classes on site, and being able to continue with classes after graduating. 18+.
Auditions
Two speeches, one modern, one Shakespeare, and a workshop.
Audition fee: £20   Fees: c£6000 for course

Richmond Drama School
The Richmond Drama school is based in the local Adult and Community College and is able to supplement it's own, rather limited, resources with theirs, notably a

theatre, library, gym and television equipment (on another site, with limited access). Students may also attend the College's wide range of adult education classes such as jazz, singing, tap, dance, mime, English Literature and so on. The drama school itself offers a continual assessment programme where students gain credits in seven modules: Study, Rehearsal and Performance of Texts (3), Improvisation and Devising, Voice, Dance and Exercise, Radio. There are also seminars with actors, writers and directors, and the school has a close link with the nearby Orange Tree Theatre. This course is meant to be an all-round training in one year, with some people leaving to go on to three year courses at other drama schools, while others leave to go straight into the profession.

Auditions
Two speeches, one Shakespeare and one modern, neither more than three minutes long.
Audition fee: £15   Fees: c.£2000 for course

St Catherine's Drama Studio

The course is based in a converted chapel on the outskirts of Guildford. Television plays a large part in the training and all students are expected to become familiar with the management of television operations and to record their own show reels. Also covered by the course is vocal work, movement, mime, improvisation and so on. Performances take place either at the school's own studio theatre or sometimes in schools.

Auditions
Two speeches required, one Shakespeare or Restoration Playwright and one other, neither more than three minutes. The audition also includes movement, improvisation, characterisation, vocal and script work.
Audition fee: £20 Fees c£5500 for course

Company Courses, Acting, Full Time

The Academy
The school has its own theatre (which operates as a fringe venue for other, outside productions), and plenty of rehearsal/classroom space. The company puts on about nine plays per year at the school's theatre. There is a separate show case, and a three week run at another fringe theatre. 30+ hours per week. The course lasts a year. No formal qualifications required, but applicants are expected to have had some previous training or reasonable experience. Each application is judged individually. 18+.
Auditions
Two contrasting speeches of not more than three minutes each, plus a workshop. About three hours.
Audition fee: £20 Fees: c£3500 per annum

Arts Educational Company
The Arts Educational Schools are well established and have long had a good reputation. The company course is Stanislavski based and extremely demanding with long hours and hard work expected of the students. Standards are high and it is not a course for slackers. The course moved location within the last few years and can now enjoy the facilities of the rest of the Arts Ed. Like many one year courses the first term is class based with performance coming in at the end of the second term.

The third term is unusually spent entirely within a repertory system so that productions may run for several weeks. These productions are usually staged at well established theatre, most recently at The Theatre Museum in Covent Garden. The course is a mix of a straightforward post-graduate/mature student course and a company. It is not as well known as it deserves to be. 21+

Auditions
Two short contrasting speeches needed (preferably one classical, one modern), a group movement class and an interview.
Audition fee: £25 Fees: c.£7000 per annum

City Lit
The Community Theatre Company at City Lit operates on Saturday afternoons. Performances are in venues such as old people's homes. The idea is to learn how to work within a company and to gain experience of playing to different audiences in unconventional spaces.
Fees: £50 concessions, £100 other.

Court Theatre Training Company
The training company came into existence when the Court Theatre Company, a touring company, started to operate workshops for young and aspiring actors. This developed into a second, training theatre company. Both companies are now based at The Courtyard Theatre, a fringe theatre in central London. The course runs from 9am to 10pm on four days a week, Thursday to Sunday inclusive (about 44 hours per week), leaving three days free to take a part time job if necessary. The duration of course varies from one term to seven, depending on the previous level of experience and development of the

actor. A feature of the CTC is that they are making a conscious effort to avoid traditional text-based theatre (although both classical and modern texts are studied) and are looking to Europe for new ideas - "a physical, visual and total theatre experience". Actors may be accepted, depending on vacancies in the company, at the start of each term i.e. January, April and September. 18+.

Auditions
Two speeches, one Shakespeare or Jacobean/Elizabethan playwright and one modern (post 1956), plus improvisation.
Audition Fee: £20 Fees: c£4000 per annum

Cygnet Training Theatre

Cygnet maintains a company of sixteen to twenty four performers in all, of which a maximum of 50% are beginners. There is no fixed length of time for anyone to be with Cygnet. However, to achieve a full training from little previous experience they estimate would take three years. Others with more extensive experience may attend for a year. Some professional actors, or recent graduates from drama schools attend for even less as they seek the polish and exposure that continuous performance gives. Productions are toured in the West Country, taken to the Edinburgh Festival and London, and there is a final showcase production for those who are leaving. The course is based on the methods of Stanislavski, St Denis, Michael Chekhov, Grotowski and Peter Brook.. There are strong links between Cygnet and Peter Brook's centre in Paris. Cygnet offers several options to take in conjunction with the Professional Acting Course. They are Music, Directing and Stage Management (there is also a full time Stage Management option).

Auditions
Two contrasting speeches of your choice, neither longer than three minutes each, plus a workshop including some improvisation. Apart from basic talent, they are looking for people who will fit into the company as it stands. Audition fee: £20 (plus optional £8 for a written assessment of your audition) Fees: c£3000 per annum

Part Time Courses

Two Year Course, Acting, Part Time

The Academy
The first school to offer a complete part time training. The school has an advantage over the majority of schools in this group in that it has its own theatre (which operates as a fringe venue for other, outside productions), and plenty of rehearsal/classroom space. The two year course takes five evenings a week, plus Saturdays and occasional Sundays. 24+ hours per week. There are at least six plays presented during the two years. The basics are covered, plus how to set up and run your own theatre company - many of the students do this after graduation. Entry requirements: No formal qualifications required, but they will need to be convinced that you have the maturity and dedication to complete such a demanding course. 19+, no maximum.

Auditions
Two contrasting speeches of not more than two minutes each, plus a workshop. About three hours.
Audition fee: £20 Fees: c£2500 per annum

The Alternative Drama School
Two years of classes held on three evenings a week and at weekends. 16 hours a week approx., plus production

weeks 2-3 times a year. Entry is on a first come, first served basis and absolute beginners are welcomed.
Fees: £40 per week

The Armstrong Arts Academy

A two year course operating on Saturdays only, 9.00am to 6.00pm. Rehearsals for public performances in the second year are held outside these hours. The course has developed from Michael Armstrong's realisation that, as a writer, director and producer, he was constantly seeing actors who were lacking in techniques which enabled them "to find and express convincingly the reality and truth of a role". He developed a series of exercises which addressed these problems. The first year concentrates exclusively on these exercises, aiming to build up understanding of the techniques involved until the process becomes effortless. Text based work is only introduced towards the end of the first year, but the second year is text and performance based, often with outside lecturers. The final term looks at the practicalities and realities of the profession - any professional actor would jump at their class on handling bad scripts and bad direction, a common fact of life that drama schools pretend don't exist (for example, the often quoted "there are no bad scripts, only bad actors"). Graduates may continue to take part in Academy showcase productions, and after taking the teacher training course in the Armstrong technique, may teach in the Academy. 17+.
Auditions:
Two contrasting speeches, one Shakespeare and one modern (19th or 20th century) neither longer than 3 minutes, plus an interview.
Audition fee: £10 Fees: c£1300 per annum.

The City Lit
The course at the City Lit runs on three evenings per week. Classes are in voice, movement and Acting (6 hours per week) in the first year, with other subjects such as improvisation, television technique, rehearsals and scene study being added in the second year (9 hours). Of course a student can add to the basic content from a huge range of classes taught at City Lit which include mime, mask work, directing, juggling, clowning, Alexander, getting a job, singing and audition technique.
Entrance by interview.
Fees: £75 for concessions, £150 others.

NW5 Theatre School
The school is small and facilities are limited. The aim is to exploit each students potential by developing their imaginative, physical and vocal skills, whilst at the same time heightening their natural talents and awareness of themselves. The course has six components: Development of imaginative skills; sensual discovery; Acting technique; Using learnt skills on text; interpretation and Performance. The course runs on three days a week.
Auditions
One, two minute speech.
Audition fees: £10   Fees: c£2000 per annum

Questors Theatre
Questors is one of the most famous of amateur theatres, well known for the very high standards of production and acting comparable to professional theatre. Most actors at Questors have had training, some on them on

the part time courses that Questors has been offering since 1946. The two year course is not seen as a training for the professional stage, although every year some students go on to drama school. The course runs on one or two evenings per week, plus Saturday afternoons and rehearsal time on other weekday evenings as required. The first year aims to make a good beginning in understanding the processes and techniques of acting and concentrates on acting exercises and improvisation with classes in movement and speech. Entrance to the second year depends on the students work and progress during the first year - about half the group continue for a year dominated by two productions which are put on in the theatre. 18+.

Auditions:
Two contrasting speeches of the students choice of about 2-3 minutes each, plus a short improvisation.
Audition fee: NONE Fees: from c£70 (concessions) to £200 per annum Some financial assistance is available.

The Poor School

The Poor School aims to offer a good training at the lowest fees possible. Luxuries such as a glossy brochure are out, essentials such as good teachers (and the staff list is good) are in. Students work four evenings a week, and all day Saturday or Sunday (about 22 hours per week). The school concentrates on the basics of acting - voice, movement, acting, and improvisation - partly because of time restrictions but also partly with the assumption that anyone who needed to do stage fighting (for example) could easily gain the necessary training. Final productions are held in a fringe theatre. Training in this way is demanding and the school's approach is probably more

intense than that of, say, the Academy. 100% attendance is required. There is no age restriction for applicants, but most are in their mid-twenties.
Auditions
Two speeches, one of which musts be Shakespeare, neither longer than two minutes. These are heard in front of a panel. Afterwards there is a group improvisation session.
Audition fee: £20 Fees: c£2500 per annum

School of the Science of Acting
The course is run in association with GITIS (The Moscow Institute of Theatre Arts) and follows its tradition of teaching inherited from the methods developed by Stanislavski. The principal has evolved his own method which is called the Science of Acting. Put simply, acting is a technique that can be taught, and this course teaches it (alongside other staples of drama school training such as dance, speech, improvisation and so on). Courses run on three evenings a week and Saturdays (about 17 hours per week).
Auditions
Applicants must present a Shakespeare speech, a fable, a piece of modern poetry or prose, a song or a dance, with none of the pieces exceeding two minutes.
Audition fee: £20 Fees: c£2500 per annum

The School also offers another one year intensive course for actors who are unhappy with their professional training. The Science of Acting is the only subject taught on two evenings a week.
Entrance by application Fees: c£1000 per annum

One Year Course, Acting, Part Time

Blair Theatre School
The school has been recently founded. The one year course runs Monday to Fridays evenings, with some Saturdays. 20+ hours per week. The course aims to prepare students for working in the profession. Areas such as television and radio are not covered. There is a presentation of the students work at the end of each term and a full play is staged using an outside director. A graduation showcase is performed at a London Theatre. 18+. There is also a foundation course for the 16+ age group.
Auditions
Two speeches, one Shakespeare, one modern, neither longer than three minutes. Also an unaccompanied song.
Audition fee: £15 Fees: c.£2000 per annum.

Academy of Performing Arts (York)
The Academy of Performing Arts is a relatively new school and one of the few that operates outside London and the South. It has a strong local presence, using local theatres for performances and staging many TIE productions and pantomimes. The course has developed from offering part time speech and drama courses and it is in this area that the school remains strongest, with areas such as musical theatre and dance hardly being studied.

Their system is so devised that the courses can be taken individually or as a whole, potentially providing the only 3 year part time course available. Each course takes approx. 20 hours a week and includes two full scale public productions.

The Acting Certificate course concentrates on voice and characterisation. Entrance requirements: A pass in English and Drama at GCSE level or a Bronze Medal in Acting. 16+.

The Actor's Diploma Course is the intermediate course. As well as the basics it also incudes elements of stage management. Entrance requirements: a pass in English and Drama at 'a' level, or a Gold Medal in Acting or the Academy's Acting Certificate. 18+.

The Teacher's Diploma is the final course. Continues on from the other courses, but adds an element of teaching and co-ordinating lessons and examination days. Students also produce a paper on teaching speech and drama. Entrance requirements: a Teachers certificate or the Academy's Actor's Diploma, or a postgraduate degree. Mature students with acting experience are also considered. 18+.

Auditions

Two speeches, one modern (post 1950) and one Shakespeare, and any published poem, none longer than two minutes each. A three minute 'entertainment', which could be a song, a dance, or a piece of drama, or anything that might entertain the panel. There will also be a sight reading test.

Audition fee: £23   Fees: c£550 per course

Central
The course aims to provide an introduction to acting for two evenings a week for three terms (seven weeks per term), plus two Saturdays each term. The work is organised into Modules. Module one is an Introduction to Acting and has open entry, Module 2 is Shakespeare and Module 3 is Contemporary Texts. Modules 2 & 3 are open to those who have complete Module 1 or have had some previous experience. Central is one of the best known and highly regarded drama schools at the moment and this course would provide a good starting point for anyone with ambitions for continuing onto the three year course.
Fees: £300 per module (£200 concessions)

Morley College
The course runs on three evenings a week and is aimed at committed students who are interested in creating theatre. Students often go on to drama schools for full time training. The first two terms are class based, with the final term being more project work leading to a final production. A bargain by anyones terms - apply early.
Auditions.
One speech required.
Fees: from £100 for concessions to £500 per annum

Mountview
This course is aimed at those students who are intending to go on to further drama training, or for those who find it difficult to fund full time training. 3 evenings per week for classes on movement, voice, acting, singing and

dance, plus two week end workshops on audition technique.
Auditions
Two speeches, a short song and a movement workshop.
Audition fee: £7.50 Fees: £700

Mountview also run an **"Introduction to Acting course"** on two evenings a week which operates at a less intensive level.
Auditions
One speech and joining in a movement class.
Audition fee: £7.50 Fees: £400

Questors Theatre

Questors is one of the most famous of amateur theatres, well known for the very high standards of production and acting comparable to professional theatre. Most actors at Questors have had training, some on them on the part time courses that Questors has been offering since 1946. The course runs on Saturday afternoons and is aimed at those who are seriously interested in acting, but are too young, or not ready to make the commitment to the two year course. The course is designed as an introduction to acting and is based on acting exercises and improvisation. Many students continue onto the two year course. 17-21

Auditions:
Two contrasting speeches of the students choice of about 2-3 minutes each, plus a short improvisation.
Audition fee: NONE Fees: from c£70 (concessions) to £200 per annum Some financial assistance is available.

Weekend/Evening Courses, Acting

The Academy
The first school to offer a complete part time training. The school has a big advantage over the other schools in this group in that it has its own theatre (which operates as a fringe venue for other, outside productions), and plenty of rehearsal/classroom space. There are several short, foundation courses. One runs on two evenings a week, and is primarily a leisure course, although some will use it as a starting point before going on to more dedicated training. 16+, all ages welcome.
Auditions
One speech of not more than two minutes, plus a short improvisation.
Audition fee: £15 Fees: c£1000 per year

The Academy's other foundation course is an on-going course, enrolling for four or eight weeks at a time and running on Saturday afternoons. Most sessions are designed as workshops which are complete in themselves. It is considered especially suitable for students who wish to audition for full time drama schools or to try out their suitability for the profession. Entry requirements: None. 14+, all ages welcome.
Fees: £60 for four sessions, £100 for eight.

The Actors Institute

The Actors Institute has been running for nearly 15 years and was originally started as a place where actors and others could explore and enhance their creativity. This developed into the Mastery, a weekend course that aims to put people - not just actors - in touch with their inner creativity. The Mastery still runs, but there are several other courses on offer, from one year and shorter foundation acting courses, evening classes and day long workshops. The 10 week acting foundation course is intended as a starting point for would-be professionals, pre drama school auditions, and those who are trying to decide if they want to embark on acting as a career. The basics are covered, and the course included audition techniques - obviously useful as many graduates succeed in going on to drama school. 3 evenings a week, with two one day workshops.

Auditions
One modern speech and a workshop
Audition fee: £15   Fees: c£550

Court Theatre Training Company

The training company came into existence when the Court Theatre Company, a touring company, started to operate workshops for young and aspiring actors. This developed into a second, training theatre company. Both companies are now based at The Courtyard Theatre, a fringe theatre in central London. The course runs on Saturdays for a year and covers movement, mime, voice, acting, audition technique and scene study. There is a production in the last term.
Audition Fee: £20 Fees: c£400 per annum

Classes

Actors Centre
Equity members only, with an allocation of spaces for Registered Graduates in their first year of registration. Lots of classes, all very specific to working in the theatre, commercials, television etc. Private sessions for 1/2 hour upwards are also available. There are two centres in London and Manchester, with other regional training programmes offered (contact Manchester for details). Well worth joining if you can.

Actors Institute
The Actors Institute has been running for nearly 15 years and was originally started as a place where actors and others could explore and enhance their creativity. This developed into the Mastery, a weekend course that aims to put people - not just actors - in touch with their inner creativity. The Mastery still runs, but there are several other courses on offer, from one year and shorter foundation acting courses, evening classes and day long workshops. Classes cover voice, singing, writing, motivation, and there are regular evening acting classes which are held Monday to Thursday, and students can join at anytime, except for "Basics" which is a series of four classes starting each month.

Anna Scher Theatre
Anna Scher is justifiably famous for the courses that she runs from 6 year upwards. Classes are usually after school and are hard to get into - the waiting list for the 6-11 year olds is 4 years long! Classes are specifically acting based and include improvisation and theatre games. The theatre is often first port of call for producers looking to cast youngsters and has its own agency (although it does not handle modelling or commercial advertising).

Boden Studio
Individual and group classes for 3-20 year olds in Acting, Speech and Drama, Singing, Dance. Full scale productions are mounted two or three times a year.

Brighton School of Music and Drama
Individual, shared and group lessons and classes in Acting, Speech and Drama, Music. Plays are presented at intervals throughout the year.

City Lit
Evening and short courses in a wide range of specialities from Mime, clowning, acting, dance and so on. Many of these are specifically designed for the actor, whether total beginner, aspiring professional or already established. For example there are courses on Auditioning for drama school (a bargain at £18, £9 concessions), singing for actors, acting for camera and timing the laugh lines.

Harlequin Theatre School
Evening and weekend classes for 3+ including drama, tap, ballet, singing, speech, and audition preparation for drama school entry.

Islington Arts Factory
Selection of classes 6+ including Ballet, yoga, Contemporary dance, flamenco, Alexander Technique, Mime, music.

Jeannine Greville Dance Academies
Selection of classes from 2 1/2 to 18 in dance (tap, Jazz, Ballet), Drama and Singing and acrobatics. Several centres.

Lee Strasberg Theatre Institute
Lee Strasberg became famous for his training of Hollywood stars such as Marilyn Monroe, Marlon Brando, Dustin Hoffman and Robert De Niro among others. The institute carries on his way of teaching, known as "The Method" based on the methods of those such as Stanislavski. The courses run for twelve weeks. At the heart are the basic acting classes, which are taken in two 4 hour blocks per week, during the day or evening. Other classes may be added, such as speech, singing, classic scene study, Building a play, Shakespeare text and so on. Taking all the classes offered would cover c32 hours per week for twelve weeks and cost c£2000.

Morley College
Hundreds of courses on different subjects, but particularly relevant are the numerous dance classes. There are

many special one day workshops, such as a day spent with an alternative theatre company, or a day with a professional dance company. Good value.

Mountview
As well as the courses listed above, Mountview also runs a teenage acting course on one evening a week, young peoples workshops during the Easter and Summer holidays for 8-14 year olds, and young peoples acting and dance lessons on Saturdays.

Stagecoach Training Centres
Stagecoach covers the main three disciplines of dance, drama and voice and students take classes in all three. Classes take place on Saturdays and in the holidays. There are six centres currently in the South and Midlands. The head office in Surrey runs a theatrical agency which students may join. 6-16.

Stardust Children's Theatre Workshop
Selection of classes on Saturdays 5 to 16 years in Ballet, tap, jazz, disco and modern dance, "Vocals", mime and theatre workshop.

White Rose Studio
A selection of individual, small group, and workshop classes in drama and speech offered evenings/weekends. Individual coaching and preparation of audition speeches is available.

Short Courses Full Time

Courses Longer than Four Week

6 Month Course, Acting
London Theatre School
The school follows the tradition methods of teaching classical acting. Aimed mainly at overseas students it includes elements such as an introduction to British dialect and phonetics, historical dance, Shakespeare text and scene study. The courses runs for two terms.
The audition procedure is the same as for the one and two year courses but may be waived if the applicant can supply other evidence of ability e.g. a letter of recommendation, reviews of work performed etc.
Fee: c£3000 for course.

12 week Course, Acting, Full Time
Lee Strasberg Theatre institute
Lee Strasberg became famous for his training of Hollywood stars such as Marilyn Monroe, Marlon Brando, Dustin Hoffman and Robert De Niro among others. The institute carries on his way of teaching, known as "The Method" based on the methods of those such as Stanislavski. The courses run for twelve weeks. At the heart are the basic acting classes, which are taken in two 4 hour blocks per week, during the day or evening. Other classes may be added, such as speech, singing, classic scene study, Building a play, Shakespeare text and so on.

Taking all the classes offered would cover c32 hours per week for twelve weeks and cost c£2000.

8 week Foundation Course, Acting, Full Time
The Actors Institute

The Actors Institute has been running for nearly 15 years and was originally started as a place where actors and others could explore and enhance their creativity. This developed into the Mastery, a weekend course that aims to put people - not just actors - in touch with their inner creativity. The Mastery still runs, but there are several other courses on offer, from one year and shorter foundation acting courses, evening classes and day long workshops.

The full time course is intended as a starting point for would-be professionals, pre drama school auditions, and those who are trying to decide if they want to embark on acting as a career. The basics are covered, and the course included audition techniques - obviously useful as many graduates succeed in going on to drama school. Fees: c£1000

Four Week Courses, Acting

Court Theatre Training Company

The training company came into existence when the Court Theatre Company, a touring company, started to operate workshops for young and aspiring actors. This

developed into a second, training theatre company. Both companies are now based at The Courtyard Theatre, a fringe theatre in central London. The course covers movement, mime, voice, acting, singing and improvisation working towards a final presentation in the Courtyard Theatre. 17+ Entry by application.
Fees: c£500 for course

Advanced Residential Theatre and Television Skillcentre International

ARTTS is the only school where students are expected to live on site, about 17 miles south of York. Accommodation is in residential units continuing dining and sitting rooms, kitchen and utility room and single study/bedrooms. A multi aspect, multi media course including Acting, Directing and Production Operation skills for all aspects of a performance from script to stage and screen.
Fees c£1000 including half board accommodation

British American Drama Academy

BADA offer three courses in their "Midsummer in Oxford" programme. Each course runs concurrently for four weeks in July/August. A feature of the course is that Acting classes are taken by well known actors and directors e.g. Jeremy Irons, Alan Rickman, Prunella Scales, Steven Berkoff, Adrian Noble. Movement, voice and improvisation classes are taken by teachers from drama courses either from Britain or the USA. Students are accommodated in Balliol College Oxford. There are excursions to see the RSC at Stratford upon Avon and the Royal National Theatre.

The Advanced Acting Program is intended for those who are aiming to become professional actors and have had previous experience. Accredited by The Juilliard School.
The Intermediate Acting Program is for students who have had some experience of acting, especially Shakespeare. Accredited by the University of California at San Diego (UCSD).
The Undergraduate Acting Program is for those who may have had limited experience of working on the British classics. Accredited by UCSD.
Audition fee: £25 Fees: £1250 + £975 for accommodation. Some scholarships available.

Central School of Speech and Drama
An intensive Shakespeare Course, aiming to give actors confidence in tackling the problems posed by Shakespearean text and performance. Mornings are spent in skill classes, voice, movement, textual studies and afternoons in rehearsals leading towards a presentation of the work. Tutorials examine specific Voice and Movement problems. Students are expected to have had some acting experience. 17+.
£725

Drama Studio London
There are two programmes, Pre-professional and Advanced which run consecutively so that a student could take one after the other is they wished. The courses covers classes in Acting, Voice, Singing, Movement, Dance, Shakespeare, Verse speaking, Stage Combat and Acting for television. There are also Studio and theatre visits and lectures and seminars by visiting directors,

actors and teachers. Each student attends rehearsal for a production at the end of the course. 18+.
Application fee: £10 Fee: £750

Guildford School of Acting
The course has two options, Shakespeare or Contemporary. The mornings are spent in basic technique classes with the afternoons working on scenes in a rehearsal situation with a director. There are also two practical master classes, one in mask making and the other on make-up.
Fees: £635

London Academy of Music and Dramatic Art
The longest established drama school of all, LAMDA is well known for its examinations in subjects such as Spoken English, taken by over 40,000 school children and students each year. This is an intensive Shakespearean programme. Classes cover the basics of voice, movement and acting and include Elizabethan music and stage combat. Trips to Stratford upon Avon and other theatre as and museums are included.
Entrance is by application with two recommendations from drama teachers or directors.
Fees: £950 (£1535 to include accomodation)

Mountview
This course is aimed at those who are considering a career in professional theatre or for those who wish to broaden their communication skills. Time is shared between classes, project rehearsals, visits to the theatre and master classes. The final presentation, which is

directed by a visiting professional director is either scenes or a complete play. Specialist tuition in singing and/or audition technique is available (at extra cost). 17+
Fees: £700

Oxford School of Drama

The course is intended for those who are intending to go drama school or university. Students generally should have had previous experience of acting and, ideally, improvisation although enthusiasm and commitment will compensate. The course covers Voice, Movement, Improvisation, Text analysis and Audition technique. At the end of the course scenes from a modern play and a Shakespeare play are presented as well as contemporary and classical audition pieces. The presentation takes place at The Old Fire Station Theatre in Oxford and is assessed by professional actors and directors (e.g. Jane Lapotaire, Diana Rigg), as well as specialist tutors from the school. There are also trips to the RSC, National Theatre or other nationally recognised theatre companies. 17+

Auditions
Two speeches, one Shakespeare and one modern.
Fees: c£650 (Accommodation at an Oxford College from £65 per week).

Webber Douglas

This course aims to be an introduction to full time professional training. The course combines class work (voice, movement, Dance, Improvisation, Shakespeare, Acting Techniques among others) with work on two

plays, one Shakespeare and one by a European playwright. Visits to London theatre are included. 17-30. Entrance by application with a written testimonial from a teacher or theatre director/actor.
Fees: £780

Two Week Courses, Acting

The Academy
The first school to offer a complete part time training. The school has a big advantage in that it has its own theatre (which operates as a fringe venue for other, outside productions), and plenty of rehearsal/classroom. 15+, all ages welcome.
Fees: £200

Advanced Residential Theatre and Television Skillcentre International
ARTTS is the only school where students are expected to live on site, about 17 miles south of York. Accommodation is in residential units continuing dining and sitting rooms, kitchen and utility room and single study/bedrooms. A multi aspect, multi media course including Acting, Directing and Production Operation skills for all aspects of a performance from script to stage and screen. Fees c£600 including half board accommodation

Guildford School of Acting

The School emphasises in its brochure how close and easily accessible Guildford is to London, but as a drama school it seems to lack the hard edge and competitive spirit of some of the London schools, being a friendly and enthusiastic place to study. The course has two options, Shakespeare or Contemporary. The day starts with a vocal or movement warm up and then the rest of the day is spent working on scenes with a director. There is a practical master class on make-up.
Fees: £350

Oxford School of Drama

The OSD runs two courses and for both it is recommended that students stay in accommodation organised by the school. The Introduction to Acting course starts with voice and movement exercises, followed by acting technique, with text work in the afternoons. Classes run Monday to Friday and on Saturday mornings. In the evenings there are lectures and workshops which cover topics such as Circus skills, Mime, Stage fighting, Improvisation. At the weekend there are other activities such as a tour of Oxford, a treasure hunt or a barbecue. There is also a trip to the RSC or the National Theatre. 14-17
Entrance by a letter explaining why they would like to attend.
Fees: c£350 (Accommodation at an Oxford College from £65 per week)

The Advanced Acting Course is intended for those with a serious interest in drama, who are perhaps thinking of a career in theatre or applying to drama school. The

course covers: Preparation and background of a character, Motivation, Physical and Imaginative Awareness, and Improvisation. There are voice and movement classes every day. In the evenings there are lectures and workshops which cover subjects such as: Shakespearean Verse, Audition Technique, Working on Character through Masks, Historical Dance, Contemporary Dance. There is also a visit to the RSC or National Theatre. 16+ Entrance by letter of recommendation from a Drama or English teacher.
Fees: c£350 (accommodation at an Oxford College from £65 per week)

School of the Science of Acting
The school is run in association with GITIS (The Moscow Institute of Theatre Arts) and follows its tradition of teaching inherited from the methods developed by Stanislavski. The principal has evolved his own method which is called the Science of Acting. Put simply, acting is a technique that can be taught, and this method teaches it (alongside other staples of drama school training such as dance, speech, improvisation and so on). This course serves as an intensive introduction into this method.
Fees: £295

One Week Courses, Acting

Central
A youth theatre course for ages 13+ at one of the best known drama schools. The course covers voice, movement, staging, physical theatre, ensemble playing and working with text leading to a final presentation.
Fees: £150

Court Theatre Training Company
The training company came into existence when the Court Theatre Company, a touring company, started to operate workshops for young and aspiring actors. This developed into a second, training theatre company. Both companies are now based at The Courtyard Theatre, a fringe theatre in central London. This course concentrates on Shakespeare and aims to make Shakespeare come alive and remove any fears.
Fees: £135

East 15
This drama school has two sites, one in Essex and one in Yorkshire where the summer courses are held. Sherriff Hutton is an extremely beautiful Jacobean house in lovely grounds and students can choose to stay there in self catering shared accommodation. East 15 has a different approach from most drama schools in that it is concentrates on the understanding of character through

text study and research. Classical texts e.g. Shakespeare, Ibsen and Chekhov are mainly studied. On the final Saturday of each course a performance of the week's work is given in full costume with lights and sound in various us rooms of the house, many of which are authentically panelled and furnished according to their period.
Fees: £180 without accommodation, £225 with accommodation (shared and self catering)

Italia Conti
Choice of two options; Performing Arts or Drama. The aim of the course is to provide a sample of what is studied on a Performing Arts or Drama course. Students are aged from 9 - 19 and are divided up into four levels from beginner to Advanced/Professional. The course culminates in a short performance at the school's theatre.
Fee £250

School of the Science of Acting
The course is run in association with GITIS (The Moscow Institute of Theatre Arts) and follows its tradition of teaching inherited from the methods developed by Stanislavski. The principal has evolved his own method which is called the Science of Acting. Put simply, acting is a technique that can be taught, and this method teaches it (alongside other staples of drama school training such as dance, speech, improvisation and so on). This course serves as an introduction to the school and, should a student subsequently be accepted onto a full time course the cost of the summer course will be deducted.
Fees: £175

5 Day Audition Course
The Academy
The Academy was the first school to offer a complete part time training and has gone on to develop a range of courses. This course is aimed at getting the would be drama student into the school of their choice and offers a money back guarantee for those who fail eight or more auditions. As there are easily eight top rank courses (including currently six degree level courses) this seems worth the money. Topics covered include choice of speech, self presentation, learning about workshop or improvisation sessions, and finishes with a mock audition, with a feedback session.

Auditions
One speech of not more than two minutes, plus an interview.
Audition fee: £10 Fees: £100

Stage School (up to 16)

Arts Educational
One of the best known and respected schools. The course balances academic studies to National Curriculum and GCSE (12 options) standards with specialist training in dance, drama, music and art. Pupils choose to specialise in dance or drama and from the fourth year opt for Dance, Drama or Musical Theatre. Students who have opted for the drama option maintain singing and dance. A serious school combining excellent vocational training with high academic standards (for example, all the teaching staff hold BA or higher degrees). Not surprisingly the school is many peoples first choice.
Auditions
A day long audition including educational tests in English and mathematics.
Audition fee: £25   Fees: c£5500 per annum

Italia Conti
Italia Conti has been established as a stage school since the beginning of the century and now takes pupils from 9 - 16. The course is accredited by the Independent Schools Joint Council. The curriculum stays in step with the National Curriculum and aims to provide a through ground work. Pupils can take a range of GCSE's. Vocational classes in Dance, Acting and Singing are arranged according to each child's ability and standard. Pupils may take part in Academy productions. The school also

has an agency. One of the best known schools with a distinguished roll call of former students.
Auditions
Two short and contrasting pieces are required for the drama section plus some sight reading. The dance section asks for a song (bring a taped accompaniment) and up to three dance style i.e. tap, ballet and modern, of not more than two minutes each. Applicants may have to take a schoolroom test, and have an interview.
Audition fee: £20   Fees c£4000 per annum

Pattison's Dancing Academy and College
Based on the fringes of Coventry, Pattison's takes children from 5-18. Boarding is available from 10 years. The junior part of the school is primarily concerned with laying a good academic foundation and basic skills training. Music Dance and Speech training are included in the curriculum in short periods from the start, with all children over the age of 7 or 8 taking part in some form of dance training after school. In the senior school children follow the national curriculum in a wide range of GCSE subjects. Dance and drama lessons are held after school and on Saturday mornings. At 16 pupils may go onto the student course, or the drama foundation course.
Fees: c£1500 - £2500 per annum.

Ravenscourt Theatre School
This school was founded on the closure of the famous Corona Academy on the retirement of its principal, and continues its traditions and format of academic studies to GCSE standard in the morning and dramatic studies in the afternoons. Dance (ballet, jazz and tap) is also studied but the emphasis is on producing actors not

dancers. The school runs its own agency and actively seeks work for its pupils - with considerable success. 5-16.
Fees: c£2500 per annum

Shandy Stage School
The Shandy Stage School is a small school which aims to cover both Academic studies and performing Arts studies with equal emphasis. GCSE's are taken in up to nine subjects and there is an emphasis on dance in the theatrical subjects.
Fees: c£2500 per annum

Sylvia Young Theatre School
The school covers ages 7-16. Academic studies continue to GCSE and pupils are expected to take at least exams five subjects, and are encouraged to take more. Dance, drama and music form the basis of the vocational studies. The school runs its own agency and many of the pupils take part in outside professional work, such as the Children's Royal Variety Performance. Singing is one of the schools strong point with a well known choir. The school also runs some outside classes.
Fees: c£3000

Van Dyke Academy
The Academy aims to provide a high standard of education combined with theatre training in dance, Speech and Drama. The school also offers part time classes from 3 years upwards.
Fees: c.£3500 per annum.

Musical Theatre Courses

Musical Theatre Courses are for those who wish to work in the area of musical theatre. For this they need to be able to dance, sing and act, usually in that order. For that reason most of the musical theatre or performers courses are based in dance schools. Recently drama schools have become interested in musical theatre and are adding courses. Usually their strengths are in acting, singing and dance, in that order. The main exception is the London Studio Centre which, because of its time-tabling system, can allow students to concentrate on one area or spread their studies widely according to their wishes. Which approach you prefer depends on your current abilities and your own ambitions. For example, someone who has been to stage school may prefer a more acting based course, or you may wish to be an actor first and foremost but as you have a good singing voice it seems a waste not to develop that talent and so a drama based musical theatre course would suit.
Auditions usually include acting speeches as well as some dance. Read the requirements carefully; some schools provide a pianist and require sheet music, whereas others expect you to have pre-recorded your accompaniment. Schools which are dance based accept students from 16 and will usually not take girls without previous dance training.

Courses which have CDET at the end of their entry are accredited by the Council for Dance Education and Training, those with NCDT are accredited by the National Council for

Drama Training. Students with places on NCDT or CDET accredited courses are more likely to recieve local authority grants. A full list of NCDT and CDET accredited courses is at the back of the book.

Three Year Courses, Musical Theatre, Full Time

The Arts Educational School
The aim of the course is to produce performers who are skilled dancers, actors and singers. Unlike most schools it benefits from being at a school where there is both a classical dance course and a straight acting course so that within the course there is no inherent emphasis on one area. The course is performance centred, and two full scale musical productions and a musical cabaret are presented at the end of each year. Students are required to stage manage productions. As well as the main and studio theatres there ore many other facilities such as a Pilates studio. 16+

Auditions:
Girls should be of elementary Ballet standard; boys should have had some previous dance training although this is not essential. Applicants attend a ballet class and stretching exercises, and perform of prepared jazz dance solo. A song (piano accompaniment) and a speech of the applicants choice is also required. Students may be given a music ear test and asked to sing scales and exercises. Audition fee: £25   Fees: c£7000 per annum.. One scholarship for a male student CDET

Doreen Bird College

The aim of the college is to give a comprehensive and balanced training in Dance and the related subjects of Singing and Drama. Students leave here as dancers who can act and sing, rather than actors or singers who can dance. Technical classes are arranged according to standard rather than year. Male students have separate Ballet, Modern and Singing classes. The first year is a foundation year where all students study all the subjects offered. After this students can specialise in classical or contemporary dance. There are opportunities for those students interested in choreography throughout the course. During the final year many students appear in professional pantomimes at Christmas and there is a final Summer showcase. The school has its own theatrical agency.

Audition fee: £25   Fees: c£7000 per annum   CDET

The Elliott-Clarke College

A traditional school primarily offering dance training, although there is a drama option on the performers training course. The aim is to produce people who can successfully work in all areas of the performing arts, with the emphasis on live theatre. Television and radio are not included in the syllabus. 'A' level Theatre Arts, History of Drama, and/or Ballet may be studied by Dance and Drama students, and they are also allowed to attend the local FE college on half day or evening release if they wish. 16+.

Auditions

Applicants are invited to attend the college for a week so that their academic and vocational ability can be as-

sessed. During the week there will be an audition and interview.
Audition fee: None Fees c£1500 per annum.

Guildford School of Acting

The course has two options, Acting and Musical Theatre, which are not confirmed until after completion of the first year. Both groups do the first year together and then separate in emphasis. It is worth pointing out that of the drama schools which now offer a musical theatre option this is the only school that covers specific dance techniques such as classical ballet, Cecchetti, jazz (including Matt Mattox) and tap. They are continually improving facilities. Final productions are put on in Guildford and London. This may become a degree course in the future.

Auditions

Applicants limited to 700 each year. Each audition takes a day and consists of classes in movement and Improvisation, and one speeches classical or modern, not more than two minutes long. Also a song is required, which will be accompanied so sheet music is required. A group song is taught at audition and a voice appraisal is made. As a policy they try not to recall. 18+, no formal maximum, but most students are in their early 20's.
Audition fee: £30 Fees: c£5500 per annum   NCDT

Hertfordshire Theatre School

The school has been recently founded and this course aims to teach both acting and musical theatre. Course work is very performance based, with three major productions a year for each year, two of which are dramatic and one of which is a musical. Apart from this the first two years are spent on projects ranging from Greek

Theatre to present day. Each project covers both musical and acting, so if a twenties play was being studied then a twenties song would be learnt. In this way the course aims to cover a variety of styles, movements, playwrights and so on. The basics of acting technique, voice and movement are studied in specific classes. All acting is based on the principles of Stanislavski. Productions take place in a local theatre and the final production showcase is in London. Hitchin itself is a pleasant rural town with cheap accommodation while having easy access to London. 18-30

Auditions

Two speeches, one from a comedy and one from a tragedy, neither longer than three minutes each, and a song which may be unaccompanied, or with a backing tape or with piano accompaniment (bring sheet music). There is also a movement and dance class

Audition fee: £25 Fees £5000 per annum or £3500 with the Sponsorship Bursary (presumably applicable for those who are unable to get a LEA grant).

Italia Conti

As a stage school Italia Conti has been established since the beginning of the century, but the 16+ courses are more recent developments. The school has its own theatrical agency to help with the business of getting work on graduation. Each time table is individually structured according to the students needs and abilities. The aim is to produce actors who can dance and sing, dancers who can sing and act and singers who can dance and act. The first year aims to provide a solid foundation to build on. A level English is also offered as an option for first year students. Any weakness in any particular area is assessed and the time table adjusted accordingly at the start of the second year. The final year concentrates on presentation and productions. 16+

Auditions
Two short and contrasting pieces are required for the drama section, with possibly some sight reading. The Dancing and singing section consists of a song (accompaniment on tape) and up to three dance styles i.e. tap, ballet and modern, none more than two minutes long plus an interview.
Audition fee: £20   Fees c£5500 per annum CDET

Laine Theatre Arts
Laine Theatre Arts is based in new purpose built studios in Epsom, a quiet town on the fringes of London. The aim is to give a balanced training in all areas of the performing arts, in order to develop versatile all-rounders. Each student receives an individual time table according to his or her specific needs. Students can opt to take the Musical Theatre course which gives equal emphasis on the three main components of Dance, Singing and Drama, but otherwise the course emphasises the dance aspect. There are male only classes. Third year students are encouraged to take the Associate teaching exams of the Imperial Society of Teachers of Dancing. Most public performances take place at the local community theatre and performances are video-taped, but there are no specific television facilities for students. The school is protective of its students and checks that accommodation is suitable. 16+

Auditions

For girls a ballet class is compulsory, followed by a modern solo dance not longer than 1 1/2 minutes (optional if the subject has not been studied before). Boys attend a ballet class if they have studied it before, or if not are assessed for their potential, and then attend a jazz class and perform a modern or jazz solo not longer than 1 1/2 minutes. Students may also present an accompanied song (bring sheet music) and a speech, up to two minutes long.

Audition fee: £25   Fees: c£7000 per annum CDET

London Studio Centre

The London Studio Centre moved into it's new premises in King's Cross about five years ago, making it one of the best equipped schools in the country (and probably Europe). At the heart of the school is its time table. Each student selects their own course from a choice of over 400 classes available a week. In theory this means that a student could study television every week for three years, or never attend a class. In practise choices are supervised so that a balance is achieved, with specialisation (if desired) only coming after a foundation year to establish a broad base of achievement. Classes are graded so that each student is working at the right level - there are for example fourteen levels of ballet. The school also benefits from having a close association with Cameron Mackintosh Ltd, and London City Ballet who are based at the LSC. For an all round training in the Performing Arts and for sheer style, enthusiasm and professionalism this course is streets ahead. 16+.

Auditions
Applicants attend classes in five areas; ballet, jazz dance, physical movement, singing and drama. A would be student should pass highly in two or more of these areas, although they will make allowances for someone who has had no dance training before.
Audition fee: £25 Fees: c£8000 per annum   CDET Scholarships available

Midlands Academy of Dance and Drama
The aim is to give students an all round theatrical training. in the third year students can also train as teachers, taking teaching certificates with the IDTA, ISTD, LAMDA, NBSD. Course work covers classical ballet, jazz, tap, modern, stagecraft, contemporary, double work, pas de deux, ballroom, Latin, Alexander technique, stage fighting, Anatomy, Acting, Improvisation, camera technique, and singing.
Audition fee: £20 Fees: c£3500 per annum

Mountview
Mountview is a professional, forward looking school, constantly adding to facilities and fine-tuning the courses it offers. Compared to a school like the Bristol Old Vic it has a large intake, which can lead to some students feeling they have been left on the sidelines. The course starts with a Foundation year giving the basics in Voice, Acting, Movement and Music and Singing which is common to all three year students. From then on students divide into a musical theatre group and an acting group. Both courses continue with the same basics but there is a greater emphasis on singing, voice, movement,

dance and musical presentation with the musical theatre group. Mountview was one of the first schools to introduce touring as a way of developing and gaining experience. Tours usually operate in Europe and the USA, with acting workshops and lectures incorporated into the schedule. The school energetically promotes its final year students. No official age constraints.

Auditions
A day long workshop consisting of four work sessions e.g. voice, movement. Two acting pieces are needed, one from a modern play and another of your choice, either modern or classical, but neither piece may be longer than two minutes. Two songs of contrasting style are also need, and one must be from a musical. The pieces are accompanied so bring sheet music for the pianist. About 50 places are offered.

Audition fee: £25 Fees: c£6500 per annum NCDT Several scholarships available.

Performers Dance College

The course aims to provide the all round training that dancers need. Unusually students are encouraged to audition for television and theatre work (at the directors discretion) at the earliest opportunity, and this emphasis on the practicalities of getting work runs through the training. Production experience is provided both by the school in end of year shows, musical evening s and drama workshops and also by local operatic societies and production groups who often request students as extra cast for their productions. Teaching qualifications can be taken in the final year. 16+. Students with considerable previous training may be recommended a one or two year course.

Auditions
Usually a ballet class followed by a jazz class. Students must perform a short dance routine lasting between one and two minutes. Any accompaniment should be on tape. Applicants may also perform a song or short dramatic piece if they wish.
Audition fees: £20 Fees: c£4500 CDET

The Urdang Academy
The Urdang Academy is a well respected dance school situated in the heart of Covent Garden, the centre of the Dance and Theatre world. There is a close association with the Bolshoi Academy, and a Bolshoi teacher takes up residency with the school annually. Many theatre, dance and production companies hold audition and rehearsals on the school's premises. The musical theatre performers course is primarily for dancers who intend to go into musicals, television, jazz and contemporary companies and groups. Dance classes predominate and include, Ballet, Jazz, Contemporary, Choreography and Tap, and there are also singing and drama classes. Final year students receive Song and Dance presentation coaching and master classes in audition technique. The course may be combined with the teachers course.

Auditions
A prepared dance not longer than one minute.
Audition fee: £15 Fees: c£6600 per annum. CDET

Two Year Course, Musical Theatre, Full Time

The Academy of Musical Theatre
A small school, recently founded. This course is intended as a foundation for those who have little or no previous experience, although some earlier dance or singing training would be an advantage. Classes taken include singing, acting techniques, voice, Dance (including Classical Ballet, Jazz and Tap), mime and Improvisation. During the second year there are full productions open to the public. 16+

Auditions
Two speeches, one Shakespeare, one modern, neither longer than three minutes each, plus a song and, if you dance, a routine (music should be recorded, or bring an accompanist).
Audition fee: £15   Fees: c£3500

London Academy of Performing Arts
Aims to produce actors who can sing and dance. The first year is linked to the two year acting course while the second year concentrates on different types of musical theatre i.e. musicals, revue, cabaret et al. They are setting up a musical theatre company which is to be a professional company staging productions in the Academy's theatre or touring the UK and abroad. This will provide

a possible third year of training and a way into the profession.
Auditions
Two speeches, on classical and one modern (which may be linked to a song from o musical or play), each lasting about two minutes, plus a song from a musical or operetta to be accompanied. There will also be a movement workshop.
Audition fee: £25 Fees: c£5000 per annum

Redroofs Theatre School
The performing arts course is based, appropriately, in the former home of Ivor Novello. Dance, acting voice and speech and singing are all covered, although Dance is optional. During the first year there is a schools tour. The second year is more production based. Productions take place at a nearby theatre run by the school as a professional company. Students are expected to stage manage shows. There is an optional extra term whereby students can take exams in drama and Dance teaching exams. Students may join the professional company on leaving. 16+.
Auditions
Two speeches, one from Shakespeare (or other classical verse play) and one modern, neither longer than four minutes plus a song. Students with previous dance training should also prepare a short dance.
Audition fee: £15 Fees: c£4000 per annum

One Year Courses, Musical Theatre, Full Time

The Academy of Musical Theatre
A small school, recently founded. This course is intended for those who have previous training or experience who reach the required standard at audition. Classes taken include singing, acting techniques, voice, Dance (including Classical Ballet, Jazz and Tap), mime and Improvisation. There should be some full productions open to the public. 16+

Auditions
Two speeches, one Shakespeare, one modern, neither longer than three minutes each, plus a song and, if you dance, a routine (music should be recorded, or bring an accompanist).
Audition fee: £15   Fees: c£3500

The Academy of Musical Theatre also offers a refresher course. This course is intended for qualified students who wish to repeat on some particular aspect of their training. Students join the school for as long as it may suit them. Classes taken include singing, acting techniques, voice, Dance (including Classical Ballet, Jazz and Tap), mime and Improvisation.

Auditions
Two speeches, one Shakespeare, one modern, neither longer than three minutes each, plus a song and, if you dance, a routine (music should be recorded, or bring an accompanist).
Audition fee: £15   Fees: c£1000 per term

Academy of Live and Recorded Arts
Of the "new" drama schools, ALRA is probably the largest and most established. It was founded to fill the gap in training students for work in television. Now almost all schools cover television, but at ALRA television work as an integral part of the course, to be taught with the same emphasis as say, voice. The performers course covers dance, voice, movement and acting. It is not clear why they consider the course to be unique, as there are many courses aiming to produce actors who can sing and dance, dancers who can act and sing etc. Final productions are held in the college which some see as being too far away from the West End to attract the large professional audience graduates hope for. 16+. Post graduate students already have some training may be considered for intensive one or two year training.

Auditions
No audition speeches required. Instead applicants take part in a day long series of classes - voice, movement, improvisation, Jazz dance and Ballet. Applicants without previous Ballet experience will be separately assessed on the day.
Audition fee: £29.37 Fees: c£7000 per annum

Mountview

Mountview is a professional, forward looking school, constantly adding to facilities and fine-tuning the courses it offers. Compared to a school like the Bristol Old Vic it has a large intake, which can lead to some students feeling they have been left on the sidelines. The first term gives a foundation in the basics of voice, Acting, Movement and Music and Singing. From then on students divide into a musical theatre group and an acting group. Both courses continue with the same basics but the acting option emphasises textual work, where the musical theatre option concentrates on voice, singing and dance. The final productions are usually held in central London theatre; the school energetically promotes its graduating students. 21+.

Auditions

A day long workshop consisting of four work sessions e.g. voice, movement. Two acting pieces are needed, one from a modern play and another of your choice, either modern or classical, but neither piece may be longer than two minutes. Two songs of contrasting style are also need, and one must be from a musical. The pieces are accompanied so bring sheet music for the pianist. About 50 places are offered.

Audition fee: £25 Fees: c£8500 per course (four terms) NCDT

Redroofs Theatre School

The performing arts course is based in the former home of Ivor Novello. Dance, acting voice and speech and singing are all covered, although Dance is optional. Productions take place at a nearby theatre run by the school as a professional company. Students are expected to stage manage shows. There is an optional extra term whereby students can take exams in drama and Dance teaching exams. Students may join the professional company on leaving. Applicants should either be drama graduates or have previous professional experience or have attended for at least one year of a similar establishment.

Auditions
Two speeches, one from Shakespeare (or other classical verse play) and one modern, neither longer than four minutes plus a song. Students with previous dance training should also prepare a short dance.
Audition fee: £15 Fees: c£4000 per annum

Short Courses

Four Week Courses, Musical Theatre

Central
A practical course aimed to increase the actor's confidence in approaching musical theatre performance. Mornings are spent developing and exploring skills such as vocal technique, movement, song and scene analysis and the afternoons spent in rehearsal for a final studio presentation of musical theatre material chosen specifically for each student's development. Solo and ensemble work included.
Fees: £725

Mountview
The course is designed for students who want to explore and experience this area of theatre. Mornings are spent on class work - singing, improvisation, dance techniques, song presentation - and the afternoons are spent working in with a musical director and choreographer in rehearsal for a project for performance on the final day.
17+
Fees: £700

Weekend Course, Musical Theatre

Court Theatre Training Company
The training company came into existence when the Court Theatre Company, a touring company, started to operate workshops for young and aspiring actors. This developed into a second, training theatre company. Both companies are now based at The Courtyard Theatre, a fringe theatre in central London. The course runs on Saturdays for a year and covers dance, movement, voice, acting, singing, and musical audition technique. There is a production in the last term.
Audition Fee: £20 Fees: c£400 per annum

Dancers

Classical ballet dancers usually start training at an early age, 12 being probably the latest, certainly for girls. Many dance schools, especially those specialising in modern or contemporary dance will accept older boys without previous training. Several of the dance schools are 'feed' schools for dance companies, and not unnaturally, these schools are very popular.
Auditions usually take the form of ballet classes, with maybe solos of other dance styles.

Courses which have CDET at the end of their entry are accredited by the Council for Dance Education and Training, those with NCDT are accredited by the National Council for Drama Training. Students with places on NCDT or CDET accredited courses are more likely to recieve local authority grants. A full list of NCDT and CDET accredited courses is at the back of the book.

Dance Schools (up to 16)

The Arts Educational School at Tring
This famous school in a former Rothschild mansion takes 270 boarders and up to 40 day girls. Facilities include a recently built theatre and an indoor swimming pool. Recently they have added a preparatory department and the age range is now 8 - 18. Dance drama and music form the course of the vocational studies. There is an emphasis on Classical Ballet within the dance department, with students taking RAD, Cecchetti, and ISTD examinations. Junior pupils are chosen to dance in various productions mounted by the English national Ballet Company. All pupils study drama, and may choose to specialise and take GCSE in drama, and may go on to the Drama Foundation course. As well as classes and individual lessons in music the school has two orchestras and a choir, which has recently was Youth Choir of the Year, among other achievements. Academic subjects are studied following the National Curriculum, with 13 subjects offered at GCSE and 11 at A level, including theatre studies, Music, English and French. Classes are also offered in Computer Studies, Dressmaking, among others.

Audition
Entry between 8 and 14 is by audition and educational test. Entry to the sixth form is by audition only, but major examinations in dance, or a good standard in drama or music, must have been obtained before admission.
Audition fee: £30   Fees: c£4000/7000 prep school (day/boarding), c£6000/£9000 (day/boarding)

Elmhurst Ballet School

The school is well established and respected in the dance world, and its graduates are to be found in dance companies all over the world. During the last ten years or so there has been considerable expansion and improvement to facilities, which is continuing. Regular visits take place to professional dance and drama performances and there are also occasional visits to the Bolshoi and Vaganova schools in Moscow and Leningrad. A few children are day pupils, but most board the third year of the student course is non-residential). Pupils begin at about 10 and most stay until they are 18 or 19. The emphasis is on achieving a general dance training combined with high academic standards until 16 when pupils may specialise. Drama, Music and Singing all play a large part within the syllabus, with regular productions of plays and concerts being given at the school's theatre. There is also a school orchestra, choir, madrigal and modern song group. Academically standards are high with a graduate teaching staff. 13 GCSE subjects are offered, and most students take 7 or 8, with 69% getting grades A-C.

Auditions

The audition nearly lasts a full day and consists of classes in ballet, modern dance, drama and a singing test.
Audition fee: £40   Fees: c£5500 + c£2000 boarding

The Hammond

The Hammond is a well established and respected school which provides high academic and dance standards. Dance training is both integrated into the time as well as after normal school hours and on Saturdays. Pupils may board. The school has a good reputation for academic studies; it is one of the few schools to provide GCSE results (as 86% of the students who sat GCSE in the last four years achieved five or more passes at grades A-C this is perhaps not surprising). Students take a wide range of subjects, and most take eight or nine GCSE's. In the past a proportion of pupils have gone elsewhere to take A levels and go on to university; the school has recently started offering A level education as well. Music is an important feature of the school, with three choirs and an orchestra. The vocational course also has good results, with many of the pupils joining to the Royal Ballet Upper school as well as Hammond's own student course.

Audition fee: £25 Fees: Education: c£3500, Dance training: c£2000, Boarding: c£4000

The Royal Ballet School

The Royal Ballet school is probably the most famous dance school in the UK, if not the world. Most of this country's principal dancers were educated here. The Lower school takes pupils from 11-16 and is based at the White Lodge in Richmond Park, a glorious setting. The school is predominantly boarding. The school aims to provide a balanced education with ballet as an important, though not dominant, part. Their philosophy is that the differing demands of dance training and academic studies are mutually beneficial in the development of the individual. Academically standards are good, with most pupils taking 7 GCSE's. Most pupils also learn a musical instrument or sing. Most students continue to the Upper School. Pupils are eligible for grants from the DES, which continue should they carry on into the Upper School.

Audition fee: NONE Fees: c£10500 + £3500 boarding per annum.

The Urdang Academy

The Urdang Academy is a well respected dance school situated in the heart of Covent Garden, the centre of the Dance and Theatre world. There is a close association with the Bolshoi Academy, and a Bolshoi teacher takes up residency with the school annually. Many theatre, dance and production companies hold audition and rehearsals on the school's premises. The lower school runs from 10-16 and aims to combine academic excellence with the training required for the future professional dancer.

Auditions

A prepared dance not longer than one minute, and academic books covering French, English and Mathematics.

Audition fee: £15 Fees: c£6000 per annum.

Dance Degrees

The College of the Royal Academy of Dancing
The degree course is to commence in September 1994, subject to validation by the University of Durham. Students will need RAD, Cecchetti, ISYD or BBO elementary Certificate and the equivalent of 2 A levels. 70% of the course is to be practical.
Fees: c£6500 per annum

BA Hons Dance Theatre
The Laban Centre
The Laban Centre is one of the leading dance institutions in the world, both for vocational courses and it's extensive post graduate research. The main characteristic is the range of study available, rather than concentrating on training in one particular technique, or for one particular company. Facilities are very good, some of the best in Europe. The aim of the course is to combine developing a high level of technical and artistic competence with versatility as a dancer and inventiveness and originality in dance making and choreography. The main part of the course is in technique classes in contemporary dance, classical ballet and choreography and performance is an integral part of the training, either through perfomances of their own work or in pieces created for them. There is a wide range of optional subjects available such as Dance analysis and apprecia-

tion, Dance History, Teaching studies, Notation, Costume, Lighting, Music, Drama and Dance Culture and Communication. There are also special workshops and lectures from visiting artists, critics and scholars. This is known as the Performance route. Recently the Centre has added an alternative course structure which is the Critical and Cultural Studies route. This has an academic emphasis and is particularly suited to those students who may be thinking of a future career in dance/art administration, dance writing/journalism. The diploma course and the BA Hons course are the same except that the degree course requires students to have 5 GCSE'S and 2 A levels. Mature students may be allowed to submit a written piece of work in lieu of qualifications.

Auditions

Last a day, and consists of practical classes in contemporary dance and classical ballet, repertory and improvisation a physical examination and an interview.

Audition fee: NONE Fees: c£7000 CDET

BA Hons Contemporary Dance
London Contemporary Dance School

One of the best schools and internationally famous for the high calibre of teaching and the high standards of its graduates. The school hopes that, while ensuring that the highest technical standards are reached, the student's imagination is stimulated to produce highly creative and imaginative dancers. The daily training involves classes in Ballet and Contemporary dance (Graham based) and there are opportunities to study other dance styles throughout the course. Students do not need a background in ballet. Other main areas of study include choreography, music and stagecraft. Other classes in-

clude T'ai Chi Ch'uan, Dance History and Community Dance. Students are streamed together for technique classes. There are also courses designed to broaden students understanding of contemporary culture, the history of dance and dance in other societies. 17+. 2 A Levels required (exemption may be granted for mature students).
Auditions
Two classes in contemporary dance and ballet, plus a prepared short solo. Applicants also sit an informal essay paper. A special paper may be set for those candidates who do not have the correct academic qualifications.
Audition fee: £30   Fees: c£350 per annum CDET

London Contemporary Dance School also offers a BA in Contemporary Dance which is taught in modules and is entirely practical. Students may transfer onto the Honours degree course after the first year if they wish.
Auditions
Two classes in contemporary dance and ballet, plus a prepared short solo. Applicants (who do not need A level qualifications) must offer four of the following eight options: A portfolio of 5 examples of artwork (e.g. photography, costume design, drawing, model making, sculpture), a practical music audition with a test piece of approx. 3 minutes length (this can include vocal, instrumental or original composition work), an A level pass (any subject), a written account of the solo shown at the audition if the student's own work (approx. 300 words), a written account of any cultural, community, physical activities or special interests where the student has a practical involvement (approx. 750 words), an example,

or examples of independent course work (total 1500-2000 words), an essay on any subject (approx. 1500, and written expressly for the purpose), an essay written under exam conditions and taken from a list of suggested topics supplied by LCDS.
Audition fee: £30   Fees: c£350 per annumm CDET

BA Performing Arts (Dance)
Northern School of Contemporary Dance

The aim of the Northern School of Contemporary Dance is of "maintain its reputation as a Centre of Excellence providing high quality educational and training opportunities in dance and dance related areas with particular concern for access and equal opportunities". It is not unusual for people with very little dance training or with disabilities to be accepted. The school is part of Leeds University and can therefore share in the benefits of belonging to a larger organisation, such as facilities and student activities. The BA course is about 75% practical dance and 25% academic work. Techniques studies include: Contemporary dance (Graham, Cunningham and Limon), Classical Ballet (Vaganove, Cecchetti and English), including pointe-work, repertoire and pas de deux, and Jazz dance. All are taught to a professional level. Over the three year course the amount of public performance increases, either at the school's theatre or venues around the country and occasionally abroad. Other subjects include Choreography, Music, Creative Arts, Health and Safety, Design, History of Dance and Dance as Educational. There are also opportunities for performing and teaching in the community.

Auditions
Two classes, one classical and one contemporary and a two minute solo, plus an interview. The school looks for commitment and potential rather than polished performances and students with very little previous experience are often accepted. Students need 5 GCSE's, 2 at A level or an equivalent qualification such as a BTEC National diploma, or to take the Special entrance examination for those without qualifications.
Audition fee: NONE Fees: c£2500 (Mandatory grants)

Three Year Courses, Dance, Full Time

Arts Educational
The course is classically based but there is a strong emphasis on contemporary dance, as many dance companies require contemporary in their repertoire or at least the ability to adapt to modern styles. It cover the disciplines of Ballet, Contemporary Dance and Jazz as well as other styles of dance. First year students are required to also stage manage productions. Performance is regarded as an integral part of the dancers training and various productions are staged throughout the year either in the studio theatre or the schools main theatre. Other facilities include a Pilates studio. Guest choreographers are invited to create works specifically for the students and there are also choreographic workshops of the students own work. Students may take RAD exams in Ballet and Cecchetti. 16+
Auditions
Applicants take part in a ballet class and prepare a solo dance. Girls must hold a pass certificate in Elementary Ballet; boys may be at any level of training.
Audition fee: £25 Fees: c£6500 per annum CDET

The Central School of Ballet
The Central School of Ballet was founded by Christopher Gable, who is also artistic director of the Northern Ballet Theatre. The aim of the school is to give equal emphasis

to the mind and body of a dancer, to develop an all round artist who combines visual and musical awareness with physical abilities and creative imagination. The course is based on the discipline of Classical Ballet, according to the system developed by Agrippina Vaganova. This system puts a particular emphasis on the basic physiological principles of classical dance. RAD examinations can be taken in addition. Contemporary dance is a major part of the course and is based on the Martha Graham technique. Jazz, choreography, mime and acting, music appreciation, dance appreciation and critical studies, singing and eurhythmics are included. All students study dance at A or AS level. A level English Literature, French and Art are also offered. The school operates a 41 week year, which is longer than some other schools.

Auditions

Students take a classical ballet class, and there may also be some Contemporary movement, Jazz and/or improvisation. There is no need to prepare a special audition exercise, nor do students need to have reached a particular grade. There may be a further audition in April/May.

Audition fee: £25   Fees: c£7500 per annum   CDET

Elmhurst Ballet School

The school is well established and respected in the dance world, and its graduates are to be found in dance companies all over the world. During the last ten years or so there has been considerable expansion and improvement to facilities, which is continuing. Regular visits take place to professional dance and drama performances and there are also occasional visits to the Bolshoi and Vaganova schools in Moscow and Leningrad. Most board until the third year of the student course which is non-residential. Many of the pupils have been at the Junior school. Students may specialise in Classical Ballet, Jazz, Modern or Musical Theatre. Drama, music and singing classes continue with many students taking part in drama productions, concerts, the school choir and orchestra. The third year of the course concentrates on performance, audition training, and general preparation for the profession. Students may study for the RAD and ISTD teaching exams. Students may also take one to three A levels from eight offered by the school, and each year a few students continue with academic studies at university. Business studies (RSA/Pitmans exams in word processing, Shorthand and/or Typing) and cookery (City and Guilds) are also offered.

Auditions
The audition nearly lasts a full day and consists of classes in ballet, modern dance, drama and a singing test.
Audition fee: £40   Fees: c£6000 + c£2500 boarding CDET

The Hammond
The Hammond school has a long history of dance teaching, originally with children, and now with the Junior and Senior dance courses. The school is well respected in the dance world and its graduates are found in dance and ballet companies throughout the world. The course provides specialised dance training in Classical Ballet and Modern Theatre, and students may also combine the course with Teacher training, gaining experience with the Hammond Associate Programme which runs classes from 3 1/2 upwards. Students may take the examinations of the RAD and the ISTD. There is one major annual production, but students gain theatre experience with

the Performing Group, which provides a range of opportunities ranging from workshop demonstrations to presentations. All are held in venues in and around Chester. Recently the school has started to offer an A level study programme as well as the dance programme. This has had successful results, and the number of A level subjects offered has increased to seven.
Audition fee: £25 Fees: c£7000 per annum CDET

The Laban Centre

The Laban Centre is one of the leading dance institutions in the world, both for vocational courses and it's extensive post graduate research. The main characteristic is the range of study available, rather than concentrating on training in one particular technique, or for one particular company. Facilities are very good, some of the best in Europe. The aim of the course is to combine developing a high level of technical and artistic competence with versatility as a dancer and inventiveness and originality in dance making and choreography. The main part of the course is in technique classes in contemporary dance, classical ballet and choreography and performance is an integral part of the training, either through performances of their own work or in pieces created for them. There is a wide range of optional subjects available such as Dance analysis and appreciation, Dance History, Teaching studies, Notation, Costume, lighting, music, Drama and Dance Culture and Communication. There are also special workshops and lectures from visiting artists, critics and scholars. This is known as the Performance route. Recently the Centre has added an alternative course structure which is the Critical and Cultural Studies route. This has an academic

emphasis and is particularly suited to those students who may be thinking of a future career in dance/art administration, dance writing/journalism. The diploma course and the BA Hons course are the same except that the degree course requires students to have 5 GCSEs and 2 A levels. Mature students may be allowed to submit a written piece of work in lieu of qualifications.
Auditions
Last a day, and consists of practical classes in contemporary dance and classical ballet, repertory and improvisation a physical examination and an interview.
Audition fee: NONE Fees: c£7000 CDET

Northern Ballet School
The Northern Ballet School was founded in 1977 to provide an alternative to the concentration of courses in London and the South East. The school recently moved into new premises with improved facilities including its own 430 seat theatre. The course has two options, Classical or Theatre, which are perhaps more differences of emphasis than two separate courses. Both have a strong balletic element. The Course syllabus covers Ballet, Classical Repertoire, Pas de Deux, Modern Theatre dance, Jazz, Contemporary, National, Tap, Make-Up and stagecraft, Singing and Drama and Audition Technique. There are also Masterclasses given by visiting professionals. The school has an arrangement with the nearby Chetham's Music School for students who wish to study for A levels.
Auditions
Entrance is by an audition class and interview.
Audition fee: £20 Fees: c£7000 per annum CDET

The Northern Ballet School also offers a dance teachers course. The course follows the professional dancers course and covers Ballet, Classical Repertoire, Pas de Deux, Modern Theatre dance, Jazz, Contemporary, National, Tap, Make-Up and stagecraft, Singing and Drama and Audition Technique. Additional subjects include A level Ballet, Teaching technique and psychology, Anatomy, Notation, Music Appreciation, and the History of Dance. Practical teaching experience is provided on the part time junior classes held by the NBS and outside and students must complete 40 hours teaching practise to qualify for the diploma. The school has an arrangement with the nearby Chetham's Music School for students who wish to study for further A levels.

Auditions
Entrance is by an audition class and interview.
Audition fee: £20 Fees: c£7000 per annum CDET

Northern School of Contemporary Dance

The aim of the Northern School of Contemporary Dance is of "maintain its reputation as a Centre of Excellence providing high quality educational and training opportunities in dance and dance related areas with particular concern for access and equal opportunities". It is not unusual for people with very little dance training or with disabilities to be accepted. The school is part of Leeds University and can therefore share in the benefits of belonging to a larger organisation, such as facilities and student activities. The diploma course follows exactly the same programme as the Degree course, but without the academic element. Techniques studies include: Contemporary dance (Graham, Cunningham and Limon), Classical Ballet (Vaganove, Cecchetti and English), including pointe-work, repertoire and pas de deux, and Jazz dance. All are taught to a professional level. Over the three year course the amount of public performance increases, either at the school's theatre or venues around the country and occasionally abroad. Other subjects include Choreography, **Music**, Creative Arts, Health and Safety, Design, History of Dance and Dance as Educational. There are also opportunities for performing and teaching in the community.

Auditions

Two classes, one classical and one contemporary and a two minute solo, plus an interview. The school looks for commitment and potential rather than polished performances and students with very little previous experience are often accepted.

Audition fee: NONE Fees: £590 per annum CDET

Rambert School
(at The West London Institute of Higher Education)

Rambert Dance Company was the first British ballet company (as Ballet Rambert). It is one of the best known in Europe and has two outstanding modern choreographers. The school aims to offer a complete training in dance, both classical ballet and contemporary. The course includes daily classes in Ballet, Contemporary Dance, Repertoire (both 19th and 20th century), Point Work, Pas de Deux, Character, Choreography and RAD Syllabus (optional). A level Dance is also offered, while it is possible to arrange further A level study with local FE colleges. There are four performance periods a year, two entirely composed of students works and two including work by professional choreographers. Performance takes up a large part of the course. The school benefits from being part of a larger institution and can take advantage of its facilities, as well as their own extensive range of studios. The institute offers courses in Art, Film and TV, Music, Drama among other Humanities subjects and there are many opportunities for students to collaborate on Arts projects.

Auditions
Comprise of a short Ballet class and contemporary dance sequences given by a member of the audition panel.
Audition fee: £20 Fees: c £600 per annum CDET

The Royal Ballet School

The Royal Ballet school is probably the most famous ballet school in the UK, if not the world. Students are accepted from 16 upwards from the Lower school and other schools from all over the world. Each student has a two year academic programme; the more able pupils usually take two A levels, while others may concentrate on GCSEs. Some students may follow an exclusively practical programme of courses such as shorthand and typing, computer skills, spoken languages and music theory. Some female students may board but the school is primarily non-residential. Dance classes in Classical Ballet, Character, Pas de Deux, contemporary dance make up a large proportion of the course, and students may also study Benesh Notation, Singing and Drama. Students are encouraged to choreograph. Graduates from the school join ballet companies through Britain and Europe, but the main purpose of the school is to provide dancers for the two Royal Ballet Companies in London and Birmingham. There are student exchanges

with the Pairs Opera School, the Royal Danish Ballet School and the Beijing Dance Academy.
Audition fee: NONE Fees: c£8500 Financial assistance available CDET

Stella Mann College

The course aims to cover all aspects of dance training and related studies. The first two terms are broad based to give the chance of an all round dance training in Ballet, Modern, Tap, Jazz, Contemporary, National and Character dancing. In the final year students concentrate on a specialised selection of subjects according to their aims. This course may be combined with the teacher training course. ISTD exams taken and the children's and major syllabi of the Royal Academy of Dancing are studied as part of the theory of teaching. Teaching practice is developed through the course, with a period of outside teaching experience. 16+

Auditions
Applicants should have reached a general elementary standard. Audition and interview.
Audition fee: £20 Fees: c£5500 per annum CDET

The Urdang Academy

The Urdang Academy is a well respected dance school situated in the heart of Covent Garden, the centre of the Dance and Theatre world. There is a close association with the Bolshoi Academy, and a Bolshoi teacher takes up residency with the school annually. Many theatre, dance and production companies hold audition and rehearsals on the school's premises. The classical performers course is intended for those who are intending to go into classical ballet companies. Classes include

Ballet, Pointe work, Repertoire, Pas de Deux, RAD majors as well as jazz and contemporary dance, tap, Drama, Singing as well as others. Final year students attend master classes given by visiting artistic directors and principal dancers, open classes with professionals, and classes in audition technique, among others. The course may be combined with the teachers course.

Auditions

A prepared dance not longer than one minute.
Audition fee: £15 Fees: c£6600 per annum. CDET

Two Year Courses, Dance, Full Time

The English National Ballet School

The English National Ballet School is the most recently founded (and smallest) of the ballet schools. The school and the ballet company share premises and it is the aim of the course that students graduate into the Company (subject to the number of contracts available that year). Students are often chosen to perform with the company while still on the course. As well as classical ballet a range of dance styles are also studied including Contemporary, Character, Repertoire, Tap, Jazz, Pas de Deux and Solo. Further education in A level subjects is available, usually Dance and French. There are also lectures in Art, Music and Drama as well as workshops with the Production and Wardrobe Departments of the ENB. 16+.

Auditions

Preliminary auditions consist of a ballet class and are held throughout the UK. The final audition is at the end of March.

Audition fee: £25 Fees: c£7000 per annum CDET

One Year Courses, Dance, Full Time

The College of the Royal Academy of Dancing
The dance teacher training course is an intensive training for the teaching of classical ballet to children of 4/5 years up to young adults of 13+. It is aimed at more mature students. The course covers, Daily ballet class, body-conditioning, class structure, analysis, vocabulary, classical theory, anatomy, history, music Composition and weekly teaching practise. Graduates are awarded the ARAD (Associate of the Royal Academy of Dancing) and the Diploma of the Professional Dancer's Teaching Course (Dip PDTC). Graduates are credited with one year of the three year Teaching course programme (which is due to become a degree course).

London Contemporary Dance School
One of the best schools and internationally famous for the high calibre of teaching and the high standards of its graduates. The school hopes that, while ensuring that the highest technical standards are reached, the student's imagination is stimulated to produce highly creative and imaginative dancers. Classes take place in contemporary dance (Graham based) and ballet daily, and there are also classes in choreography, repertory, music stagecraft, movement studies and teaching dance. Students may also take classes scheduled for the three year degree courses. Certificate students may join the

degree course. Students should have had previous training in dance. Most will be mature or post graduate students. 20+
Auditions
Two classes in contemporary dance and ballet, plus a prepared short solo.
Audition fee: £30 Fees: c£7000 per course CDET

The Northern School of Contemporary Dance

The aim of the Northern School of Contemporary Dance is of "maintain its reputation as a Centre of Excellence providing high quality educational and training opportunities in dance and dance related areas with particular concern for access and equal opportunities". It is not unusual for people with very little dance training or with disabilities to be accepted. The school is part of Leeds University and can therefore share in the benefits of belonging to a larger organisation, such as facilities and student activities. This course leads to a Foundation Certificate in Dance performance awarded by the RSA and is also an access course to degree level study. The course give a basic training in Contemporary, Classical and Jazz dance, with a programme of Creative and Performance studies. Students may continue to vocational dance or performing arts courses, at degree level if desire.
Fees: £590 per annum

The Benesh Institute

The Benesh institute, formerly the Institute of Coreology is the only centre in the world that teaches Benesh Movement Notation to professional level. Coreology is the scientific study of dance, but can be used to notate all

forms of human movement. It can be used in many areas, such as anthropology, but is most commonly used to record dance works, and the Benesh system is the most widely used. The main aim of the course is to equip students with the skills necessary to undertake proficiently the recording and reconstruction of all forms of dance. The course lasts for four terms. Terms 1,2 and 3 correspond to Elementary, Intermediate and Advanced levels. Classical ballet, contemporary dance, partner work and group work are studied. In the last term students undertake external project work in an area of their own choice, such as an apprenticeship to a dance company or notating a work in a professional company. Students should have advance level dance qualifications or professional dance experience. Many are likely to be former dancers who, whether be age or accident, are having to leave the dance profession, but wish to stay within that world. Some scholarships are available. Entrance is by audition.
Fees: c£9000 per course

The Laban Centre

The Laban Centre is one of the leading dance institutions in the world, both for vocational courses and it's extensive post graduate research. The main characteristic is the range of study available, rather than concentrating on training in one particular technique, or for one particular company. Facilities are very good, some of the best in Europe. Mature students study dance and related subjects at a level appropriate to their skills and experience. The programme of study is individually constructed to be suitable to the students needs and aspirations. Students must take the core areas of Contempo-

rary Dance, Choreography and Choreological studies. They may continue to study in these areas or select from a list of options which can include: Arts Administration, Classical Ballet, Community Studies, Dance Appreciation, Dance History, Dance in Education, Music for Dance, Teaching Studies, Improvisation among others.
Auditions
Students attend an interview and practical class.
Audition fee: NONE Fees: c£7000 CDET

There is also a one year programme for US students who may spend their Junior year abroad at the Laban Centre. Successful students receive full credits and the programme of study can be planned to suit the individual needs of the student.
Audition fee: NONE Fees: c£7000

Another one year course offered is the Professional Diploma in Dance Studies. The course is centred on a broad range of common core subjects which includes: Contemporary Dance, Choreography, Choreological Studies, Arts Administration, and Technical Production. Options may include Improvisation, African and Indian Dance, Music, Aspects of Dance Production and Teaching Studies. There is also a placement with a Community Dance Project. Students should be either graduates or have considerable professional experience (neither degree subject or experience need be in the field of dance). Mature students who have neither a degree or appropriate experience may be eligible to take the course over two years full time.

Auditions
Students attend an interview and a practical class. The Centre will consider applicants with physical disabilities.
Audition fee: NONE Fees: c£7000 CDET

The Advanced Performance Course is for dancers who wish to perfect their technique whilst at the same time gaining professional company experience. Each year the company commissions three or four new works, and they also tour for three to four months in the UK and abroad. There are daily classes in ballet and contemporary dance. Other elements include improvisation and choreographic workshops, teaching skills, repertory, technical production and dance administration. Students must have completed a three year full time professional dance course.
Auditions
An audition of an interview and practical classes followed by a recall audition in summer.
Audition fee: NONE Fees: c£7000 CDET

Short Courses

The Benesh Institute
The Benesh institute, formerly the Institute of Coreology is the only centre in the world that teaches Benesh Movement Notation to professional level. Coreology is the scientific study of dance, but can be used to notate all forms of human movement. It can be used in many areas, such as anthropology, but is most commonly used to record dance works, and the Benesh system is the most widely used. The 2 and 5 day short courses are an introduction to Benesh. Students should have advance level dance qualifications or professional dance experience. Many are likely to be former dancers who, whether be age or accident, are having to leave the dance profession, but wish to stay within that world.
Fees: from £40 (concessions) to £100 other.

London Contemporary Dance School
The LCDS offers during Easter and Summer a variety of courses over six days which can be taken singly or combined to make a full day (for example, Body Conditioning, followed by Contemporary Dance, followed by Massage for Relaxation). They also offer evening classes in contemporary dance.
£31+ per course.

The Royal Ballet School

The **two week summer course** is designed to give students an opportunity to study at the Royal Ballet School. Classes include Classical Ballet, Solo variations, Repertoire, Character, Pas de Deux as well as in Music, Choreography and improvisation. New ballets are choreographed especially for the group and this, and other works are presented at the end of the course. The course is residential. Financial assistance is available. 15 - 17
Audition fee: NONE Fees: c£450

The **one week Course** is a residential course for children between 10 and 12 (boys up to 14). Students stay at the White Lodge in Richmond Park and have a chance to study at the Royal Ballet Lower School. Classes taught include classical Ballet, National Dance, Eurhythmics, Movement, Choreography, Improvisation, Mime and classical Greek dance. The course includes other informal lectures and a visit to the Ballet. Financial assistance is available.
Audition fee: NONE Fees: c£250

Other Performers and Skills

Alexander Technique
The Alexander Technique was developed by an actor to help with vocal problems, but is used on a wide range of problems such as chronic back pain, migraine, nervous tension. It should be initially taught in a series of frequent one-to-one lessons, but as the teaching becomes incorporated into daily life the need for lessons diminishes. Many drama schools include Alexander in their curriculum.

The Alexander Institute at Danceworks
Offers one-to-one lessons, introductory workshops and courses.

The Bloomsbury Alexander Centre
Offers one-to-one lessons, introductory workshops and courses.

The East London Alexander Centre at Bodywise
One to one sessions and introductory workshops.

The Society of Teachers of the Alexander Technique
Can put you in touch with an Alexander teacher in your area. Write (SAE please) or phone.

Clowning and Physical Theatre

Central School of Speech and Drama
Rapidly expanding, Central must be the most dynamic drama school at the moment; it has always been one of the best. This

one year physical theatre course concentrates on the practical study of movement work for actors and aims to train specialist teachers for drama schools and theatres. Students are expected to have a basic understanding of movement studies and relevant work experience. Entrance by interview.
Fees: c£3000 per annum   CDS

City Lit
Several evening, short and Saturday courses are available including Juggling (beginners and advanced) and Clowning at a variety of levels.
Fees: £19 concessions, £38 others.

Fool Time
Fool Time has developed from offering a series of classes and short courses in clowning skills to being the major UK provider of serious professional training in this rapidly increasing field. The premises are being expanded and will eventually include residential facilities as well as an aerial hall and performance space, studio theatre, gym and swimming pool, library and catering. The studios for rehearsals etc. have already been completed. The final aim is for the school to offer a degree course in performance arts. Several courses are currently offered:
a one year foundation course for beginners covering areas such as Equilibristics (tightrope walking, unicycle etc.), manipulation (juggling etc.), Acrobatics (tumbling, balances) and Aerial skills (trapeze etc.), plus physical awareness and conditioning, movement studies and performance studies.
Fees c £3000 per annum;
Four one year specialist courses for those with some experience in Equilibristics, manipulation, acrobatics and aerial skills c £3500 per annum;

three month "clowns, eccentrics and fools" course developing comic techniques and comical performances fees c £1000

Mime

City Lit
The City Lit offers several evening, short and Saturday courses in mime and physical theatre
including Mime technique and improvisation, Mask and the actor, Discovering mime, performing beyond naturalism
Fees: from £19 to £100

Desmond Jones School of Mime
The School is the longest established school of Mime in Britain. The Foundation course runs on Monday to Friday afternoons for three months and is based on the technique of Etienne Decroux, although it draws from a variety of sources. Most students are complete beginners and come from a variety of backgrounds. Advanced work (optional) continues for a further three terms. Entrance is by interview. 18-35.
Interview fee: £5 Fees: c£600 for course

Radio

City Lit
An introductory course on one evening a week leading to practical skills in radio reporting and interviewing, leading to feature making.

Morley College
The college offers two courses for potential technicians/journalists; "basic radio production" for beginners and "Radio Production Workshop" for those who have attended the basic course, or have previous experience. Skills learnt start with interviewing, writing scripts, tape-editing and develop to producing magazine and feature programmes, and further technical skills. Entrance by interview.

Radio School of Drama
There are three courses available, Introduction, Intermediate and Advanced, which run all year round, each lasting a week. The Introduction course assumes no previous knowledge and aims to teach basic microphone technique, the Intermediate course develops techniques and prepares individual audition speeches, and the Advanced concentrates on selecting and perfecting audition speeches which are recorded onto a tape at the end of the course. The aim is for training to equip graduates with the techniques necessary for professional work in radio drama, broadcast or voice-over.
Fees: from £175.01 (Introduction) to £233.83 (Advanced) (inc. VAT) per course.

Voice

Central School of Speech and Drama
Rapidly expanding, Central must be the most dynamic drama school at the moment; it has always been one of the best. Voice has always been a strong component of Central's courses. This one year course aims to train future teachers, especially at drama schools. The first part of the training looks at the study

of voice and phonetic theory, and the speaking of a wide range of texts (poetry, prose and dramatic). The second part of the course is spent on a placement at leading schools such as Guildhall, Rose Bruford and Central itself. Students are expected to have relevant professional experience, e.g. as actors, speech therapists, speech and drama teachers or be able to demonstrate a knowledge of voice e.g. trained singers. A basic understanding of voice and two years work experience are essential.
Entrance by interview.
Fees: c£3000 per annum   CDS NCDT

Central also offer a one term evening course on English Pronunciation for Japanese speakers taught by phonetic and linguistic specialists. Includes individual tutorials.

City Lit
Lots of different evening classes in aspects of voice training and other related subjects such as Speaking Shakespeare, text and the actor, Voice and Verse and so on.
Fees: £14 to £80

Guildford School of Acting
The one week singing course is for anyone who wants to improve their singing, with the emphasis on modern theatre demands. Other disciplines relating to voice will be studied such as speech, movement and acting.
Fees:

Voice Overs
A one day workshop in professional recording studios on the art of the voice-over. Does not include demo-tape. £117.50

Voiceworks
Evening and weekend workshops and classes on subjects relating to voice e.g. Singing and Public speaking as well as basic voice classes. Founded by one of the most respected and influential voice teachers, Patsy Rodenberg.

Presenter and Announcers

Announcers
Announcers (also known as Continuity Announcers) provide the link between programmes. They may also be required to introduce the next programme, preview future programmes, read news bulletins and so on. They must also be prepared to ad-lib should anything happen to the programme transmission. They will reflect the style of independent television companies and so a local accent may be preferable.. Applicants normally have previous experience within the industry, often as a performer.

Presenter
There is such a wide range of presenters that it would be impossible to give any one particular route into this career. However, news and current affairs presenters often have a background in journalism, documentaries are often presented by experts on the subject, sports presenters are often former players, music and 'youth' programme presenters may be former disc jockeys and so on. Very occasionally there are open auditions for presenters. Many presenters start in children's television and use it as an opportunity to move onto other presenting work.

Positive Productions
A one day course featuring a guided tour of a television studio, leaning to use an autocue, a 'live' outside

broadcast news report, your own chat show, and some technical experience such as camera and autocue operation. Would-be presenters also get an information pack, including "How do I find work as a presenter", and a 20 minute show reel of their 'best bits'. Total cost £229.13.

The Performers World

Everyone you meet, whether in or out of the profession will advise you not to become a performer. And because everyone gives the same advice it is somehow easier to dismiss them, because you can see that not all performers are out of work, you read about the money that some of them make, how glamourous the profession seems, how easy the work seems. Of course for some performers this may be true, for some of the time, but generally performers do not seem to have a long working life, whether actors, dancers or presenters. An actor may play a leading role in a popular series, but that may be the high point of their career; such an opportunity may never come again. A dancer may have their working life cut short through injury. Presenters seem the main staple of 'Where are they now?' programmes.

It is only a few who manage to have a 'career' as a performer in the sense of a job that lasts a working life.

The nature of the business dictates that the majority move in to some other career by their thirties. After all, it is easy to live away from home in digs for low wages (£160 a week is average for repertory theatre) when you have few personal or financial commitments. It is much harder when going involves leaving family for a wage that will hardly
covers the mortgage.

For this reason look through the courses available in the next section. A drama school diploma means very little to the outside world but a degree or a BTEC qualification will stand you in good stead should (or perhaps, when) you need a real job.

Section II

General Courses

Degree Courses

Degree course information has been simplified into four sections: Drama, Film, Media, Photography. A degree in Performance Arts or Theatre Studies will come under the Drama section, one in Communications will be under the Media section and so on.

Each section is sub-divided into further sections:
   Single subject
   Combined subjects
   Combined subject index
   Post graduate study (where appropriate)

Within each course there are varying levels of vocational studies for example, the Film Studies degree at the University of Kent has no practical film making at, whereas that at Newport School of Art and Design is two-thirds practical. As a showreel is an important part of gaining employment within the film industry this may affect the choice of course.

Degrees which are very specific, such as in Theatre Design or drama school courses which have recently become validated as degrees, are listed in their respective career section

DRAMA

BA Hons Drama
University College of Wales, Aberystwyth
"Drama at Aberystwyth is characterised academically by its emphasis on the indivisibility of theory and practice. Practical work is seen as illumination and deepening the student's understanding of the written text; similarly, theoretical approaches are tested in the workshop of creative work. There is an emphasis on perspectives on directing and on methodology of discussing performance. Aberystwyth Drama also offers a remarkably extensive range of practical options, with a unique emphasis on lighting design and sound and enjoys a strong reputation for its acting work."

Year 1: Introduction year to variety of teaching methods and requirements. Practical work.
Years 2 & 3: Theory options include: Shakespearean Drama,. Classical Tragedy, the Modern European Theatre, American Theatre and British and Irish Political Theatre. Critical study of Television. Production options include: Acting and Directing (theory and practice), lighting, sound and stage management, costume and set design, and Theatre in Education.

Grades: BCC / 20 points

Also available as Joint Honours with: American Studies, Art, Art History, Classical Studies, Education, English, French,

Geography, German, Information and Library Studies, Irish, Italian, Pure Mathematics, Spanish, Welsh, Welsh History.

BA Drama + Theatre Arts
University of Birmingham

"The Department is a leader in the field of practical drama, having pioneered a course which puts at its centre the actor in performance. At the core are complementary Dramatic Medium and Theatre Practise courses which all students follow, and from this stem the optional courses which aim to develop more specialised skills."

Year 1: Courses on: Stanislavsky, Building a Scenario, Speaking a Text, Modern Dance Language through practise and dance notation, Technical work (including costume and wardrobe, prop making and theatre crafts), Dance Theatre, Music Theatre.

Years 2 & 3: Theatre practice course based on a theme e.g. Madness and Folly, Sex, Society and the Stage, Crime and Punishment. Options include Encounter and Text, Biomechanics, Total Theatre, Choreography, Music Theatre, Design, Playwriting, lighting and Sound, theatre administration. The Dramatic Medium Course includes Style and Culture, Modernism, Style and Form, Shakespearean Style. The Drama tic Form course includes Tragedy, Comedy, Epic, etc. Other options cove a range of drama and theatre and may be by specific country (e.g. Italy, Ireland, Nigeria), specific author (e.g. Shakespeare, Pinter), theatrical movements (e.g. expression, theatre of the absurd), types of theatre (e.g. the American Musical, melodrama) or the relationship of the theatre to society at large (e.g. TIE, community theatre).

Grades: BBC

May be combined as Joint Honours with East Mediterranean History, English, French Studies, German Studies, Greek (Ancient), Greek (Modern), Hispanic Studies, History, History of Art, Italian, Latin, Media and Cultural Studies, Music, Portuguese, Russian, Sport and Recreation Studies.

BA Hons Drama (Theatre, Film, Television) University of Bristol

"The Drama Department approaches theatre, film and television across the three years in a comprehensive and broadly based way, regarding them as much more that branches of literature. Plays and films are studied in the light of their historical background and the cultural conditions of their production and presentation. Students are given solid grounding in the technical and craft aspects of theatre and video, to enable them to explore creative and aesthetic questions through productions, classes and workshops."

Year 1: Approaches to Theatre, Film and Television; Performance Studies; Film and Television Production Studies; Text/Rehearsal/Production; Voice Workshops; Theatre Technical Classes.
Year 2: Critical Perspectives; Choice from: 20th Century Avant-Garde; Film Styles and Conventions; Elizabethan and Jacobean Drama; Performance Studies; Film and Television Production Studies; American Theatre; Aspects of Medieval Drama and Theatre; Drama and Television; Epic and Parable; Futurism; the New Woman in the Theatre; Perspectives of Drama and Theatre in Africa; Playwriting.

Year 3: Critical Theory and Analysis. Choices from: Medieval, Tudor, Stuart Drama and Theatre; Performance Studies,; Film and Television Production Studies; Film and Television; Dissertation; British Theatre since 1968.

Grades: BCC

Also available as Joint Honours with English, French, German, Italian or Spanish.

BA Theatre
Dartington College of Arts

"Study of Theatre at Dartington is based on innovative practice and rigorous critical debate. It provides intensive experience in performance and composition. The performance work is physically based, and encourages the development of an intelligent and resourceful body and voice. In order to make theatre, students are helped to develop skills in perception, direction, writing, devising, choreography and scenography. research skills also from and essential part of the development of a student's critical language."

Also available with Music, Visual Performance and Arts Management.

BA Performing Arts
De Montfort University

"The study of Performing Arts - which covers theatre, dance and music - involves students in a broad range of approaches. Each of the performance areas has distinctive disciplines and practices on which theory is based, and each contributes to a study of theory of performance. The courses Dance/Music/

Theatre: The State of the Art are central to all study. Students learn to investigate and experience performance, to understand the context in which the performance is produced and its effect on the product, and to appreciate the best innovatory practise."

Courses available include: Introduction to the Alexander technique, Contemporary Dance Practice, Dance innovators, Musicianship and Analytical skills, Music history, Percussion studies, choir, Orchestra, Contemporary theatre practice, 20th Century theatre, Theatre, Symbols and Ritual, Script, Text and Performance, Performance Technology, Choreography in context, Writing about bodies: Dance Criticism and Analysis, Music History, Analysis and Technology, Performance Theatre, Gender and Theatre, Performance and Politics, Devising and Directing, Theatre Performance.

Also available as Joint Hons with Arts Management, Visual Arts, History of Art and Design, Media Studies, English, History, Politics.

BA Hons Drama
University of East Anglia
"This programme teaches Drama with a strong practical emphasis. You study the theory, history and social significance of Drama. Close attention is paid to the development of personal and technical skills. The work is complemented by detailed study of dramatic literature, productions, and a wide variety of project work."

Courses include: Theories of Drama, Theatre History, Classical drama, Drama to Marlowe, Shakespearean and Jacobean drama, Restoration Drama,. Melodrama, Contemporary British and European Drama, Creative Writing, Theatre Directing, Critical Practice, as well as practical work in stagecraft, voice and movement.

Also available with: English Literature, English History, American Literature, Comparative Literature, Linguistics Film Studies.

BA Hons Drama
University of Exeter

"Drama at Exeter is taught largely through studio sessions. That is to say that the subject is practised at the same time as it is learned. The relationship between theory and practice is more like a Science course, with necessarily long periods of laboratory work, than a lecture-based Arts degree. The course centres round a sequence of group projects, lasting 1-6 weeks. Some, but not all, of these projects conclude with a presentation. All drama students get equal opportunities and challenges to act, to direct and to write or otherwise create dramatic events."

Year 1: Introduction to the languages of drama and performance, Pre-texts, Contexts and Resources.
Year 2: Projects, Stagecraft, Textual Interpretation.
Year 3: Courses available include: Theatre Practice; Directing; Devising; the Creative Actor; Practical essay; Theatre Research; Dissertation; Special subjects; Technical specialisation; Textual Interpretation.

Also available as BA Combined Hons degree with English, German and Spanish.

BA Theatre and Media Drama
University of Glamorgan
"The course aims to provide a thorough grounding in practical and theoretical drama in theatre, television and radio, and open varied choice of careers in drama for its graduates. It combines a strong blend of practical, creative experience with a sound analytical training." Offered in association with the Welsh College of Music and Drama.

Core strands: Performance, Production, Textual Studies, Cultural and Critical Studies.
Options include: Scriptwriting for Theatre, TV and Radio; Directing; American, European and Third World Cinema; Contemporary TV and Radio Drama. Third year specialisations are: Directing, Acting, Management and Administration.

May be studies as combined Hons degree with some 40 subjects including: Art, Communication Studies, English Literature, French, Geography, German, Philosophy, Psychology, Religious Studies, Sociology, Spanish, Welsh, Women's studies.

BA Dramatic Studies
Glasgow University
(in association with the Royal Scottish Academy of Music and Drama)
Dramatic Studies (3 Years)
"The specifically practical classes in Voice and Movement Studies, Drama in Education, Theatre Arts, and Drama Studies (Acting and Directing) are taught at the School of Drama, and the more theoretical work at the University. You soon

discover, however, that the theoretical and the practical elements of the course overlap a great deal."

The degree at Glasgow is modular with a wide choice of subjects and degree type - Single, Joint, Ordinary, Honours - depending on courses studied during the four years.

Theatre Studies (4 Years)
"You study the present and past theatre practice by examining the various arts of the theatre, such as directing, play construction and play spaces, theoretically and critically and in their historical and sociological contexts, focusing in the Ordinary class on contemporary British Theatre. The Higher Ordinary class continues these studies, focusing on contemporary European theatre. Seminars in both classes include practical exploration of concepts introduced in the lecture courses and critical discussion of productions presented in local theatres. Before going on to the Advanced Ordinary or Honours classes, you are required to attend a practical vacation course."

Theatre Studies may be paired with one of 30 subjects for an Honours degree including English, Film and Television Studies, French, Geography, German. Hispanic Studies, History, History of Art, Italian, Music, Philosophy, Politics, Psychology, Sociology, Theatre Studies.

BA Drama and Theatre Arts
Goldsmith's College, London University
"This degree offers a broadly-based study of theatre, radio, TV/Film, arts administration, community and ethnic drama. The structure of the programme caters for those who wish to acquire a broad practical and intellectual perception of the

whole field, as well as those who wish to specialise in a specific area in considerable detail."

Years 1-3: English Theatre to 1642, History of Western Theatre, Modern and Contemporary Theatre, Dramaturgy, Popular and Applied Dramatic Forms, The Practice of Contemporary Theatre, Radio, Television and Film. Options may be selected from within this core and may vary from lectures and seminars to workshop-based practical classes. Two individual Special Subjects are constructed by individual students.

Also available with English or Education.

BA Hons Drama
University of Hull

"This course concentrates on the study of drama in all its aspects, literary, historical, aesthetic and presentational, with an equal stress on formal teaching and practical work."

Year 1: Introductory survey of theatre forms and conventions and the sources of dramatic inspiration.
Years 2 & 3: Options chosen from a list of between 40 and 50 covering many aspects of European theatre history and dramatic literature e.g. Classical Theatre, Moliere, Shakespeare, Ibsen, Contemporary theatre, Oriental Theatre, practical performance, direction, design, technical theatre, the media.
Also available as Joint Honours with American Studies, English, French, German, Italian, Music, Theology.

BA Hons Drama: Theatre Studies
John Moores University

"The aims of the course are to offer a syntheses of practical and theoretical approaches to enable students both to engage in drama and to understand how it is done. To develop creative and craft skills in dramatic expression at the same time as extending critical understanding of the significance of drama as a social art and the role of theatre in culture."

Year 1: Drama; practice and performance, methods in the humanities; multidisciplinary perspectives on the practices of reading and interpreting texts. Options include: movement, mask and the actor, drama: from page to stage, theatre in context, contemporary theatre as a cultural practice plus modules from other departments.
Year 2: Technical and performance skills in different modes of theatrical presentation, theory of understanding the performed play in a variety of cultural and historical contexts, radio and television drama production.
Year 3: Performance style, the role of the Director, drama in the community, European Avant-Garde Theatre, Political Theatre, Women's theatre, Black Theatre.

Grades: CC

Also available as Joint honours with some 40 plus subjects including Business, Dance, European Studies, Art, French, German, History, Japanese, Law, Media and Cultural Studies, Philosophy, Politics, Russian, Sociology, Spanish, Women's Studies, Environmental Science and Policy, Sports Science.

BA Hons Drama and Theatre Studies
University of Kent

"Studying drama at university acquaints you with a wide range of theatrical and dramatic theory and history, and it develops your understanding of theatre practice. What makes the Single Honours programme at Kent unique is its fourth year, which provides an opportunity to concentrate on practical work in a specific option, such as Directing, Devising or Theatre Administration. The fourth year allows you to bring together and apply what you have previously studied: theatre history and theory, technology, design, writing and performance."

Year 1: Stage Technology; Postwar British Theatre in Performance.

Year 2: Either Introduction to Performance or Advanced Stage Technology and choice of three Options from: Origins of European Theatre; Drama and Society in the Age of Shakespeare; Italian Comedy and its Influence; American Drama; Twentieth Century British Drama; Theatre and the Woman Question 1880-1918; English Theatre 1660-1800; European Tragedy.

Year 3: Options from Text, Image, Performance: Literature and Drama 1780-1880; Stage Design; Radio Drama; Women in the Theatre; Farce; Theatre Systems and their Funding; Modern European Theatre; Playwriting; Practical Project; European Tragedy.

Year 4: Directing or Devising or Theatre Adminstration.

Grades: BBC

Also available as Combined Honours with : African & Caribbean Studies, Classical Civilisation; Comparative Literary

Studies, English and American Literature, English Language, Film Studies, French, German, Greek, History, Italian, Latin, Linguistics, Philosophy, Theology and Religious Studies, Computing.

BA Hons Drama, Theatre and Television Studies King Alfred's College

"In this course students will study Drama as a process rather than as a series of dramatic products. The student will be part of that process; students will learn by doing. Working within a group students will make television programmes, and create live performances, developing their own texts or using the texts of plays already written. The work will cover fiction and documentary. Students will have opportunities to develop imaginative, vocal, visual and bodily flexibility, individually and within large and small groups. The course places emphasis on academic analysis. Students will be required to read widely, come to terms with new concepts and ideas and develop their own analytical writing."

Year 1: Study of myth, dramatic theory and semiotics; Medieval European Drama; African drama and the drama of other worlds; Contemporary drama and television; Narrative, Metaphor and Image in live performance and through making videotapes; Project work in drama and documentary.
Year 2: Community drama; Documentary and documentary drama; video documentary project; Popular tradition and the Elizabethan playhouse; Modernism in European drama.
Year 3: Contemporary aesthetic theory for drama on television and in live performance; Dissertation; group projects in live and recorded media exhibited publicly.

Grades: 20 - 24 points

Drama may also be taken as a modular BA Hons degree with American Studies, Computing, Education Studies, English Studies, Environmental Studies, Geography, History, History of Art, Japanese studies, Language, Communication and Writing, Religious Studies, Social, Economic and Political Studies.

BA Hons Theatre Studies
Lancaster University

"We believe that practical and production work is the best way to generate knowledge about theatre and performance, and consequently we expect our students to engage with theoretical and critical issues through workshops and performances. We see such activities as being central to the academic process. Our approach involves practical training in theatre techniques and performance skills, although we do not provide preparation specifically for a career in professional theatre."

Year 1: Basics of performance skills and theory, technical theatre practice, theatre forms and expressions.
Year 2: Two from: acting, directing, playwriting, lighting and sound, design, theatre administration, devising. Two from: Stanislavski and Brecht, Ritual Theatre, Medieval English Theatre.
Year 3: Choice from: Television Drama, Shakespeare in the 20th Century, Popular Theatre.

Grades BBC

Also available as a combined degree with Education Studies, English, French, German, Italian, Religious Studies.

BA Hons Drama (Theatre Arts, Dramatic Arts or Theatre Crafts)
University of Leeds (Bretton Hall)

"There are three distinct routes leading to the Honours degree in Drama. Common to all three is the view that Drama and Theatre operate as inextricable agents with both expressive and performance elements. The expressive releases the potential of the person and the artist, the performance controls and disciplines through specific communicative and interpretative skills. Also common to all three is the view that creativity and spontaneity are best triggered and effectively used through application of the intellect."

Theatre Arts
"For those wishing to make performance as thinking actors their main emphasis"

Year 1: Basic coarses in: vocal and physical expression, improvisation, acting techniques, foundations of drama, dramatic criticism, stage techniques, group work methods. Workshops on major figures in acting theory and practice developed into productions and a workshop performance of a Greek Drama based on Laban Principles.

Year 2: More intense training in voice and Movement including period movement, song and dance. Acting and Improvisation: Commedia dell'Arte; the classical text; Workshops by a visiting director. Theatre background studies.

Year 3: Studies undertaken in a professional theatre context, as a member of a company.

Dramatic Arts
"For those wishing to develop performance and instigatory skills in professional devised theatre practice."

Year 1: Basic course in vocal and physical expression and improvisation leading to Narrative Theatre techniques; background studies in Stanislavski and Brecht; Theatre of Fact - devising, techniques, educational; Theatre of Issue; Supporting studies.
Year 2: Continuation of vocal and physical skills and development of practice in educative theatre; Deconstruction Theatre techniques centring on the Jacobean period plus historical social background. Supporting studies.
Year 3: Work within a professional context; performances in regional theatre in the round and other venues. Individual and group devised pieces, study of play text and further applied improvisation projects. Supporting studies.

Theatre Crafts
"For those wishing to develop creative skills in technical theatre, theatre design, back-stage or front of house."
Year 1: An introduction to Stage and Theatre Management; practical and theoretical course in principle aspects contemporary theatre; History and background to space, lighting and sound. Supporting studies.
Year 2: Further aspects of theatre communication studied in practice and theory; prop-making and theatre crafts, light and sound design. Study of a number of key pioneers in some aspects of theatre. Supporting studies.
Year 3: Further experience and professional practice through a series of group and individual projects designed to enable the practice and theory of years 1 and 2 to be undertaken in a more total theatre context. Supporting studies may be taken.

BA Hons Drama
Loughborough University

"This course is designed to offer you the opportunity of studying drama both in. theory and practice. The two approaches are seen not merely as complementary but as indivisible in the study of a performance art. The mina teaching mode is of linked seminar discussions and practical workshop sessions which explore play text, theoretical writings, performance traditions and techniques, and examine the theatre's role and function in society throughout history. European and American theatre as well as British theatre are considered. Technical theatre (lighting, sound, wardrobe) and radio and television drama are also available as areas in which students may specialise."

Year 1: Introduction to theoretical and practical areas, Critical studies, Analysis and Criticism, Workshops on the drama and theatre of Classical Greece and Medieval England leading to performance.

Years 2 & 3: British Drama 1550-1709. Theatre Practice and Group Project. Options from: Television Studies, Advanced Technical Theatre, Classical Theatre, Theories of Drama, 19th European Drama, 20th Century European Drama, Melodrama and 19th Century British Theatre, 20th Century British Theatre, 20th Century American Drama, Women's Theatre and Modernism.

Also available as a Joint Honours degree with English.

BA Hons Drama
University of Manchester

"We are concerned with the study of the play in performance as well as on the printed page, which makes us different from other disciplines which study dramatic literature. Our courses are designed to help us understand the various social, philosophical, religious and political conditions that inspire the production of theatrical activity in its many and varied forms. But we must also consider the audience for which a play was written, the type of theatre in which it was intended to be performed, and the various technical problems the play might present to actors and directors. We must also make comparison with similar kinds of theatre in other cultures and countries."

Year 1: Foundation year covering basic concepts, a survey of key plays selected from an historical period, a survey of selected key ideas about theatre and its function in society, the practical exploration of performance methods and theatre crafts,
Years 2 & 3: Choice from range of options which may include, for example, Theatre in Education; Film; Cross Dressing in the Theatre; Nineteenth Century Popular Theatre; Radical Theatre 1920/40; Quasi-Theatrical Leisure; Performance Studies; Theatre Design.

Grades: BB/BCC

Also available with English or French as Double Honours (4 Years) or with German or Italian as Joint Honours degrees, Grades BBC.

BA Hons Drama and Theatre Studies
Middlesex University

"This award allows students the opportunity to engage in an intensive specialist study of modern drama and theatre as a living art form offering the possibility of more extensive practical exploration of a wide range of material than is possible on the multidisciplinary programme. Drama is approached as a subject which enhances and illuminates personal experience and expression, concentrating on the period from the late nineteenth century to the present day. Theatre forms are studied in depth, with some examination of television film and radio drama."

Courses include: Introductory and foundation course; Theatre production; Modern drama in theory and practice; Shakespeare and his contemporaries; Contemporary theatre; Modern American drama; Contemporary American theatre; Contemporary television drama,; Comedy; Black theatre; Approaches to physical theatre; The director and the stage; Creative self-expression; Proposition module; Acting; Vocal skills; Broadcasting skills; storytelling; Directing skills; Intensive theatre project; Theatre design; Technical theatre; Theatre arts internship.

BA Hons Performing Arts
University of Northumbria

"The Performing Arts Course focuses on the arts and their relationship to culture and society. It is intended to provide opportunities for students to explore the practice of the arts, with emphasis on a particular art form, and to formulate views of the roles and potential of the arts in the community, in the lives of individuals and in contemporary society generally. This is achieved through practical work, both within the institution and in the community, informed by cultural studies relating the arts to social contexts, and providing a framework against which personal philosophy and practice can develop."

Year 1: Development of appropriate creative and analytical skills relevant to future work in selected locations. Examining codes of communication and Course concerns. Establishing shred practical and critical vocabularies/codes, informed by student experiences and interests of relevance to the Course.
Year 2: Taking art to/making arts for communities - through the further development of skills and understandings appropriate to community based arts work. Examining art practices and contexts. Investigating the relationships between the arts and the contexts in which they are practised.
Year 3: Making art for/with communities - through the mounting of substantial student designed community based projects. Examining professional practices relevant to the Course. Exploring the implications of/in practice of selected 'models' of professional work in the design/operation of community-based arts projects.

BA Hons Drama & Theatre Studies
Roehampton Institute

"The study of Drama at degree level must be both academic and practical. Throughout the programme you will meet theoretical questions about the nature of drama and theatre. Why do we have performers, audiences, theatre? What are the functions of drama as a medium of communication within a culture or a society? What distinguishes the study of drama from the study of other kinds of written or verbal communication, or other kinds of performance art? What is the relationship between the drama of the past and that of the present? What are the uses of drama and theatre in education and society? Above all, if we are to derive maximum advantage from Drama's almost unique ability among traditional arts subjects to offer training in both individual inquiry of high academic rigour and sustained group exploration of practical activities, then a consistent emphasis must be placed on their interdependence throughout a student's educational career. We therefore approach academic, historical, theoretical and practical forms of study as complementary methods of gaining and articulating a knowledge of drama."

Foundation courses: Approaches to Drama, Dramaturgy and Textual Analysis, Theatre and Society, Performance Analysis, Performance Project, Film and Television Analysis.
Options from: Applied drama and theatre skills, Modern and Renaissance theatre studies, Community Theatre, Writing for the Theatre and Associated Media, New Developments in American Theatre, Representing Women: Feminist Perspectives, Revolutionary Theatre, Contemporary Television Drama, Television Drama Production, Aspects of Design and Technical Theatre, Special Study in theatre Practice.

Also available as a Joint Honours degree with: Art, Biology, Business Studies, Dance, Education, English, English Language, Environmental Studies, French, Geography, History, Music, Psychology, Sociology, Theology and Religions Studies, Women's Studies.

BA Drama + Theatre Studies
Royal Holloway and Bedford New College, University of London

"The course is grounded in the belief that students do their best work when challenged to develop imaginative and practical abilities alongside their critical and analytical skills.. The location of the teaching rooms, studio theatre and workshops under the same roof makes for maximum efficiency in the integration of theoretical and practical work. All students participate in workshops and in departmental productions, where they are encouraged to develop their understanding and appreciation of widely differing traditions of dramatic performance."

Courses include: Origins of Drama (this, uniquely, includes Oriental theatre such as Japanese Noh), Shakespeare or Renaissance Theatre, Popular Theatre, Modern Drama, History of Film and a Special subject Option, which could include Adaptations of Shakespeare on Stage and Film, Study of a special author, school, director or theatrical innovator, Music and Theatre, Dance Drama, Scene Design, Costume and Masks, Lighting, Electronics and Sound, Television Drama, Theory and Practise of Performance, Directors' Course, Playwrights' Course.

Grades: ABC

BA Joint Honours, Drama and Theatre Studies plus English, Music, French or Classical Studies

BA Hons Drama
St Mary's College

"The overall objective of the courses is to provide and integrated programme of practical and theoretical studies which form a strong basis for a wide variety of careers. The Department has a modern and versatile theatre and a reputation for imaginative and adventurous productions. Strong links are maintained with the professional theatre and the Department engages distinguished professional visiting lecturers to the various courses. Professional companies perform in College and lectures, seminars and practical workshops follow visits to the theatre."

Year 1: Practical Foundation Course, Drama Foundation Course, Production
Year 2: Art and Techniques of Theatre and Television, Critical Theory, The Living Theatre, Shakespeare in Performance, British Television Drama.
Year 3: The Actor as Dramaturge, Practical Direction for Television, Avant-Garde Theatre, Gender and Sexual Politics in Contemporary Theatre, Popular Theatre, Theatre of Commitment, American Drama 1920-60, Chekhov, Stanislavsky and Meyerhold, Farce, Tragedy, Policy and Strategies for the Contemporary Theatre, Creative Writing, Dramatic Criticism and Dissertation.

Grades: CC

BA Hons Combined Honours Drama + English, Mathematics, Irish Studies, Geography, Theology and Religious Studies, Chemistry, Classical Studies, Sociology, Sport Science/Physical Education

BA Hons Theatre Studies
University of Ulster
"The programme places strong emphasis on the value of teamwork and enterprise. Over the duration of the course students progressively assume individual and collective responsibilities, where the processes of making and managing theatre constitute a central focus fro the expressive and creative energies of the students. A salient feature of the course is the wide range of assessments used in helping a student to build up a lively profile; and the ideal 'theatre' students is one who learns to devise and apply resourceful and intelligent solutions to theoretical and practical problems. Students can expect to develop a level of practical proficiency with specialist options in Stage Management, Theatre Technologies, Theatre Administration and Press, Publicity and Print."

Also available BA Humanities Combined: Theatre Studies plus Asian Studies, English, European Studies, French, Geography, German, History, Irish, Media Studies, Philosophy.

BA Theatre Studies and Dramatic Arts
University of Warwick
"At undergraduate level, one of the distinguishing features of Theatre Studies at Warwick is the strong emphasis placed on the study of the modern period. Students are introduced to the work of modern theatre practitioners and playwrights and are encouraged to build their own critical and creative responses to the contemporary theatre and tits achievements. At the same time, a comprehensive grounding is offered in the discipline of European theatre history and dramatic criticism so that judgements may be made in the context of historical

development and change. The course down not attempt to provide comprehensive coverage of theatre history and the development of the drama. it does, however, examine drama and performance outside the bounds of conventional literary studies. The aim is specifically to provide students with the abilities needed to investigate, analyse and criticise the theatre of our time, and more generally provide a thorough basis for the understanding and critical appreciation of a wide variety of theatrical experience."

Year 1: Playhouse and Performance (I); Theatre and its context; Modern British Theatre; Introduction to Performance Skills.
Year 2: Playhouse and production (II); Experimental and Innovative theatre (I), Options from Texts and Performance, Theatre in the Community; Television Studio Performance, or an outside course.
Year 3: Experimental and Innovative Theatre (II), Options from courses that may include The Musical since 1939; Radio Drama; Ancient drama on the Modern Stage; Theatre in Education, Drama and the Scripted play; American Experimental performance.

Grades: BBC

Available in Joint honours with English, French, Italian.

BA Hons Theatre Studies
University of Wolverhampton
Courses available include: Performance skills and the Language of Theatre; Twentieth Century Practitioners; Drama and Mass Communication; Devising for the Theatre; World Theatre; TV Drama in Production; Applied Drama; Projects

and Ply Productions; Renaissance Drama in Performance; Modern Drama; Critical Issues in Drama and Theatre.

Also available as part of a combined course with some 83 options including: American Studies, Business, Computer Aided Design, Dance, English, French, German. History, Media and Communications, Music, Photography, Russian, Spanish.

BA Combined Studies
(Drama not available as a single subject)

BA Hons Visual and Performing Arts
University of Brighton

"This original and imaginative course consists of three complementary areas of study which are entitled Visual Art, Performance and Historical and Related Subjects. The setting of these three course components in coincidence with each other will provide students with opportunities to: investigate some of the possibilities that can arise from various relationships between the arts; appreciate the general mutuality of theoretical and practical work in the arts and the importance of practice on the course that is informed and supported by knowledge of History and Theory; co-operate with other students in group activities and take responsibility for their own individual programmes of work."

Years 1-3: Visual Art: induction courses in drawing, painting, print-making, three dimensional structures, video/audio media. Historical Studies. Dance Option: taken within visual imagery, projected lighting and sound of dance theatre. Includes dance composition, performance and critical study. Music Option: Includes Musical skills, ensemble work, recording and electronic techniques. Theatre Option: Includes performance, production, critical analysis.

BA Hons Combined Subjects
Chester College

"Emphasis is placed upon student-directed investigation and areas of particular student interest and/or strength. Modes of assessment are varied, allowing fusion of the theoretical and the practical."

Years 1-3: Fundamentals: Communication skills & Dramatic form.
Playwright and Practitioner: Realist/Naturalist approaches, Alternative approaches, Drama and Theatre in the Community (includes introduction to TV methods).
Culminations: Shakespeare, Study of a Playwright, Movement, Practitioner or Genre, Options chosen from Ply-writing, Directing, Design, Improvisation, Dissertation.

Grades: 12 points minimum

To be combined with Art, Biological Studies, Computer Science and Information Technology, English Literature, French, Geography, History, Maths, Psychology, Theology and Religious Studies, Physical Education and Sports Sciences.

BA Hons Creative Arts
Crewe and Alsager CHE

"This art course affords students the opportunity to pursue normally TWO of the Creative Arts subjects (Dance, Drama, Music, Visual Arts and Writing) but it is distinguished by a common core - the equivalent of a third subject- known as Integrated Arts. An emphasis is placed upon the relationship between theory and practice in the arts and their is room for students to devise their own work."

Years 1 & 2: Drama Workshop (Practical) - vocal and physical techniques, performance conventions from a range of contrasting periods, Stanislavski, Classical Naturalism. Options from designing for the theatre, directing for the theatre, writing for the theatre. Theatre Studies (Theory) - modern playscripts and their cultural context, period plays in performance. Performance analysis and criticism.
Year 3: Drama Workshop (Practical) - Physical and Visual Theatre, documentary/political theatre, Directing for the theatre. Television Drama Studies. Theatre Studies (Theory) - Post 1956 British and European theatre plus options.

BA Theatre Studies and Communication Arts University of Huddersfield

"BA Communication Arts is an interdisciplinary degree course offering students a choice of four programmes of study. The students from the different programmes work together in the common Core Studies that have two major aims: to provide a detailed understanding of the processes of human communications; and to develop a wide range of individual skills through practical activities. These skills include the analysis, organisation and presentation of information and ideas in the form of writing, speech, and pictures; the use of a wide variety of media technologies; and direct awareness of the responsibilities and roles of professional communicators."

Year 1: Language in Use, Media Studies, Writing and Performance, Technology and Information, study in unfamiliar language (e.g. Italian, Spanish, Japanese), Theatre Form, Approaches to Acting.
Year 2: Language in Use, Media Studies, Writing and Performance, Technology and Information, Drama and Society, Theories and Models of Theatrical Production.

Year 3: Media and Communication Policy, Media and Communication Theory, Applied Studies, Work related Project, Theatrical means and Performance Style, Dramatic Essays.

BA Hons Visual and Performed Arts
University of Kent

"This is a combined subjects course specially designed for students who have a broad interest in the arts and who do not wish to restrict their studies to any one discipline."

Year 1-3: Core courses: Reading the Image, Patronage and Cultural Organisation in Twentieth Century Britain. Selection of courses from History and Theory of Art with either selection of courses from Film Studies or Drama degree programmes.

Grades: BCC

BA Hons Performance Arts
Middlesex University

"The course is designed chiefly for those who wish to study one performance art (dance, drama or music) in depth while developing their skills in the other two. Additionally, interdisciplinary study stresses the interdependence of the performance arts and emphasises creative and experimental work. Students may also extend their study of performance into related areas such as visual arts, mime, media (including video production), arts in education, literature, community work and arts management."

Performance Studies: taken by all students and includes taught courses and a programme of performances. They may

include: choreography, costume, stage management, composition, accompaniment, business or hours management.
Drama: Approaches to acting and the technical arts. Study of Dramatic literature and modern practitioners. Final year options.
Dance: Choreography, performance and appreciation. Dance technique classes - classical ballet, Cunningham, Humpphrey-based, Graham-based, Release, Pilates and jazz. Critical studies. Final year options, which could include dance performance, choreography and dance in society.
Music: Performing, composing and analytical study. Tuition on two instruments,. Specialist final year options could include composition, performance and aesthetic appreciation and criticism.
Supporting Studies: Could include: visual arts, mime, media, literature, community work, arts in education and administration.

BA Hons Combined Studies
Nene College

"Drama offers a unique blend of academic study and practical experience; it encourages enquiry and invites active participation. The question 'What make theatre alive?' is the central concern, and some of the answers are provided through practical activities which involve movement, dance, language, song and design, and which are used to discover dramatic forms in action. Some of the answers come through a study of theatre history combined with work on play-texts to offer evidence for the re-creation of living performances."

Level 1: Induction course; examination of play-texts seen in performance; experimentation through practical work with

theatrical styles and performance techniques. Drama on Television.
Level 2: Courses include Dramatic Genres and Styles, Jacobean Theatre, Naturalism in 19th Century Theatre, Women's Plays since 1968. Techniques of Composition, Group devised performances.
Level 3: Developments in Modern and European Drama from 1900 to the Present Day. Practical work is student led or devised.

Recommended combinations include English Studies, American Studies, Art and Design, Music, Sport and Recreation Studies, Psychology, Media and Popular Culture.

BA Hons Creative Arts
Nottingham Polytechnic

"Creative Arts, as the name suggests, is primarily about contemporary 'creativity' and the course places a considerable emphasis upon original and innovative practical work in each of its three main disciplines (music, visual arts, performance). 'Artists' (in the general sense of the word, be they writer, painter, composer, sculptor, performer, director, etc.) are not isolated individuals working outside of an historical and cultural context, but are sensitive and reactive to the issues of the day, seeking means to express their thoughts, emotions, fears and visions through a variety of media and art forms. This course offers artists who wish to learn about and express their creativity through media of music, performance and visual arts, the opportunity to develop their creative ideas, their skills and techniques and their understanding of the place of the arts in our present and future society."

Year 1 & 2: All students study two of the three major subject areas. Critical studies.
Year 3: Students opt to specialise in one area. Critical studies.

BA Combined Studies
Queen Mary and Westfield College
in association with the Central School of Speech and Drama

"Drama, is taught in collaboration with the Central School of Speech and Drama. Students are registered as undergraduates of the University of London, but also have the privileges of membership of the Central School. Speech and movement, acting, directing and design are studied in relation to plays of different periods and styles. There are general courses on the history of the theatre from classical to modern times and on dramatic theory and criticism. Special subjects are chosen for concentrated study, and there is great emphasis on project work individually selected by each undergraduate."

Courses available: English and Drama, French and Drama, German and Drama, Hispanic Studies and Drama, Russian and Drama.

Grades required: 20 points

BA Combined Arts
University of Plymouth

"The syllabus for this study area has been created with the aim of giving students and staff the opportunity to explore the relationship between a wide spectrum of performance traditions. Theatre Arts and Drama is about creativity, analysis and practical performance. While it explores work in the theatre, dance, film and video, ritual circus and community arts, etc., its essence lies in evaluating the relationship between performer and audience so that "Performance" is the organising concept for our syllabus. We try to blur the boundaries of disciplines and develop new ways of thinking about performance. Our perspective is inter-cultural. Areas of concentration include elements of performance, structures of performance arts in the community, practical issues in performance, cross cultural studies, advanced performance."

Courses available: Theatre Arts and Drama with English, Contemporary History, Media, Design Arts, Art History, Education Studies.

BA Hons Drama and Television
University College of Ripon and York St John

"Practical work is essential to all our courses. You learn Through practice. at the same time, you are expected to evaluate what you do in the light of critical studies of theory and the work of established practitioners. Our courses are more about understanding the nature of drama and television than about acquiring technical skills."

Year 1: Making Images: moving imagery, live performance, still imagery, project.
Drama Option:
Year 2 & 3: Making theatre and making television. Theatre forms, Theatre Practice, New Theatre
Television Option:
Years 2 & 3: Making theatre and making television. Making TV for an audience, Making Documentaries or Making Television Drama, Independent Video.

The course may be combined with American Studies, Art, English or Physical Education.

BA Hons English with Theatre Studies
University of Sussex

"This is a new degree in the School of English and American Studies. It gives prominence to drama, emphasising the importance of considering plays as works from performance in the theatre, and not merely texts to be read in private."

Year 1: Introduction to Theatre Studies, Approaches to English.
Year 2: Drama (practical workshop element), Period of English Literature.
Year 3: Shakespeare or Special Author, or Special Subject, American Drama or Theory, Performance and Representation.

BA Humanities
West London Institute

"The major in Modern Drama Studies is a specialist course in twentieth century performance. The work explores a range of naturalistic and non-naturalistic approaches. There is a strong emphasis on the European repertoire, although you are encouraged to pursue interests relating to other modern cultures."

Courses include: a year long acting course with intensive training in voice and movement skills, a year long course in directing, acting and design within specially formed companies, and a final production where students mainly specialise

in either directing or acting (but could include design or writing for example).
Options include: laboratory theatre, critical studies, work placements in theatre management, local authority centres and companies.

The UK Centre for EAST, the European Association of Students of Theatre is based at the Institute. European work and contacts are a key part of development activity.

Degree may be taken with choice of options from Art, American Studies, Business Studies, Computer Studies, Earth Sciences, English, Film and TV Studies, Geography and Environmental issues, Geology, History, Leisure Management, Music, Religious Studies.

BA Combined Studies
Worcester College
"The course has three main feature: textual analysis, study of original performance contexts; and practical exploration of drama in performance."

Courses include: Basic practical course; study of post-war British plays; Elizabethan/Jacobean drama, the Women's movement in twentieth century theatre, late nineteenth century naturalism, twentieth century documentary drama, Shakespeare.

Two component courses are studied for three years, and one for two years. Courses include: Aspects of Modern World History, Biological Perspectives, Computer Applications, Education Studies, General Psychology, Geography: Earth Studies or Human Studies, Literary Perspectives (English

Literature), Literature and Life in Shakespeare's England, Nineteenth Century Literature, Sociology, Studies in British History, the Musical Experience.

Combined Courses Index
Drama +....

BA DRAMA + AFRICAN & CARIBBEAN STUDIES
University of Kent

BA DRAMA + AMERICAN STUDIES
University College of Wales, Aberystwyth
University of East Anglia
University of Hull
University of Kent
King Alfred's College
Nene College
University College of Ripon and York St John
West London Institute
University of Wolverhampton

BA DRAMA + ART
University College of Wales, Aberystwyth
Chester College
De Montfort University
University of Glamorgan
John Moores University
Nene College
University College of Ripon and York St John
Roehampton Institute
West London Institute

BA DRAMA + ART HISTORY
University College of Wales, Aberystwyth

University of Birmingham
De Montfort University
Glasgow University
King Alfred's College
University of Plymouth

DRAMA + ARTS MANAGEMENT
Dartington College of Arts
De Montfort University

DRAMA + ASIAN STUDIES
University of Ulster

DRAMA + BIOLOGY
Chester College
Roehampton Institute
Worcester College

DRAMA + BUSINESS
John Moores University
Roehampton Institute
West London Institute
University of Wolverhampton

DRAMA + CLASSICAL STUDIES
University College of Wales, Aberystwyth
University of Kent
St Mary's College

DRAMA + COMPUTING
Chester College
University of Kent
King Alfred's College

West London Institute
Worcester College

DRAMA + COMPUTER AIDED DESIGN
University of Wolverhampton

DRAMA + DANCE
John Moores University
Middlesex University
Roehampton Institute

DRAMA + DESIGN
University of Plymouth

DRAMA + EARTH SCIENCES
West London Institute

DRAMA + EDUCATION
University College of Wales, Aberystwyth
Goldsmiths' College
King Alfred's College
Lancaster University
Roehampton Institute
University of Plymouth
Worcester College

DRAMA + ENGLISH
University College of Wales, Aberystwyth
University of Birmingham
University of Bristol
Central/Queen Mary and Westfield
Chester College
De Montfort University

University of East Anglia
University of Exeter
University of Glamorgan
Glasgow University
Goldsmiths' College
University of Hull
University of Kent
King Alfred's College
Lancaster University
Loughborough University
University of Manchester
Nene College
University of Plymouth
University College of Ripon and York St John
Roehampton Institute
St Mary's College
University of Ulster
West London Institute
University of Wolverhampton
Worcester College

DRAMA + ENVIRONMENTAL STUDIES
John Moores University
King Alfred's College
Roehampton Institute

DRAMA + EUROPEAN STUDIES
John Moores University
University of Ulster

DRAMA + FILM
University of East Anglia
Glasgow University

University of Kent
King Alfred's College
West London Institute

DRAMA + FRENCH
University College of Wales, Aberystwyth
University of Birmingham
University of Bristol
Central/Queen Mary and Westfield
Chester College
University of Glamorgan
Glasgow University
University of Hull
John Moores University
University of Kent
Lancaster University
University of Manchester
Roehampton Institute
University of Ulster
University of Wolverhampton

DRAMA + GEOGRAPHY
University College of Wales, Aberystwyth
Chester College
University of Glamorgan
Glasgow University
King Alfred's College
Roehampton Institute
St Mary's College
University of Ulster
West London Institute
Worcester College

DRAMA + GEOLOGY
West London Institute

DRAMA + GERMAN
University College of Wales, Aberystwyth
University of Birmingham
University of Bristol
Central/Queen Mary and Westfield
University of Exeter
University of Glamorgan
Glasgow University
University of Hull
John Moores University
University of Kent
Lancaster University
University of Manchester
University of Ulster
University of Wolverhampton

DRAMA + GREEK
University of Birmingham
University of Kent

DRAMA + HISTORY
University College of Wales, Aberystwyth
University of Birmingham
Chester College
De Montfort University
University of East Anglia
Glasgow University
John Moores University
University of Kent
King Alfred's College

University of Plymouth
Roehampton Institute
University of Ulster
West London Institute
University of Wolverhampton
Worcester College

DRAMA + INFORMATION AND LIBRARY STUDIES
University College of Wales, Aberystwyth

DRAMA + IRISH
University College of Wales, Aberystwyth
St Mary's College
University of Ulster

DRAMA + ITALIAN
University College of Wales, Aberystwyth
University of Birmingham
University of Bristol
Glasgow University
University of Hull
University of Kent
Lancaster University
University of Manchester

DRAMA + JAPANESE
John Moores University
King Alfred's College

DRAMA + LATIN
University of Birmingham
University of Kent

DRAMA + LAW
John Moores University

DRAMA + LEISURE STUDIES
West London Institute

DRAMA + MATHEMATICS
University College of Wales, Aberystwyth
Chester College
St Mary's College

DRAMA + MEDIA STUDIES
University of Birmingham
University of Glamorgan
University of Hull
John Moores University
King Alfred's College
Nene College
University of Plymouth
University of Ulster
University of Wolverhampton

DRAMA + MUSIC
University of Birmingham
Dartington College of Arts
Glasgow University
University of Hull
Nene College
Roehampton Institute
West London Institute
University of Wolverhampton
Worcester College

DRAMA + PHILOSOPHY
University of Glamorgan
Glasgow University
John Moores University
University of Kent
University of Ulster

DRAMA + PHOTOGRAPHY
University of Wolverhampton

DRAMA + POLITICS
De Montfort University
Glasgow University
John Moores University
King Alfred's College

DRAMA + PORTUGUESE
University of Birmingham

DRAMA + PSYCHOLOGY
Chester College
University of Glamorgan
Glasgow University
Nene College
Roehampton Institute
Worcester College

DRAMA + RELIGIOUS STUDIES
Chester College
University of Glamorgan
University of Hull
University of Kent
King Alfred's College

Lancaster University
Roehampton Institute
St Mary's College
West London Institute

DRAMA + RUSSIAN
University of Birmingham
Central/Queen Mary and Westfield
John Moores University
University of Wolverhampton

DRAMA + SOCIOLOGY
University of Glamorgan
Glasgow University
John Moores University
Roehampton Institute
St Mary's College
Worcester College

DRAMA + SPANISH
University College of Wales Aberystwyth
University of Birmingham
University of Bristol
Central/Queen Mary Westfield
University of Exeter
University of Glamorgan
John Moores University
University of Wolverhampton

DRAMA + SPORT
University of Birmingham
Chester College
John Moores University

Nene College
University College of Ripon and York St John
St Mary's College

DRAMA + VISUAL PERFORMANCE
Dartington College of Arts

DRAMA + WELSH
BA Drama + Welsh
University College of Wales Aberystwyth
University of Glamorgan

DRAMA + WOMEN'S STUDIES
University of Glamorgan
John Moores University
Roehampton Institute

FILM STUDIES

BA Hons Photographic Studies
University of Derby
"The degree is a practical visual arts course, with photography and allied subjects as the principal means of expression. The main concern of the course is image-making; you will be encouraged to work creatively with all aspects of photography to include film/video, printmaking, audio-visual, experimental and historical photographic processes."

Years 1/2: Concentrates on the acquisition of knowledge and skills of the photographic arts. Critical Studies: Film, History of Photography, Philosophical approaches to Art and Language, Photographic Theory.
Years 2/3: Individual study of an area of photographic arts.
Options:
Academic Route: Concentration on critical studies and theoretical issues.
Film and Video: Provides the major component of studies from start of the degree.

BA Hons History and Theory of Film and Visual Media
Manchester Metropolitan University
"A modular programme offering historical and critical study of film and of photography, graphics, book illustration, magazine design and prints, advertising, cartooning and comics etc. The visual media are studied in the context of social and

political history in Europe and American and related to artistic and cultural traditions."

Years 1-3: Placements and practical projects. Extensive use of the exceptional study resources for film and the media in the University and the region.

BA Hons Illustration and Animation
Manchester Metropolitan University

"The course offers students the opportunity to explore, experience and research the field of image creation and generation and their impact on communication problem solving. The course will present opportunities for students to work with and alongside students from other related disciplines in art and design. Other levels will develop skills and abilities in model-making and various forms of animation. Great significance is attached to the importance of contextual and professional studies."

BA Hons Television Production and Design
Manchester Metropolitan University

"The course aims to provide a basic foundation of experience in the principles of direction and production design through practice in the arts and skills of television. This is done principally by interpreting a given message and presenting a statement for a defined audience. The course is structured to develop the students ability to organise and direct the production or design of programmes, who can initiate and realise ideas and respond to the ideas of others in an intelligent, sensitive and imaginative way. Students are encouraged to develop their intellectual and imaginative potential through broadly based theoretical studies and creative practice. Technical and operational skills are developed to support this but are not seen as the main aim of the course."

BA Hons Photography, Film and Television
Napier University

"The course prepares graduates to enter the profession of photography or the film and television industry and related areas. Great emphasis is laid on using these medium as a form of visual expression and communication. While it is important in a course of this nature for students to develop high levels of professional skill, it is also recognised that the development of individual creativity is of equal importance. The course is broad in nature and encompasses the study of the wide range of visual media including stills photography, film, television, multivision and graphic design. Other subjects studied within the course include communication studies, historical studies and business studies. The course has a common first year and then follows two separate pathways; one with the Still Image and the other with the Moving Image."

Year 1: Photographic studies, communication studio, audio visual media, graphic design, historical studies, video production.
Year 2: Film and television production, computer graphics, electronic imaging, communication studies, historical studies.
Year 3: Film and television production, communication studies, computer graphics, electronic imaging, historical studies, business studies.
Year 4: Film and television production, communication studies, computer graphics, electronic imaging, historical studies, business studies.

Grades CD plus portfolio or showreel.

BA Hons Film and Photography
Newport School of Art and Design
(Gwent College of Higher Education)

"Film, Photography and the associated new technologies of moving and still video imaging are the principal concerns of the degree. It is recognised that the acquisition of practical skills and the development of a visual vocabulary results from consistent practice and critical evaluation. With this in mind, the programme examines and develops related issues in film, photography, video and digital imagery."

Students must choose two Studio subjects which include: Animation, Biovisual Studies (Wildlife Film and Illustration), Documentary Photography, Film and Video, Photomedia, Telemedia (Computing in Art, Video, Sound and Light Systems), Writing and Publishing, and one Theory subject from: Design Theory and History, Film and Cinema Studies, Media Theory and History, History and Theory of Photography. Students may choose to take Documentary Photography or Film and Video as double studio subjects.

BA Film and Drama
University of Reading

"The course ranges across the history of the cinema and of the drama of the corresponding period (approximately the last hundred years) with a particular focus on European and American Traditions. The central aim is to develop critical understanding. The emphasis is therefore on the close study of films and plays and on consideration of critical debates and competing theories which have influenced discussion of film and drama."

Years 1 & 2: Core subjects: Studies of European film and drama from naturalism to modernism, issues of authorship in film, drama and television. Options: American cinema, American theatre, British cinema, British Theatre. Plus practical work in film and drama.

Year 3: Core subjects: Alternative forms in film and drama, the problems posed by the concept of realism. Options: documentary, Irish Theatre, third world cinema, east European theatre, television drama. Plus practical work in film and drama including independent project e.g. a dissertation, drama production, film, video or a combination of practical presentation and critical writing.

BA Combined Hons Film and Drama with:
English, Sociology, French, Italian or German

Grades: BBC. English Literature or Theatre Studies preferred.

BA Hons Drama and Television
University College of Ripon and York St John

"Practical work is essential to all our courses. You learn Through practice. at the same time, you are expected to evaluate what you do in the light of critical studies of theory and the work of established practitioners. Our courses are more about understanding the nature of drama and television than about acquiring technical skills."

Year 1: Making Images: moving imagery, live performance, still imagery, project.

Drama Option:
Year 2 & 3: Making theatre and making television. Theatre forms, Theatre Practice, New Theatre
Television Option:
Years 2 & 3: Making theatre and making television. Making TV for an audience, Making Documentaries or Making Television Drama, Independent Video.

The course may be combined with American Studies, Art, English or Physical Education.

BA Hons Television and Radio
University of Salford
"This course comprises a common core of three major fields of study extending throughout the three years: Media, Culture and Society; Production Theory and Practice; Projects - Production and Analysis. There is a strong emphasis upon practical work much of which is broadcast oriented. Towards the end of the second year students choose academic options to feed into the third year dissertation and practical work. The final year allows greater specialisation and an individual choice of study with emphasis on student-led work."

BA Hons Film Studies
Sheffield City Polytechnic
"The aims are to enable students to develop a detailed understanding of the history and development of the cinema, both as a distinctive form of cultural production and as an important component of the mass media, and to acquire a basic level of expertise in film production."

Year 1: Film and Media Contexts, Theories of Textual Analysis, Applied Textual Analysis, Introduction to Film History, Media Production, Skills.
Year 2: International Perspectives on the Media, Perspectives on Hollywood, Alternative Cinemas, Option, Film Production, Writing Skills.
Year 3: Film and Business, Special Study: British Cinema, Dissertation, Writing for the Media, Film Production, Arts and Media Administration.
Options can also be chosen from a range offered by other degree such as History of Art, Design and Film.

BA Film, Television and Radio Studies
Staffordshire University
"The main concern of the course is to promote the critical understanding of the media through a detailed analysis of the forms and processes of individual films, television programmes and radio programmes."

Year 1: History of Film, Television and Radio, Mass media Institutions, Formal and Critical Analysis, Writing for the Mass Media, Studio based project.
Year 2 : History of Film, Television and Radio, Mass Media Institutions, Writing for the Mass Media, Documentary News and Current Affairs, Representation and Stereotyping, Music and the Audio Visual Media, Art Cinema and the Tradition of Quality, Popular Film Television and Radio Comedy, Television and Advertising. 5 week Industrial/Professional Placement.
Year 3: Contemporary Mass Media: Issues of Professional Practice. Two Options chosen from: British Popular film and Broadcast drama; Culture, Imperialism and the Developing

World; Politics, Film and the Media in East/Central Europe; Dissertation or Script Writing Project.

BA Hons Film and Media Studies
University of Stirling

"Teaching of the subject at Stirling concentrates on critical and theoretical work centring on film, television, radio and the press. A limited amount of practical work is available."

Year 1: Elements of Communication; The moving Image; The British Media.

Year 2 & 3: Media Theory I: Concepts and Methods; Media Theory II: Realism and Narrative; Sociology of Journalism. Options selected from: Authorship in the cinema; Genre in Hollywood (the Western); John Grierson and documentary analysis; Television and Radio drama; Advertising; Print journalism and the UK press; the new German Cinema; Psychoanalysis and cinema; Radio: industry and culture; Elements of radio journalism; Research methodology; Elements of television journalism; Contemporary cultural theory; Documentary production among others.

May be taken as a combined honours course with: Business Studies, Economics, English Studies, French, German, History, Japanese Language, Marketing, Philosophy, Political Studies, Psychology, Religious Studies, Sociology, Spanish.

BA Hons Film and Video
West Surrey College of Art and Design

"This lively and exciting course combines practical training in the use of film and video with a strong theoretical component. Creative and technical developments and subjects of current debate in this fast moving area are taken into account., Initiative, independent study and creative ability are emphasised throughout the course."

Courses include: Research techniques and budgeting, Scriptwriting, 16mm and Video cameras, Sync Sound recording and Mixing, Set design and Construction, Studio and Location Lighting, Directing of Actors, Picture and Sound Editing, Viewing and Analysis of Rushes, All aspects of Post-Production, Information Technology, Film, Television and Video History, Theory and Criticism an cultural Studies, Business, Professional, Legal and Employment Studies.

Accredited by ACTT (graduates become full members on getting a job).
Recognised by BKSTS.

BA Hons Film and Literature
Warwick University
"The cinema was the first great new art from of the twentieth century; it has also, especially in its popular, commercial areas, been of central significance in the development of Western culture. Part of the aim of this degree is to define and explore the creative potentialities of the film, examining critically the achievements of its major practitioners and the various theories of film that have been elaborated. There is also consideration of the sociological and ideological aspects of cinema, relating films to the particular cultures and period in which they were produced exploring the significance of genres and stars and the role of technology and economics. The literature courses offer a broad coverage of English, European and American literature, primarily of the nineteenth and twentieth centuries, with works selected from mass and popular litera-

ture as well as established literary tradition. The major emphasis is place on critical training in the reading of poetry, prose and drama and the theoretical and methodological issues raised by the study of literary texts."

Year 1: Film studies, Basic Issues and Methods; Introduction to Literary Studies; Aspects of Modern French an German Literature.
Year 2: The Hollywood Cinema; Aspects of European Cinema; Forms of Narrative; American Literature.
Year 3: Film Aesthetics; Naturalism; Options in Film and Literature.

Grades: BBB

Also available as Joint Hons with French and Italian.

BA Film Video and Photographic Arts
University of Westminster
"This is essentially a joint course in the creative practice and theoretical and critical study of either film and television or photography and multi-media. By their nature, the two pathways are multi disciplinary, and have characteristics which relate them to traditions in both the arts and the mass media. They are broad based, with concerns which range from the practical and technical skills to consideration of cultural and, social and critical issues of production, consumption and interpretation. The principal aim is to provide you with a sound academic knowledge and understanding of the film and photographic media, together with confident practical abilities to produce and communicate through them. The u underlying assumptions of this theory and practice course are that media practice requires full aware awareness of critical

and theoretical issues, and that media study need to be related to the processes and constraints of practice."

Recognised by BECTU/ACTT, giving full ACTT member status to graduates on obtaining an ACTT grade job.

BA Hons Animation
West Surrey College of Art and Design
"This is the first degree course in animation in Europe. The course aims to train students to become practising animators capable of working in many different fields of the animation industry. The course is essentially practical, although theoretical studies are undertaken and closely related to practical work. Graduates are encouraged to produce clear, critical writing, to develop the ability to work with others and make informed decisions about their future careers, as well as contributing to an industry which is at an exciting stage of its development."

Courses include: History and Theory, Cultural Studies, Information Technology, Life Drawing, 2D and 3D animation, Computer Animation, Professional and Business Awareness.

Accredited by the ACTT (Graduates may become full members once they are offered employment).

BA Combined Studies
(where Film can not be studied as a single subject)

BA Hons Audio Visual Media Studies combined with another subject
University of Central Lancashire
"This course offers an opportunity to study such media as photography, tape/slide and video on a practical, workshop basis, with an equal proportion of lecture-based work. It is primarily Arts-oriented. Its aim is to enable students to study the Audio-Visual Media from a variety of viewpoints and in a number of contexts. For example, there are opportunities to examine the practice of making photographs and video programmes, as well as to explore the ways in which different groups in society use these media, and react to their presence in the world."

May only be taken as a joint or minor subject with some 50 plus subjects, including American Studies, Astronomy, Business, Languages, Design Studies, Education Studies, English, History, Journalism, Law, Management, Politics, Psychology, Public Relations, Sociology, Women's Studies.

BA Hons Modular Degree Scheme
University of Derby
"Film with Television Studies complements studies in the arts, humanities and social sciences. The emphasis is very much on

critique of films and so well developed skills in written communication are essential"

BA Hons Film and English Studies
University of East Anglia
"This programme allows you to combine the specialist study of film and television with an exploration of the cultural contexts within which these media developed in Britain."

English Studies e.g. Renaissance Culture, Eighteenth Century Writings, Austen, Popular Narratives, Romance and the Woman Writer, Contemporary Cultural Theories, Television.
Film Studies e.g.: Cinema before 1930, Classical Hollywood, Study of British cinema and television, Practical instruction in video and 8mm film leading to either an individual project or a critical dissertation.

BA Hons Film and American Studies (4 Years)
University of East Anglia
"This new programme allows you to combine the specialist study of film with an exploration of the literary, historical and political context within which it developed in America."

American Studies e.g.: The American City, The American 1920's, the Black American, Women in American Society, American Photography, The American Dram, American Cinema and its Genres.
Film Studies e.g.: Early American Cinema, Classical Hollywood Cinema, American Film and Society in the 1980s, Practical instruction in video and 8mm film leading to either an individual project or a dissertation.

MA Joint Hons Film and Television Studies
Glasgow University
The degree at Glasgow is modular with a wide choice of subjects and degree type - Single, Joint, Ordinary, Honours - depending on courses studied during the four years.

"This subject studies cinema and television as major forces within 20th century culture. The Ordinary class provides an introduction to techniques of film and television analysis, to aspects of film and television theory and form and to the changing structures of cinema and television as industries. The Higher Ordinary class extends this study with more specific topics, including authorship and genre in film and television, and the relationship of British cinema and television to questions of national culture. An introduction to video production techniques is available to students in this class. The Honours programme involves a combination of specialist options and compulsory 'core' courses, including a project-based practical element. All years of the course involve regular screenings which students are expected to attend."

Film and television Studies may be paired with one of 30 subjects for an Honours degree including English, French, Geography, German. Hispanic Studies, History, History of Art, Italian, Music, Philosophy, Politics, Psychology, Sociology, Theatre Studies.

BA Hons Joint/Combined degree Film and Video Studies
John Moores University
"Aims: To provide a critical and aesthetic understanding of film and video media. To develop students' analytical skills

in t the study of a wide range of film, and TV and video texts and the industries that produce them. To develop students' organisational, technical and creative skills in production."

Years 1-3: Core and option modules offered at three levels of specialisation in the areas of film studies and theory, television studies and theory, video production.

Preferred combinations are with Literature, Life and Thought, Drama, and Media and Cultural Studies although others are available.

BA Film Studies
University of Kent
"Film studies at Kent centre on the potentialities of cinema and its theoretical implications. Although we provide no practical traingin in the making of films, the programme offers you an ideal academic background for a career in any of the mass media."

Year 1-3: Narrative Cinema. The courses cover early, classic and recent films from all over the world. We put particular emphases on British and American cinema, and on the special aesthetic, political, commercial and industrial problems of an art of collective production and consumption.

Grades: BBC/BCC

Available as Combined Honours with : African & Caribbean Studies, Classical Civilisation; Comparative Literary Studies, Drama, English and American Literature, French, German, Greek, History, Italian, Latin, Linguistics, Philosophy, Theology and Religious Studies, Computing.

BA Hons Design
Staffordshire University
"You will specialise in one of eight options - either glass, ceramics, surface pattern, graphics, product design, photography, audio-visual communication or electronic instructional media - with the opportunity to work in the other options as appropriate. The wide range of staff and facilities provides a stimulating shared environment in which your design abilities can be developed, and encourages a wider and more imaginative approach to specialised work than would be the case on single subject course. As well as developing design abilities by project work, you learn how to exploit production methods, to provide for market needs, to perceive the historical and social context of design, to communicate ideas verbally and visually, and to understand the industrial and financial aspects of a professional career in design. It is possible to take European language studies in French, German or Italian as part of your course."

Photography includes: photojournalism, advertising, still life, fashion and landscape.

Audio visual communication aims to train flexible people who can work in entertainment, social or commercial persuasion, education and training.

BA Humanities - Film and Television Studies
West London Institute
"The courses combine to develop and promote theoretical and conceptual understanding as well as critical, creative and some practical skills. In addition, some of the modules are

designed to accommodate and even encourage a degree of analytical and practical cross-fertilisation between disciplines (for example the Visual Arts)."

Courses include: foundation studies, the language of the visual image, film production analysis, practical work (including still photography and desk top publishing) culminating in a video based project, Television as a critical study, film as an art form.

Can be taken as a minor subject with the major in American Studies, Business Studies, Drama, Earth Sciences or English.

Combined Studies Index - Film + ...

FILM + AFRICAN & CARIBBEAN STUDIES
University of Kent

FILM + AMERICAN STUDIES
University of East Anglia
University of Kent
University College of Ripon and York St John
West London Institute

FILM + ART
University College of Ripon and York St John

FILM + BUSINESS STUDIES
Stirling University
West London Institute

FILM + CLASSICS
University of Kent

FILM + COMPUTING
University of Kent

FILM + DRAMA
University of East Anglia
John Moores University
University of Kent
West London Institute

FILM + EARTH SCIENCES
West London Institute

FILM + ECONOMICS
Stirling University

FILM + ENGLISH
University of East Anglia
Glasgow University
University of Kent
University College of Ripon and York St John
University of Reading
Stirling University
University of Warwick
West London Institute

FILM + FRENCH
Glasgow University
University of Kent
University of Reading
Stirling University
University of Warwick

FILM + GERMAN
Glasgow University
University of Kent
University of Reading
Stirling University

FILM + GREEK
University of Kent

FILM + HISTORY
University of East Anglia
Glasgow University
University of Kent
Stirling University

FILM + ITALIAN
Glasgow University
University of Kent
University of Reading
University of Warwick

FILM + JAPANESE
Stirling University

FILM + LATIN
University of Kent

FILM + MARKETING
Stirling University

FILM + MEDIA
John Moores University

FILM + MUSIC
Glasgow University

FILM + PHILOSOPHY
Glasgow University
University of Kent
Stirling University

FILM + POLITICS
Glasgow University
Stirling University

FILM + PSYCHOLOGY
Glasgow University
Stirling University

FILM + RELIGIOUS STUDIES
University of Kent
Stirling University

FILM + SOCIOLOGY
Glasgow University
University of Reading
Stirling University

FILM + SPANISH
Glasgow University
Stirling University

FILM + SPORTS
University College of Ripon and York St John

Post-Graduate Diplomas

MA Cinema and Television Studies
Birkbeck College

"This course is offered in co-operation with the British Film Institute. It is designed to provide students with a sound grasp of the best in current scholarly and critical work in moving image studies, and to involve them in the full range o the BFI's activities towards the promotion of an active, forward-looking moving image culture in the UK."

Topics studied include: Textual analysis; the expanded and contracted text; virtue, value and institutions; contemporary documentary; Third Cinema, the Avant-Garde; audiences; and comparative historical studies - e.g. Russian cinema before and after 1917, the French New Wave. Placement at the BFI.

MA, Post graduate Certificate/Diploma Film and Television Studies
University of Derby

"The course is a taught, academic programme concerned with the study of film and television, and the institutions of cinema and broadcasting. Emphasis is given to the textual and contextual studies of the two media, and a thorough grounding in research methodology is provided.

Post-graduate Certificate: Critical Approaches to Classical Film and Television; Classical, Modernist and post-Classical Narration in Film and Television.

Post-graduate Diploma: Two options from: Audiences and Prime-Time Television; Early Cinema; Melodrama and Soaps; Other Practices, Other Readings; Television Drama, Series and Serials.

Masters: The above plus dissertation.

MLitt/MPhil Media Culture
John Logie Baird Centre
Universities of Glasgow and Strathclyde

"The study of contemporary media, involving both text and context, is an interdisciplinary field, drawing, at its most effective, on both the social sciences and the humanities for its theoretical perspectives and methodologies. Correspondingly, the Media and Culture Course is interdisciplinary in its intellectual direction, drawing principally on film and television theory, cultural studies, political economy and sociology, but offering students the opportunity to follow courses in literary theory, feminist studies, theatre studies and linguistics. Students are encouraged to develop not only an academic understanding of specific media (cinema, broadcasting, popular music, press) and the theoretical fields associated with them, but also a practical understanding of media institutions, production processes, and research methods. Within the limits of resources, the course offers some opportunity for practical work of video or super-8 film, and a central component of the course is an applied research project. Optional courses allow students to study particular topics in depth."

MA Video
Middlesex University

"This course enquires into the processes and outcome of professional video practice, providing the opportunity to think creatively and critically about video production in a rapidly changing industry. The course is designed to offer a programme of study in video fro graduates of any discipline; however prior video production experience is a necessary prerequisite for entry." The course comprises of four successive study areas: the Video Medium (systems of production, sound, image, editing and electronic processing), the Video Context (professional practices), the Video Production, the Creative Video Script.

MA/PG Dip Television Features and Documentary Production
University of Salford (in Association with Granada Television)

""""Despite the rapid commercialisation of so much of television Britain continues to produce documentaries and features of the highest calibre. However, in order to maintain these standards programme makers of the future have to be trained. This new programme is structured to allow applicants to specialise in one aspect of production - Camera, Sound or Editing or to focus on developing their skills as Director/ Producers or Researchers. The course focuses on the organisation, development and filming of six documentaries/features which will be broadcast by Granada TV should professional standards by meet. All students also attend modules on the changing shape of features and documentary and on production determinates."

MA/Post Graduate Diploma in Film Production (Fiction)
Sheffield City Polytechnic

"The course is primarily intended for students who have completed an undergraduate degree involving film and video practice, or some related activity (e.g. business studies for production, or theatre studies for direction). It is also for those already working in 'the industry' who wish to have further technical and creative development in theory chosen field."

The course accepts students in one of the following specialisation:
Director, Producer/Production Manager, Lighting Camera, Art Direction, Sound, Editing
The culmination of the course is the production of two short fiction films. This is sponsored by Yorkshire Television and are broadcast (if suitable). Additionally, six other 15-20 minute films are produced by the students over the year. For the MA the student must also submit a dissertation.

Media/Communication Studies

BSocSc Media, Culture and Society
University of Birmingham

"This degree is interdisciplinary in character and stands at a meeting point between the humanities and social sciences. It should appeal to people with broad and diverse interests in the contemporary world and a wide variety of backgrounds and qualifications will be welcomed in admissions. We seek to offer a broad introduction to the shape of contemporary society (including its historical formation and the various lines of its possible future development), and to some key issues within it."

Year 1: Photography project including camera work, narrative, observation and field work plus wide ranging introductory courses.

Year 2 & 3: Video project. Core courses on culture and ideology, media, gender and race issues plus options include: social and cultural history, contemporary media production, arts, cultural policy; comparative studies with other cultures including some Third World cultures, political debates to which cultural issues are central.

Grades: BBC

Also available as a BA Combined Honours of Media and Cultural Studies with African Studies, American Studies, Drama, English, French, German Studies, Greek (Modern), Hispanic Studies, History, Italian, Music, Philosophy, Portuguese, Russian, Theology.

BSc Communication and Information Studies
Brunel University

"This course is designed to give students a mature understanding of the social, intellectual and practical dimensions of the new technologies - to teach them, both theoretically and with hands-on experience, how they work, what their limits are and what the consequences of their use might be. The course is broad-based and multi-disciplinary. It demands a high standard of qualification and achievement. The intention is to train graduates to think critically about, and be prepared to manage, the new technologies in industry and commerce and the media. Students receive practical training in computing and video production, but the course is not designed to be a specialist training in wither Information Technology or Film and Television Production."

Years 1-3: Courses include: Sociology, psychology, anthropology, computing, information technology, video production, mass communications. Students may specialise in computing or video in the third year for project work.

Grades: BCC

Also available with Sociology.

BA Media Studies
De Montfort University

"The courses promote an understanding of media institutions and industries, their organisational forms and respective socio-political context. This is combined with the analysis of changing forms of media output, considering their codes and conventions, the social representations they offer and the ways in which audiences use and relate to these forms. Practical production work is designed to extend critical and theoretical understanding, develop students' technical and creative skills and provide vocational possibilities. Overall, the approach aims to combine aesthetic, social, political and creative concerns."

Courses available include: Mass Media, Introduction to Film studies, Introduction to Photography and Video Practical, Introduction to the History of Photography, Introduction to Cultural Studies: Issues in Class, Gender and Race, Seeing and thinking Photographically, Video Production: Documentary, Hollywood, Women and the media, Race and the Media: India, The origins of modern photography, Women watching television: Femininity and Subjectivity, Documentary and propaganda, Advanced video production, Placement, Men, Masculinity and the Media, British Cinema, European Cinema, Forms and Practices of Radio, Practical Journalism.

May also be a Joint Hons degree with Performing Arts, Arts Management, Visual Arts, History of Art and Design, English, History or Politics.

BA Hons Communication Studies
University of Glamorgan

"Our course brings together a variety of approaches to the study of Communication. It draws upon the insights provided by a range of different disciplines and approaches using Psychology, Sociology, History, Linguistics, media and Cultural Studies."

Year 1: Foundation courses in Culture Forms and Social Relations, The Individual, the Social and the Sign; The Anatomy and Context of Language; Media Institutions and the Modern World.

Year 2: Any three from: Cultural Regulation and informal Cultures; Identities and Social Relations; The Meaning and Use of Language; Media Theory, Forms and Practices. One practical from: Cultural Documentation; Data Gathering and Processing Techniques; Syntactic, Semantic, and Discourse Analysis; Techniques, Codes and Conventions of TV Production; Desktop Publishing.

Year 3: Any four from: Design, Culture and Environment; Musical Cultures; Sex, Gender and Social Relations; Literacy, Politics, Society; Contemporary Political Analysis; The Social and Historical Contexts of New Technology; Madness and Society; Cognition and Communication; Language and Society; Alternative Approaches to Meaning; Introduction to Language Breakdown; Language in the Mind; Television Forms and Social Relations; Forms and Practices of Radio; The International Cultural economy; Celtic Identities; Literacy Studies: Critical Practice and Literary Theory; Teaching English as a Second/Foreign Language.

May be studies as combined Hons degree with some 40 subjects including: Art, English Literature, French, Geography, German, Philosophy, Psychology, Religious Studies, Sociology, Spanish, Theatre Studies, Welsh, Women's studies.

BA Communications
Goldsmiths College, University of London
"This degree offers a combination of communications theory and media practice. It provides you with both a solid basis of

practical experience in media production, and an understanding or how the media function, drawing upon a wide range of theoretical disciplines. The practice and theory components are intended to work in conjunction, providing insights and understanding for each other."

Year 1: Media Production: Introduction to Options from Creative writing (fiction), electronic graphics and animation, photography, print journalism, radio, scriptwriting and television production. Two options selected for further study. Communications Theory: Courses in Society, Culture and Communications, Foundation in Communication Studies, Media History and Politics, Cultural Studies, Semiotics.
Year 2: Media Production: Advanced course in one of chosen options. Media Management course. Communications Theory: Courses in Culture and Communications, Psychology of Communications, Media Sociology.
Year 3: Media Production: Complete production work in chosen option. Communications Theory: Choice of options, including courses from other departments.

Also available BA Communication Studies and Sociology.

BA Hons Media and Cultural Studies
John Moores University
"Aims: To provide students with analytical skills to study a wide range of media texts including television, film, video, photography, popular literature (e.g. science fiction), and to understand cultural practices and experiences (leisure, tourism, heritage, theme parks, enterprise and culture and popular culture). To analyse the media industry, media and cultural policy and development."

Year 1: Reading the media, Producing the media, methods for research. Options available in photography, cinema history, radio and television.
Year 2: Theory and methods, mass communications, film studies, history of popular culture. Options in journalism and independent study which could involve work experience.
Year 3: Contemporary popular culture, television drama, broadcast and newspaper news and information, popular fiction. Options in film, photography and ethnography. Dissertation (optional).

Planned additions include programmes in film and video, journalism and photographic studies.

Grades: 12 - 16 points

May be combined with some 40 plus subjects which include Business studies, Dance, Drama, European Studies, Art, French, German, History, Japanese, Law, Philosophy, Politics, Russian, Sociology, Spanish, Women's Studies, Environmental Studies, Sports science.

BA Hons Culture and Communication
Lancaster University

"This new degree combines perspective from a number of different disciplines concerned with the study of Society, language, visual representation, media, marketing and the individual. The degree is designed to offer students a wide range of choice together with a firm foundation in one or more major disciplines."

Core subjects, with choice of courses, include: Contemporary culture - Sociology of popular culture, Human rights, Computing and society, Gender and the law; Cultural Anthropology - Meaning and symbol, Introduction to anthropology, Religion and the martial arts, Myth; Language and Social Life - language in society, discourse analysis, Grammar, genre and social context; Sociology and psychology of communication - Topic in psychology, Sociology of interpersonal relations; Visual representation - Art in the late 20th century, Modernism, Criticism and historiography; Media - Media sociology, the representation of women in film; Marketing - Marketing behaviour, Consumerism.

BSc Communications and Society
Leicester University
"This course adopts a multi-disciplinary approach to the study of mass communication. Although the filed of mass communications will be the main focus of study throughout the three years of the degree, the Sociology courses will complement the courses provided by the Centre for Mass Communication Research."

Year 1: Mass Communications, Media Studies, Understanding Societies.
Year 2: Images, institutions and Influences; Analysing Communication Processes; Sociological Analysis; Social Psychology.
Year 3: Popular Culture: Theory and Perspectives, Popular Culture and the Mass Media; Audiences and Influences. Choice form: Policy and Politics; the International Context of Communication; Power, consensus and Conflict; The media and Gender; Communications Policy; Communication Technologies.

Grades BBC

BA Hons Communication Studies
London Guildhall University
Year 1: Broadly-based courses in Sociology, the sociology of the media, cultural history. Some studio based practical work.
Years 2 & 3: Courses chosen from range of options including, video, photography, computer graphics and animation, social science, cultural studies. Course from other departments e.g. marketing, languages, computer studies may also be taken.

Also available as Joint Hons with Art and Design, Business Studies, Modern Languages, Politics and Government, Psychology, Sociology.

BA Hons Cultural and Critical Studies
Newport School of Art and Design
"Film, Photography and the associated new technologies of moving and still video imaging are the principal concerns of the degree. It is recognised that the acquisition of practical skills and the development of a visual vocabulary results from consistent practice and critical evaluation. With this in mind, the programme examines and develops related issues in film, photography, video and digital imagery."

Students must choose one Studio subject which include: Animation, Biovisual Studies (Wildlife Film and Illustration), Documentary Photography, Film and Video, Graphic Communication, Photomedia, Telemedia (Computing in Art, Video, Sound and Light Systems), Writing and Publishing, and two Theory subjects from: Design Theory and History, Film and Cinema Studies, Media Theory and History, History and Theory of Photography.

BA Hons Media Production
University of Northumbria
"The course offer a rich and direverse route of study. The aim of the course is to provide graduates: who have at least a basic technical and industrial efficiency; who are well informed in the historical, theoretical and critical aspects of their practice; who are skilled in developing ideas and confident in the analysis of their own work; who are flexible in approach and aware of the financial and legal constraints of media work; who understand the ideological implications of their work and are aware of their social and cultural responsibilities."

Year 1: Introduction to Media Practice and Theory.
Years 1/2: Core programme of media theory and history. Choice from either Fiction Scriptwriting or Film/Video Production.
Years 2/3: Idividual programme.

BA Hons Communications Studies
Nottingham Polytechnic
"This degree is designed for students whose interest is in the wide field of communication studies , with special reference to contemporary problems and issues. Its main aim is to develop in the students a keen and critical understanding of communication as a dynamic process, and of its importance for society as we know it. The course also equips students with basic practical skills in media work and provides opportunities for extending these outside college."

Year 1: Culture and Society, Text and Society, Language, Experience and Action, The Mass Media and Communication Practices.

Year 2: Choice of three from Culture and Society, Text and Society, Language, Experience and Action. Communication Practices includes Problems and Issues in Contemporary Culture, four week place placement and an option from Text and Cultural Practice, Computing and Information Technology, the Craft of Writing.

Year 3: Choice from wide range of options including: Stylistics, Language and Power, Psycholinguistics, Communication, Emancipation and the Public Sphere; Mass Communication and the Political Process; Advanced Topics in Psychology; Post-war Women and Cultural Production; Images of Britain; Modern African Literature; War and Representation; Cultural Imperialism; Modernity and Post Modernity; Cultural Policy; Dissertation.

One term may be spent studying in the United States.

Grades: 14 points

BA Hons Broadcast Journalism
Nottingham Polytechnic

"This degree has been designed fro students who wish to follow a career in television and/or radio broadcasting. The course will develop the practical and organisational skills required in the collection, writing up and dissemination of news and a critical understanding of the role of the media in society."

Year 1: Cultural Studies, craft of writing, basic broadcast engineering, the media in society, studio practice, communication practices (e.g. interviewing, microphone techniques, editing).

Year 2: Public affairs. media and the law, problems and issues in contemporary communication. Media based project. Placement of six weeks intensive training in broadcast practise and four weeks practice at either a television or radio station.

Year 3: Two options from mass communication, stylistics, language and power, and cultural policies. Dissertation. Practical work in running a 24 hour newsroom on Polytechnic site.

Grades: BC

BA Hons Media and Design
University of Portsmouth

"The course aims to develop the student's competence in a design or media specialism within a multidisciplinary environment. The aim is to heighten the student's qualitative sensibilities by developing their critical faculties, and to inform the student of the historical and theoretical context of present and future design practice. The relationship of these practical and theoretical subjects is considered to be unique; and to provide students with design education appropriate to the current and future needs of design practice."

Years 1 - 3: Choice of four specialisations: Graphic Information, Video and Film, Three-dimensional Design; Historical and Theoretical Studies.

BA Communication Studies
Queen Margaret College

"The departments courses are geared to employment opportunities in organisational communication, the cultural industries and information management. Commerce, Industry and the public services depend increasingly on co-ordinated action and technologically sophisticated systems of information handling. The courses stresses the importance of an understanding of interpersonal relations and information technology for successful professionals in all walks of life."

Subjects:
Media Studies: television, film, photography, video and advertising.
Information Studies: information technology applications, social effects of IT.
Cultural Studies: communication and culture, communication and social institutions.
Human Communication: Individual human behaviour, behaviour in groups, persuasion and change.
Management Studies: marketing practices, and organisation communication.
Communications Policy: advertising standards, European media policy, freedom of information, data protection.
Practical Skills & Research.

BA Media Arts
Royal Holloway and Bedford New College, University of London

"This course approaches the study of the media from a perspective which is based on understanding, critically evaluating, acquiring and using an audio-visual language. Students explore and examine the nature and role of the modern communications media learning to relate specific contents to relevant forms in the process of translating factual and symbolic material into audio-visual communication."

The course is based in three main strands:
Media Practice, the acquisition of practical skills and could include post-production video editing, television studio recording processes, screen writing and directing, culminating in a substantial video programme written and directed by the students.
Film, Television and Video Studies, the study of existing media texts, and could include The French New Wave, Russian silent cinema, the Hollywood maternal melodrama, televised drama analysis (soaps, series, serials), specific writers, directors, performers, producers and designers.
Cultural Theory, the theoretical framework for producing and analysing media texts, and could cultural studies, Marx, FR Leavis, Mathew Arnold, Barthes.
Special Options could include The History and Practise of Animation, Computer Graphics, Video Poetry, Film and Photography, Radio and so on.

BA Hons Media, Language and Business
University of Salford

"The combination of media production skills and understanding with language and business training is designed to produce graduates with a high level of usefulness in the rapidly changing and burgeoning filed of media in which Europeanisation and management acumen plat increasingly vital roles in programme making."

Courses include: Production (video and audio)practice and analysis, video and audio projects; media in society and mass communication; international and European media; Accounting and law; management and business strategy including marketing and management of people; media management including costing; gender and sexuality in the media; new media technologies; comparative media analysis; European media.

The languages usually studied in depth are French, German or Spanish, although it may be possible to study other languages such as Arabic or Russian.

BA Hons Media and Performance
University of Salford

"This course allows students to integrate elements of the Centre's strengths in media production and dramatic performance. The course integrates key aspects of performance activity with practical media production and performance. Students develop practical working skills in performance and production workshops accompanied by the critical study of media and performance in society."

BA Hons Media and Popular Music
University of Salford

"This course draws upon the Centre's strengths in both Media and Popular Music to provide an integrated programme of study embracing key aspects of both. Emphasis is placed upon the development of a broad understanding of media and popular music, and on the development of imagination and creativity in the use of media and music technology. Students select modules in theoretical and practical aspects of media and music in order to prepare them for careers in the broadcasting, popular music, recording, leisure and entertainment industries."

BA Hons Communication Studies
Sheffield City Polytechnic

"The overall aim of the degree is to present a broad interdisciplinary approach to the study of human communication, based on a range of contributory disciplines including linguistics, psychology, sociology, literature and media studies. More specifically the course aims to develop students' understanding of the processes, uses and limitations of human communication, in the particular context of modern British society. The degree also aims to develop students' practical skills in a number of areas, such as the use of audio, video and microcomputing equipment."

Year 1: Verbal Communication, Interpersonal Communication, the Sociology of Mass Culture, Communication and Social Processes, Descriptive Linguistics, Introduction to Popular Culture, Skills.

Year 2: Language: Discourse and Situation, Communication and Social Identity, Mass Communication and Ideology, Communication Technology, Skill Project.

Year 3: Theoretical Issues in Communication Studies, Communication and Prejudice, Applications, the Analysis of Texts, Options, Skills.

BA Media Studies
Sheffield City Polytechnic

"This course aims to provide a grounding in both practical and analytical skills together with an understanding of the development of the mass media and its economic, political, social and aesthetic significance. The course pursues three main strands: the study of the social, political and economic context of the media; the analysis of media texts; the acquisition of practical skills in media production."

Year 1: Courses include: Film and Media Contexts, Theories of Textual Analysis, Applied Textual Analysis, Sociology of Mass Culture, Media Production, Skills.
Year 2: Courses include: International Perspectives on the Media, Mass Communication and Ideology, Applied Media Studies, Media Production, Skills.
Year 3: Courses include: Contemporary media, Policy and Practise/Problems of Text and Audience; Dissertation, Writing for the Media, Media Production, Arts and Media Administration.
Options can be taken from a range from other degrees, e.g. Film Studies or Communication Studies.

BA Hons Fine Art (Media)
The Slade School of Fine Art

One of the most famous art schools in the world, the Slade is now part of London University. The first year of the course is a general foundation year where students study various aspects of drawing and basic workshop practises and techniques. Workshops are arranged throughout the year to support the needs or each student as they arise and may include workshops in sculpture, video, photography, printmaking and theatre design. After the first year most students choose to specialise in either painting, sculpture or Media. The media department offers technical facilities and programmes in photography, film, video and sound. Students also take an option from the courses offered by University College. These have included Anatomy, Astronomy, Psychology and literature. Students are able to attend any other of the lectures and courses according to their interests. There is also an exchange agreement in the third year with a number of colleges and universities in Europe and the United States. Entrance is by submission of portfolio and interview.

BA Hons Communication Studies
University of Sunderland

"The degree aims to introduce students to a range of communication processes and systems; to familiarise them with the disciplines and methodologies by which communication may be studies; and to enable them to communicate effectively in a variety of situations and through a variety of media."

Year 1: Courses include: Media and Cultural Studies (Foundation), Social Science (Foundation), Radio, Video, Photography, Computing, Perception and Representation, the Individual in Society.

Year 2: Courses include: Social Science, Media and Cultural Studies, Language, Computing, Practical Video, Radio Production, Principles and Practise of Radio Journalism.

Year 3: The programme of this year allows for detailed study of selected areas such as film, music, computer language etc.

BA Hons Media Studies
University of Ulster

"This interdisciplinary Course is designed to promote the critical study of the mass media. Its main concerns are with film, television, radio and the press. The course combines sociological, historical and critical analysis of the mass media with media production work and research studies."

Year 1: Six required modules which introduce students to the concepts and methods of analysis central to the study of mass media.

Years 2 & 3: Students engage in theoretical studies and in media practice and are able to focus on specific media through either an academic or practical emphasis. Students are required to spend up to one-third of their time on practical projects in radio, television and film and to complete a dissertation in the final year.

All students have a period of placement in their second year, or may opt to spend a term at an European University chosen from Amsterdam, Ghent, Uppsala, Barcelona.

Also available, BA Hons Humanities Combined. Media Studies plus Asian Studies, English, European Studies, French, Geography, German,. History, Irish, Philosophy, Theatre Studies.

BA Hons Media Studies
University of Sussex

"The degree course in Media Studies at Sussex enables you to develop a critical understanding of television, cinema, radio and the press in Britain, as well as in an international and comparative perspective. The media are studies in their historical development, as social and economic institutions, technologies and cultural forms. The Major in Media Studies is taught in two Schools of Studies - Cultural and Community Studies and European Studies. Different School courses accompany it according to the school. The pattern o the Major courses is common to both schools."

Year 1: Introduction to Media Studies, History and Theory of Media.
Year 2: Choice from British press or Radio or Contemporary European Media or Advertising. Television and Film Analysis.
Year 3: Changing Media Environments, Media and Cultural Identities.

Grades: BBB

The European Studies is a four year course, involving the study of a modern European language (French, German, Italian, Russian or Spanish) and a year abroad in Europe between the second and final year.

BA Contemporary Media Practise
University of Westminster
"The degree is designed to offer you production experience in a broad range of media, and should prepare you on graduation for the continuing rapid changes in media technology. The programme is centred on the development of ideas which you will generate, and which will be expressed through the most appropriate medium or media, ranging from still photography through film and video to computer systems. You can specialise within the programme is you wish, but this is not required or expressly encouraged. The programme content and student centred teaching method are intended to develop creativity and critical ability within a framework of practical and academic skills."

BA Hons Media Studies
University of Westminster

"The course aims to make you aware of the possibilities and limitations of the media, both practically and theoretically; to develop the ability to criticise the productions of the media; to clarify the relationship between these media and society and, finally, to equip you for an active use of communication, in whatever filed you should choose as a career."

Year 1: Academic Studies: Introduction to Media Analysis, Mass Media Institutions and their publics. Practical Studies: Basis practical skills of print journalism, radio and video.
Year 2: Academic Studies: The Political and Social Context of the British Mass Media, Media Analysis. Practical Studies: Research, Print Journalism, Radio Journalism, Video. 3 week work attachment.
Year 3: Academic studies: Contemporary Media Policy, Theories of Modernity. Practical Studies: A series of publications, radio and video programmes; individual projects of a high standard e.g. a feature article, a radio documentary, a video documentary or studio production. A dissertation.

BA Hons Design and Media Arts
University of Westminster

"The course will allow you a very wide range of art, design and media options available through combinations of modules offered across the School of Design and Media. The aim of the course is to encourage an exploratory approach to a range of project assignments and studies. Student pathways are established by negotiation to provide initial breadth, followed by in-depth specialisation in one of the three major tracks; two dimensional, three dimensional and time-based studies. In each case, practical experimentation will be supported by historical, theoretical and critical studies, which will provide you with a range of both specific and transferable skills."

BA Hons Media Studies
West Surrey College of Art and Design

"The media informs and influences public opinion, politics, legislation, social and cultural attitudes. This theoretical course sets out to analyse how it works. As well as analysis, industrial skills and professional knowledge of a European language are taught and a comparative study is made of media products and practices in the rest of Europe. Cultural studies can also be taken".

Subjects covered: Culture and Criticism, Professional Studies, European Studies, Information Technology, Professional Practice, Production of Media Culture, Mass Media and Social Change, Media Audiences, Politics of Representation, Cultural Studies.

BA Hons Media & Communications
University of Wolverhampton

"Media and Communications looks at the interrelation between forms of culture, their consumers and their producers. It investigates the role of the media and communications industries in providing entertainment and information. The subject also offers some opportunities for practical work with video, and industrial experience through work placements."

Courses include: Communication studies, Production Methods, Communication, culture and Society, The cultural industries; Visual Communication; Audiences, Markets and Consumers; Broadcasting and the Pan-European Market; Cultural Policy and Planning. Practical modules in television production may be available.

Also available as part of a combined course with some 83 other subjects including: American Studies, Business, Computer Aided Design, Dance, English, French studies, German, History, Music, Photography, Russian studies, Spanish studies, Theatre studies.

BA Combined Studies
(Media not available as a single subject)

BSc Sociology/Media Studies
City University
The degree in a modular one, with courses in Economics, Philosophy, Psychology, Health, Sociology, Systems Science, Mathematics, Accountancy, Computer Science available. There are four Media Studies Courses:
The Media in Britain, News in Society, World Media Industry and media and Cultural Production.

BA Hons Modular Degree
King Alfred's College
Language Communication and Writing
"Language, Communication and Writing, as an interdisciplinary field, draws together work from a number of disciplines: Film and Media Studies, Cultural Studies and Cultural History, Linguistics, English Studies, Education and Creative Writing. Its main aim is to introduce students to the theoretical and practical analysis of a broad spectrum of written, spoken and visual texts. With this in view, course modules have been designed both to familiarise students with the theoretical debates that presently surround academic work in these area and, through case studies and projects, to provide them with opportunities to see and experience the implications of those debates in practice."

Year 1: Foundation year. Introduction to Communications, Introduction to Film Studies, Introduction to the Study of the English Language.

Years 2 & 3: Communication and Media Studies theories, the politics of representation, national cinemas, the British independent film sector, language and gender, language policy in education, creative writing.

May be combined with: American Studies, Archaeology, Computing, Drama Studies, Education Studies, English Studies, Environmental Studies, Geography, History of Art, Japanese Studies, Mathematics and its applications, Religious Studies, Social, Economic and Political studies.

BA Combined Arts
University of Plymouth

"The course addresses a range of central issues and debates through practical work in film/video, photography and page media (including desk top publishing). You will explore the similarities and differences between various media practices by placing these within broad historical and critical contexts. The course encourages the development of a broadly based approach to critical practice, emphasising the value of learning by practical investigation supported by informed critical and historical awareness."

Courses available: Media with English, Contemporary History, Theatre Arts and Drama, Design Arts, Art History, Education Studies.

Combined Studies Index
Media/Communications +....

MEDIA + AFRICAN STUDIES
University of Birmingham

MEDIA + AMERICAN STUDIES
University of Birmingham
King Alfred's College
University of Wolverhampton

MEDIA + ARCHAEOLOGY
King Alfred's College

MEDIA + ART HISTORY
De Montfort University
King Alfred's College
University of Plymouth

MEDIA + ARTS MANAGEMENT
De Montfort University

MEDIA + ASIAN STUDIES
University of Ulster

MEDIA + BUSINESS
John Moores University
London Guildhall University
University of Wolverhampton

MEDIA + COMPUTER STUDIES
King Alfred's College
University of Wolverhampton

MEDIA + CULTURAL STUDIES
John Moores University

MEDIA + DANCE
John Moores University
University of Wolverhampton

MEDIA + DESIGN
De Montfort University
University of Plymouth
University of Portsmouth
University of Westminster

MEDIA + DRAMA
University of Birmingham
De Montfort University
University of Glamorgan
John Moores University
King Alfred's College
University of Plymouth
University of Ulster
University of Wolverhampton

MEDIA + EDUCATION
King Alfred's College
University of Plymouth

MEDIA + ENGLISH
University of Birmingham
De Montfort University
University of Glamorgan
King Alfred's College
University of Plymouth
University of Ulster
University of Wolverhampton

MEDIA + ENVIRONMENT
John Moores University
King Alfred's College

MEDIA + EUROPEAN STUDIES
John Moores University
London Guildhall University
University of Ulster

MEDIA + FRENCH
University of Birmingham
University of Glamorgan
John Moores University
University of Sussex
University of Ulster
University of Wolverhampton

MEDIA + GEOGRAPHY
University of Glamorgan
King Alfred's College
University of Ulster

MEDIA + GERMAN
University of Birmingham
University of Glamorgan
John Moores University
University of Sussex
University of Ulster

MEDIA + GREEK
University of Birmingham

MEDIA + HISTORY
University of Birmingham
De Montfort University
John Moores University
University of Plymouth
University of Ulster
University of Wolverhampton

MEDIA + IRISH
University of Ulster

MEDIA + ITALIAN
University of Birmingham
University of Sussex

MEDIA + JAPANESE
John Moores University
King Alfred's College

MEDIA + LAW
John Moores University

MEDIA + MATHEMATICS
King Alfred's College

MEDIA + MUSIC
University of Birmingham
University of Wolverhampton

MEDIA + PHILOSOPHY
University of Birmingham
University of Glamorgan
John Moores University
University of Ulster

MEDIA + PHOTOGRAPHY
University of Wolverhampton

MEDIA + POLITICS
De Montfort University
John Moores University
King Alfred's College
London Guildhall University

MEDIA + PORTUGUESE
University of Birmingham

MEDIA + PSYCHOLOGY
University of Glamorgan
London Guildhall University

MEDIA + RELIGIOUS STUDIES
University of Birmingham
University of Glamorgan
King Alfred's College

MEDIA + RUSSIAN
University of Birmingham
John Moores University
University of Sussex
University of Wolverhampton

MEDIA + SOCIOLOGY
Brunel University
City University
University of Glamorgan
Goldsmiths College, University of London
John Moores University
London Guildhall University

MEDIA + SPANISH
University of Birmingham
University of Glamorgan
John Moores University
University of Sussex
University of Wolverhampton

MEDIA + SPORTS
John Moores University

MEDIA + WELSH
University of Glamorgan

MEDIA + WOMEN'S STUDIES
University of Glamorgan
John Moores University

Post-Graduate Studies

Higher Diploma/MA in Fine Art (Media)
The Slade School of Fine Art

The teaching programme includes introductions to photography, film, video and sound, with advanced technical knowledge being acquired on an individual basis. Students join on the basis of ability to initiate and develop specific researches. For the Higher Diploma, students submit work, normally in the form of an exhibition. In addition, for the MA, students submit two reports, one of 5000 words and the other of 10,000 words.

Photography

BA Hons Editorial Photography
University of Brighton

"This is a project based course. As the course progresses, students will be encouraged to define their own projects in liaison with tutors supported by lectures, seminars, exhibitions, group discussions, visits, guest presentations, etc. Theoretical and critical studies are considered within each project rather than as separate experiences. The course ensures that students are fully aware of professional opportunities with the discipline."

Years 1-3: Editorial Selection, Pictorial Decision Making, Research and Documentation, Description and Analysis, Critical Assessment, Electronic Imaging, New Technologies.

BA Hons Photographic Studies
University of Derby

"The degree is a practical visual arts course, with photography and allied subjects as the principal means of expression. The main concern of the course is image-making; you will be encouraged to work creatively with all aspects of photography to include film/video, printmaking, audio-visual, experimental and historical photographic processes."

Years 1/2: Concentrates on the acquisition of knowledge and skills of the photographic arts. Critical Studies: Film, History of Photography, Philosophical approaches to Art and Language, Photographic Theory.
Years 2/3: Individual study of an area of photographic arts.
Options:
Academic Route: Concentration on critical studies and theoretical issues.
Film and Video: Provides the major component of studies from start of the degree.

BA/BSc Hons Imaging
Manchester Metropolitan University

"The course is designed to offer a unique opportunity to marry the creative strengths and traditions of photography with the rapidly developing new imaging technologies. Students are recruited from either a science or arts background and this interaction is relected in common core units especially at level/year one. This level provides an introductory opportunity to research, explore and experience creative photography, imaging, its technologies and techniques. The course will present opportunites for students to work with and alongside students from other related disciplines. Students are given thorough preparation to succeed in a business and technological environment. Great significance is attached to the importance of contextual and professional studies."

BA Hons Photography, Film and Television
Napier University

"The course prepares graduates to enter the profession of photography or the film and television industry and related areas. Great emphasis is laid on using these medium as a form of visual expression and communication. While it is important in a course of this nature for students to develop high levels of professional skill, it is also recognised that the development of individual creativity is of equal importance. The course is broad in nature and encompasses the study of the wide range of visual media including stills photography, film, television, multivision and graphic design. Other subjects studied within the course include communication studies, historical studies and business studies. The course has a common first year and then follows two separate pathways; one with the Still Image and the other with the Moving Image."

Year 1: Photographic studies, communication studies, audio visual media, graphic design, historical studies, video production.
Year 2: Photographic Studies, communication studies, audio visual media, computer graphics, electronic imaging, historical studies.
Year 3: Photographic studies, communication studies, audio visual media, computer graphics, electronic imaging, historical studies, business studies.
Year 4: Photographic studies, communication studies, audio visual media, computer graphics, electronic imaging, historical studies, business studies.

Grades CD plus portfolio or showreel.

BA Hons Film and Photography
Newport School of Art and Design
"Film, Photography and the associated new technologies of moving and still video imaging are the principal concerns of the degree. It is recognised that the acquisition of practical

skills and the development of a visual vocabulary results from consistent practice and critical evaluation. With this in mind, the programme examines and develops related issues in film, photography, video and digital imagery."

Students must choose two Studio subjects which include: Animation, Biovisual Studies (Wildlife Film and Illustration), Documentary Photography, Film and Video, Photomedia, Telemedia (Computing in Art, Video, Sound and Light Systems), Writing and Publishing, and one Theory subject from: Design Theory and History, Film and Cinema Studies, Media Theory and History, History and Theory of Photography. Students may choose to take Documentary Photography or Film and Video as double studio subjects.

BA Hons Photography
Nottingham Polytechnic

"Photography is approached as one of the visual arts, and investigated with intellectual rigour, combined with all skills appropriate to the task. Students are encouraged to find and follow their own routes through the many varieties of photographic practice, and so discover the eventual destination best suited to their ambitions."

Year 1: Courses to ensure all round competence in technical and conceptual skills.
Years 1/2: Structured opportunities to extend skills and knowledge.
Years 2/3: Individual programmes of study leading to degree show.

BA Hons Design
Staffordshire University
"You will specialise in one of eight options - either glass, ceramics, surface pattern, graphics, product design, photography, audio-visual communication or electronic instructional media - with the opportunity to work in the other options as appropriate. The wide range of staff and facilities provides a stimulating shared environment in which your design abilities can be developed, and encourages a wider and more imaginative approach to specialised work than would be the case on single subject course. As well as developing design abilities by project work, you learn how to exploit production methods, to provide for market needs, to perceive the historical and social context of design, to communicate ideas verbally and visually, and to understand the industrial and financial aspects of a professional career in design. It is possible to take European language studies in French, German or Italian as part of your course."

Photography includes: photojournalism, advertising, still life, fashion and landscape.

Audio visual communication aims to train flexible people who can work in entertainment, social or commercial persuasion, education and training.

BA Hons Photography (4 Years Part-time)
University of Westminster
"The aims of the course are: to provide you with a broad-based education if you are already working in connection with photography, to expand your knowledge and understanding of the media in which you work; to produce graduates

equipped with a range of intellectual and imaginative powers necessary for your own career development, as well as the ability to make a contribution to the advancement of photography as a means of communication, business or self expression; to develop your understanding and inventiveness in the creative practice of photography; to widen and enhance your ability to execute your own visual ideas as well as understanding the potential of future developments within the media; to encourage a critical understanding of the cultural, commercial and social contexts in which photographers operate, and to provide you with an intellectual basis of critical theories of photography on which to build your own photographic practice and study of the medium."

BA Hons Photography
West Surrey College of Art and Design

"This course provides an understanding of the theory and practise of photography in its historical and social context. It also aims to develop students' visual and verbal communication skills, creativity, initiative and independence, so providing a sound basis for postgraduate study or for a career in the highly competitive world of professional photography."

Years 1-3: Subjects covered include: Photographic Practice, History and Theory, Cultural Studies, Electronic Imaging and Publishing, Professional and Business Awareness.

Post-Graduate Courses

MA Photographic Studies
University of Derby
"This is a practical course based on a critical approach to photography, which follows an interdisciplinary tradition where the practices of photography, theory and criticism inform one another. Its aim is to produce an awareness of the links between practice and theoretical positions. This is a course for artists and photographers whose work has achieved a degree of maturity and who wish to develop their knowledge and practice by working in a more structured and self-critical manner that is possible in isolation. The Master's Degree is a taught coarse which comprises the programme of work, the seminar, the group critique and the tutorial."

Photography (2 Years)
Royal College of Art
"While the theoretical concepts of visual communication cannot be ignored, Photography is predominately a practical medium. Our aim is to encourage photographers with imaginative and adventurous ideas to develop an individual, practical approach. The course is therefore designed to encourage self- reliance by offering flexibility and freedom to enable students to carry through their own professional projects. At the same time we offer the latest technology."

Year 1: Short structured courses including basic introduction, studio lighting, colour printing, retouching and handwork, practical audio-visual and computerised image manipulation. Experimentation with various approaches and techniques.

Year 2: Major project and related schemes of work. Business studies course.

BTEC Courses

General Information

Entry requirements
National - A BTEC First qualification OR four GCSE's at grade C or above OR an equivalent qualification. Design courses also require a portfolio of recent work.
Higher National - A BTEC National qualification in a relevant subject OR at least one A level and GCSEs at grade C or above OR an equivalent qualification. Design courses also require a portfolio of recent work.

Course format
All courses follow a format of Core subjects and specialist options. All colleges will offer the core subjects. Specialist options available vary from college to college.

Assessment
Assessment may include assignments, projects, case studies, practical exercises and examinations.

Higher Education
Holders of BTEC Higher National Qualifications can often be admitted to the third year of CNAA degree courses in a related subject.

Course Duration
National Diploma courses normally take two years full time and three years part time. Certificate courses normally take

two years part time. Certificate and Diploma courses are equal in standard and status, although Diploma courses include more option subjects to prepare students for a broader range of careers.

Higher National Diploma courses normally take two years full time. Certificate courses (when available) usually take two years part time.

Fees

BTEC full time courses are usually free to students under 19 (or sometimes under 18). The Local Grant Authority may insist that the student attends the course nearest to his or her home to be eligible. Part time course fees are usually paid by the student's employer.

BTEC Performing Arts Courses

The BTEC Performing Arts courses are offered at First, National and Higher National Diploma Levels. They are aimed at young people either already working with a performance company, or those who want to work in drama, dance, stage management or arts administration. The main strength of these courses is the breadth that they cover. A student will have a basic knowledge of performance, stage management, technical and management skills that will stand them in good stead should they become involved in small-scale theatre - perhaps their own company while they get started. The drawback is that, realistically a BTEC will not get you far in the real, highly competative world of performance arts where qualifications are largely irrelevant. Employers generally rely on interviews, auditions, and which drama school for their employees. On the other hand someone who has completed a BTEC course must stand a better chance at interview or audition for a drama school or college, not because of having a qualification but because of having more experience. Many former BTEC students will also be surprised at the lack of equipment at some drama schools, especially the more recently established private schools.

BTEC First Diploma
Core Subjects:
Common Skills - a broad range of general skills, including communicationg and working with others, and applying business and administrative skills to the planning and organisation of performances.
Performance Processes - develops skills in working as a member of a performance group, such as administrative skills,

eg preparing budgets, publicity, and Front of House (box office/ticket sales). Production skills are also learnt, such as using technical equipment such as lighting, microphones, tape recorders and so on.

Performance Project - bringing together the skills learnt on the course in the preparation and presentation of a performance.
Options include: Understanding Drama, Drama Performance, Understanding Dance, Dance Performance, Understanding Music, Music Performance, Understanding Performance Technology, Stage Management for Performance.

The West Country
Bridgwater College
South Bristol College
South Devon College of Arts and Technology

Greater London
Dagenham Priory Comprehensive School
Leyton Sixth Form College
Mulberry School for Girls
Newham Sixth Form College
North London College

Yorkshire & Humberside
Barnsley College
Harrogate College of Arts and Technology
Hopwood Hall College
North Lindsay College
St Wilfrids Catholic High School

Northern Ireland
Belfast Institute of Further and Higher Education
Omagh College of Further Education

Thames and Chilterns
West Herts College

North West
Preston College
The South Manchester College
Tameside College of Technology
Walsall College of Art
Wigan and Leigh College

The North
Cumbria College of Art and Design
Morton Comprehensive School
Newcastle College
North Tyneside College of Further Education
South Tyneside College

Wales
Crosskeys College

Central
The Blake High School
Burton upon Trent Technical College
Mid Warwickshire College of Further Education
Stoke on Trent College

East Midlands
Boston College
Charles Keene College of Further Education
South East Derbyshire College

East Anglia
Harlow College
South East Essex College of Arts and Technology

South of England
Chichester College of Technology
Eastleigh College
Mid Kent College of Higher and Further Education
South Downs College of Further Education
Southlands School

BTEC National Diploma

Core Subjects:
Arts in Society - a background understanding of the way in which the performed arts have developed and how they interact with society. From this base specialised areas of performance are developed.
Arts Administration - the business side of performing, including financial, legal and administrative aspects.
Production Techniques - an understanding of the venue and its opportunities and restrictions, and a working knowledge of essential performance design and technology skills.
Performance Workshop - to develop a performance using aquired skills in music dance and drama, while working as a team.
Production project - combining administrative skills with the artistic side of performance enabling students to mount a large scale performance.
Options include:
Dance - Composition and Choreography, Dance Improvisation, Dance Techniques, Language of Dance, Movement Studies.
Drama Options - Acting techniques, Directing, Language of Theatre, Voice and Speech, Writing and Devising.
Music Options - Composition and Arrangement, Introduction to Music Technology, Language of Music, Music Performance Techniques, Recording Techniques, Singing.
Stagecraft Options - Costume Construction and Wardrobe, Costume for Performance, Make-up, Management, Performance Technology, Setting for Performance.

BTEC National Diploma Performing Arts Courses

The West Country
Bridgwater College
City Of Bath College
Cornwall College
Filton College
Mid Cornwall College
New College
North Devon College
Penwith College
Salisbury College of Technology
South Devon College of Arts and Technology
Strode College
Weston Super-Mare College of Further Education
Weymouth College
Yeovil College

Greater London
Acton College
Barking College of Technology
Barnet College of Further Education
City and East London College
Croydon College
Elm Park College
Hackney College
Hammersmith and West London College
Kingsway College
Lewisham College
Performing Arts and Technology School
Redbridge Technical College
Southwark College

Tower Hamlets College
Waltham Forest College

Yorkshire & Humberside
Barnsley College
Dewsbury College
Doncaster College
Grimsby College of Technology and Arts
Harrogate College of Arts and Technology
Hopwood Hall College
Hull College of Further Education
Norton College
Oldham College
Oulder Hill Community School
Park Lane College
Thomas Danby College
Wakefield District College

Northern Ireland
Belfast Institute of Further and Higher Education
Newtownabbey College of Further Education
North Antrim College of Further Education
North Down and Ards College of Further Education
North West College of Technology, Londonderry

Thames and Chilterns
Amersham and Wycombe College
Langley College of Further Education
Newbury College
North Hertfordshire College
North Oxfordshire College and School of Art
Oxford College of Further Education
Stantonbury Campus
West Herts College

North West
Accrington and Rossendale College
Bolton Metropolitan College
Bury Metropolitan College
Calderdale College
Knowsley Community College
Nelson and Colne College
The Ridge College
Rotherham College of Arts and Technology
St Helens Community College
The South Manchester College
Southport College of Art and Technology
Tameside College of Technology
Walsall College of Art
West Cheshire College
Wigan and Leigh College

The North
Cleveland College of Further Education
Cumbria College of Art and Design
Gateshead College
Monkwearmouth College
New College
Newcastle College
North Tyneside College of Further Education
South Tyneside College
Stockton and Billingham Technical College
Ulverston Victoria High School

Wales
Afan College
Coleg Glan Hafren
Coleg Powys
Crosskeys College

Gwynedd Technical College
Gorseinon College
Llandrillo Technical College
Neath College
North East Wales Institute of Higher Education
Swansea College

Central

Bilston Community College
Coventry Centre for the Performing Arts
East Warwickshire College of Further Education
Newcastle under Lyme College
South Warwickshire College of Further Education
Stafford College
Stoke on Trent College

East Midlands

Charles Keene College of Further Education
Chesterfield College of Technology and Arts
Clarendon College of Further Education
Derby Tertiary College
Lutterworth Grammar Scgool
Melton Mowbray College of Further Education
Northampton College
North Nottinghamshire College of Further Education
North Derbyshire Tertiary College
South East Derbyshire College

East Anglia

Cambridge Regional College
Epping Forest College
Harlow College
Lowestoft College
Norfolk College of Arts and Technology
South East Essex College of Arts and Technology

Suffolk College of Higher and Further Education
South of England
Brooklands Technical College
Chichester College of Technology
Cricklade Tertiary College
Fareham College
Farnborough College of Technology
Northbrook College
North East Surrey College of Technology
North West Kent College of Technology
The Regional Centre at Queen Mary's College
South Downs College of Further Education
West Kent College of Further Education

Perfoming Arts Higher National Diploma

The North
Newcastle College

Perfoming Arts Higher National Diploma (Stage Management)

West Country
Bristol Old Vic Theatre School
Central
Coventry Polytechnic
South of England
South Downs College of Further Education
North West
Salford College of Technology

Performing Arts Higher National Diploma (Dance)

Central
Coventry Polytechnic
The North
Newcastle College

BTEC Design

BTEC Higher National Diploma in Graphic Design (Advertising)

Core subjects:
Basic visual and design theory and techniques
The history and traditions of design
The business and professional aspects of design practice
Verbal and written communication skills
Specialist core subjects:
Visualisation techniques - ensures that students develop a wide range of visualisation skills, in preparation for professional practice. Students are encouraged to work to the kinds of deadlines they will meet in real life.
Campaign development - reflects the move by advertisers towards campaigns, rather than one-off advertisements. Students learn the importance of adapting a campaign to suit difference advertising media. They are encouraged to work in creative teams, normally as art director and copywriter, in order to fully exploit the relationship between word and image.
Market identification - stresses the connection between effective advertising and a good brief. Students are encouraged to clarify the marketing and business needs of the client/product before the creative process begins.
Specialist Options:
Art Direction
Audio-Visual Skills
Copywriting

Film and Video
Illustration
Photography
Typography

BTEC National Diploma in Design

Core subjects:
Basic visual and design theory and techniques
The history and traditions of art and design
The business and professional aspects of design practice
Verbal and written communication skills
Specialist Options
Graphic design - includes illustration, typography, packaging and printing
Photography and Audio Visual Studios
Textile Studies - the theory and practice of textile design
Three dimensional Studies - include ceramics, jewellery, silversmithing and industrial design.

Design (Film and Television)

BTEC National Diploma

The North
Cleveland College of Art and Design

BTEC Higher National Diploma

The West Country
Bournemouth and Poole College of Art and Design

Wales
Gwent College of Higher Education
South of England
Farnborough College of Technology

Design (Model Making)

BTEC National Diploma

Greater London
Barking College of Technology
The West Country
South Devon College of Arts and Technology

BTEC Higher National Diploma

The West Country
Bournemouth and Poole College of Art and Design
Thames & Chilterns
Hertfordshire College of Art and Design
Rycotewood College
South of England
Kent Institute of Art and Design

Design (Theatre Studies)

BTEC National Diploma

The North
Cleveland College of Art and Design

South of England
Northbrook College
The North West
Oldham College

BTEC Higher National Diploma

South of England
Croydon College
Northbrook College
The North West
City of Liverpool Community College
Greater London
London College of Fashion, The London Institute

BTEC Higher National Diploma in Design

Core subjects
Basic visual and design theory and techniques
The history and traditions of art and design
The business and professional aspects of design practice
Verbal and written communication skills
Specialist Options
Graphic design - includes illustration, typography, packaging and printing
Photography and Audio Visual Studios
Textile Studies - the theory and practice of textile design
Three dimensional Studies - include ceramics, jewellery, silversmithing and industrial design.

BTEC Higher National Diploma

Central
Birmingham Poly
Wales
Cardiff Institute of Higher Education
West Country
Portsmouth College of Art Design and Further Education
North West
Salford College of Technology
Stockport College of Technology
Northern Ireland
University of Ulster

BTEC National Course in Audio Visual Design

Core subjects
Basic visual and design theory and techniques
The history and traditions of art and design
The business and professional aspects of design practice
Verbal and written communication skills
Specialist Options
Design Skills - introduces and develops, usually through projects, the specific skills needed to work as an audio visual design technician. The practical work provides experience in all areas of audio visual activity.
Technology - covers the technology associate with audio-visual production
Production - covers the full range of production techniques associated with visual aids, photography, television and video and film and animation. This could include scripting, record-

ing storyboarding, production, editing and post production work.
Design in context - ensures that students understand the importance of business and marketing skills in audio visual work.

BTEC National Diploma

West Country
Bournemouth and Poole College of Art and Design
Brunel College of Technology
Thames and Chilterns
Dunstable College
The North
Longlands College of Further Education
Wales
North East Wales Institute of Higher Education
Central
Kidderminster College of Further Education
North Warwickshire College of Technology and Art
Sandwell College of Further and Higher Education
Yorkshire & Humberside
Dewsbury College
London
South Thames College
Southwark College
The North West
Manchester College of Arts and Technology
The South Manchester College
South of England
Epsom School of Art and Design

BTEC Higher National Diploma

London
South Thames College
South of England
Northbrook College

BTEC Courses in Media/Communications

BTEC National Diploma in Communications

Core subjects
Basic visual and design theory and techniques
The history and traditions of art and design
The business and professional aspects of design practice
Verbal and written communication skills
Specialist subjects
Computer graphic, typesetting and desktop publishing
Editing and production
Illustration, drawing and layout
Journalism and reporting
Photography, video and animation
Scriptwriting and storyboarding
Sound recording and camera operation

BTEC Higher National Diploma in Communications

Core subjects
Basic visual and design theory and techniques
The history and traditions of art and design
The business and professional aspects of design practice
Verbal and written communication skills
Specialist Subjects
Computer aided design
Desktop publishing
Drawing, illustration and general graphics

Editing and other production skills
Journalism
Photography
Production planning
Sound recording, lighting and camera work
Storyboarding and scripting
Typography
Video, electronic imaging and animation

Design (Communications)

BTEC National Diploma

East Anglia
Lowestoft College
South East Essex College of Arts and Technology
Central
Gloucestershire College of Arts and Technology
Herefordshire College of Art and Design
Shrewsbury College of Arts and Technology
Solihull College of Technology
Mid Warwickshhire College of Further Education
South of England
Highbury College of Technology
Portsmouth College of Art, Design and Further Education
Richmond upon Thames College
West Kent College of Further Education
Thames & Chilterns
West Herts College
Greater London
Kingsway College
North London College

Yorkshire & Humberside
Harrogate College of Arts and Technology
East Midlands
South Nottinghamshire College of Further Education
The North West
Salford College of Technology
South Trafford College of Further Education

BTEC National Courses in Media

Core Subjects
Media in context
Media Images
Working practises in the Media
Media Workshop
Media Production
Specialist Options
Audio-visual Practices
Audio-visual presentation
Design in Media
Interview and presentation skills
Marketing and the Media
Media Administration
Media performance
Moving images
The Music Industry
Presentations and Exhibitions
Print Editing
Print origination and Production
Radio and tape production
Recording for Tape and radio

Sound Industries
Television, film and video production
Writing for film and television.

BTEC National Diploma in Media

West Country
Chippenham Technical College
Cornwall College
New College
South Bristol College
Weymouth College

Greater London
Barking College of Technology
Ealing Tertiary College
Greenhill College
Hammersmith and West London College
Havering College of Further and Higher Education
Hounslow Borough College
South Thames College
Southgate College

Yorkshire & Humberside
Barnsley College
Grimsby College of Technology and Arts
Hopwood Hall College
Hull College of Further Education
Kitson College of Technology
North Lindsay College
Norton College
Oulder Hill Community School
Thomas Danby College
Wakefield District College

Thames and the Chilterns
Amersham and Wycombe College
East Berkshire College
Milton Keynes College
North Oxfordshire College and School of Art
Oaklands College
Oxford College of Further Education

Central
Gloucestershire College of Arts and Technology
Henley College Coventry
South Warwickshire College of Further Education
Stoke on Trent College
Stroud College of Further Education
Sutton Coldfield College of Further Education
Tile Hill College of Further Education
Wulfrun College of Further Education

North West
Accrington and Rossendale College
Blackburn College
Burnley College
City of Liverpool Community College
Oldham College
Preston College
Rotherham College of Arts and Technology
Shena Simon College
Skelmersdale College
Southport College of Art and Technology
Walsall College of Art
West Cheshire College
Wigan and Leigh College

The North
Cleveland College of Art and Design

Cumbria College of Art and Design
Darlington College of Technology
Gateshead College
Kirby College of Further Education
Longlands College of Further Education
Monkwearmouth College

Wales
Coleg Glan Hafren
Coleg Powys
Crosskeys College
Pontypool and Usk College
Swansea College
Ysgol Emrys Ap Iwan
Ystrad Mynach College of Further Education

South of England
Basingstoke College of Technology
Brighton College of Technology
Chichester College of Technology
Eastbourne College of Arts and Technology
Eastleigh College
East Surrey College
Kingston College of Further Education
Northbrook College
Performing Arts and Technology School
South Downs College of Further Education

East Midlands
Hinckley College of Further Education
Newark and Sherwood College
Northampton College
Southfields College of Further Education
South East Derbyshire College
Tresham Institute of further and Higher Education

East Anglia
Norwich City College of Further and Higher Education
Redbridge Technical College
South East Essex College of Arts and Technology
Suffolk College of Higher and Further Education

Northern Ireland
Banbridge College of Further Education
Newcastle College of Further Education
Newtownabbey College of Further Education
North Antrim College of Further Education
North West Institute of Further and Higher Education
Omagh College of Further Education

BTEC Photography Courses

BTEC National Diploma in Photography

Core subjects
Visual Studies - develops visual awareness and good design sense
Historical and Contextual Studies
Business Management and Professional Practice studies
Communication studies
The Theory and Practice of Photography

BTEC National Diploma Design (Photography)

Greater London
Barking College of Technology
City of Westminster College
Kingsway College
Richmond upon Thames College
Thames and Chilterns
Barnfield College, Luton
Berkshire College of Art and Design
Hertford Regional College
West Herts College
Central
Herefordshire College of Art and Design
Sandwell College of Further and Higher Education
Solihull College of Technology
Stoke on Trent College
University of Central England in Birmingham

The North West
Mid Cheshire College of Further Education
Blackburn College
City of Liverpool Community College
Southport College of Art and Technology
Stockport College of Further and Higher Education
Wirral Metropolitan College
The North
Longlands College of Further Education
Newcastle College
West Country
Falmouth School of Art and Design
Plymouth College of Art and Design
Bournemouth and Poole College of Art and Design
Wales
Crosskeys College
Swansea College
Swansea Institute of Higher Education
South of England
Brighton College of Technology
Guildford College of Technology
North East Surrey College of Technology
Yorkshire & Humberside
Dewsbury College
Kitson College of Technology
Harrogate College of Arts and Technology
Wigan and Leigh College
East Midlands
Southfields College of Further Education
South Nottinghamshire College of Further Education

East Anglia
Norfolk College of Arts and Technology

BTEC Higher National Diploma in Photography

Core subjects
Basic visual and design theory and techniques
The history and traditions of art and design
The business and professional aspects of design practice
Verbal and written communication skills
The Theory and Practice of Photography
Specialist Options
Advertising Photography
Audio-visual media
Documentary Photography
Film and Television
Medical Photography
Photographic Technology

BTEC Design Higher National Diploma (Photography)

Greater London
City of Westminster College
Richmond upon Thames College
Thames and Chilterns
Berkshire College of Art and Design
Central
Sandwell College of Further and Higher Education

The North West
Blackpool and the Fylde College
The North
Cleveland College of Art and Design
Newcastle College
West Country
Salisbury College
University of Plymouth
Bournemouth and Poole College of Art and Design
Wales
Gwent College of Higher Education
Swansea Institute of Higher Education
South of England
Kent Institute of Art and Design

BTEC Fashion and Beauty Courses

BTEC National Diploma in Fashion and Clothing

BTEC Higher National Diploma in Fashion and Clothing

Please refer to the Costume/Wardrobe section

BTEC National Diploma in Beauty Therapy

Please refer to the Make-up Section

Film & Television

Within this section are listed courses and training schemes specific to film and television. The addresses are to be found in the address section towards the end of the book.

Courses and Training Schemes

Two Year Courses/Schemes

Film and Television Production Training Scheme
Film and Television Freelance Training (ft2)

ft2 was formerly JOBFIT. The idea is that training is the equivalent to an apprentice ship with trainees being attached to various productions over the training period. On the job experiences are supplemented by specially commissioned intensive short courses. Trainees all attend a basic induction course and work as crew on productions. After that they specialise and should leave able to go straight into junior grades of their chosen specialisation. As the scheme is industry based and therefore dependent on production levels for the range and variety of attachments, application times for entry can vary.

Training is offered in the following areas:
Camera Assistant/Clapper Loader, Assistant Editor/VTOps/Post-Production, Sound Assistant, Art Department Assistant, Location Assistant, Production Assistant, Assistant Script Supervisor, 3rd Assistant Director, Grips, Make-Up/Hair Assistant, Research Assistant.

Training is not offered for Directors, Producers or Script writers.

Entrance is by interview. Applicants must be able to demonstrate commitment and enthusiasm for film and television production, good communication skills, a strong visual sense, all round literacy and manual dexterity. ft2 is committed to an equal opportunities policy and aims to recruit one half of its intake from women and one third from ethnic minorities. All places are heavily over subscribed.

Trainees are paid a training allowance and certain travel expenses are met.

Film Course
London International Film School

Together with the National Film and Television School, LIFS is probably the most respected film school in the country. The course lasts for two years, and students may start at the beginning of any term. Students are not expected to specialise on this course but gain an all round understanding of the film industry and the processes involved. Each term is based around a film exercise of the students own work. In this way students cover all aspects of film including scripting, organisation and production, directing and acting, photography, Lenses, Camera, Lighting and Special effects, Animation and titling, Projection and presentation, sound, music, art department and design, make-up and Wardrobe, Film analysis and appreciation. Practical and oral tests are given each term and must be passed before continuing. There is also a final written dissertation. Hours run from 10-5 on weekdays, but students are expected to attend evening and weekend lectures. Shooting may also take place at the weekends. Facilities include 35mm as well as 16mm cameras, two studios, two cinemas, editing suite and photography dark room.

Entrance by interview. Students must submit a 300 + work critique of a film and a short film script of twenty to thirty shots, lasting approx. 3 minutes. Each shot must be illustrated

by a sketch or photograph. Students should also bring with them any examples of their work, be it film, video, photographic, art or literary.
Application fee: £25   Fees: c £11,000 per annum

Film and Television Course
The National Film and Television School
At the time of writing the NFTS was in a state of flux with entry to the three year course being closed for at least a year. Critics maintained that the school was out of touch and old fashioned; supporters held that the school had an international reputation for excellence. Whichever are right, changes are likely in response to crisis of confidence and funding. At the moment the school aims to offer a short course programme, probably in the following areas: Animation, Art Direction, Camera, Directing, Documentary, Editing, Music Composition, Producing and Sound. Each course will last between 2-3 months.

Professional Course in Film and TV Production
The North East Media Training Centre
NEMTC is a charity supported by Tyne Tees TV, Channel 4, several Training and Enterprise councils and the European Social Fund. The centre offers tailor-made and short courses but is probably of most interest for the 2 year NEMTEC Professional Course in Film and TV Production. It is expected that once industry standards are agreed on this will be equivalent to NVQ/SVQ level 4. The course is mainly practical. The foundation year aims to give a broad base in the technical, production and organisational skills required in film, video and television production. In the second year students may choose two specialist areas from Sound, Editing, Camera/Lighting, Production (Direction), Production (Production

Management) and Production (Scriptwriting). Students should be able to leave and obtain jobs at the Assistant level in Sound recording, Studio sound, Editing (on-line and off-line) and Camera (including Lighting skills). Students also leave with a show reel of at least two broadcast-standard productions. Facilities include two TV studios, viewing theatre, sound studio, editing suites, camera equipment etc. Only 16mm is available.

Entrance by interview and submission of work showing an aptitude for working with visual images, sound or the work written for TV/film. Supporting material could include Video Productions, Films, Photographs, Drawings and designs, Scripts and so on. Students need to show evidence of dedicated personal interest and commitment to working in the media.

Fees: c£5000 per annum (EEC), c£10,000 (non-EEC).

BTEC HND: Television Programme Operations Ravensbourne College of Design and Communication

"The course gives students the opportunities for developing talent in the art and technical skill of programme-making. Prog Ops is a crucial team activity in the world of professional television. It gives skills in the operation of cameras, lighting sound, vision-mixing, editing, videotape recording, and telecine. Understanding of budgeting, studio and location management, and planning techniques. Awareness of the fundamentals of staging, graphic design, script writing and production organisation. The Prog Ops course team believes that the flair and imagination to make attention-grabbing pictures and sounds goes hand-in-hand with a craft understanding of 'how equipment works." The course includes a minimum six week work placement during the Summer Vacation between years one and two.

BTEC HND: Television Studio Systems Engineering
Ravensbourne College of Design and Communication

The course gives the fundamental engineering expertise for maintaining and developing hardware and software and keeping a television station on air or a facilities company in business. The TSS course programme is a unit-based modular structure. All parts of the course are composed of two strands; theoretical studies in electronics, audio and video theory, engineering systems and industrial studies; and 'hands on' engineering application in the laboratories, television studios, video and audio computerised edit suites, maintenance and other practical work areas in the School of Television and Broadcasting. The course includes maintenance of the two professional television studios, computer controlled lighting rigs, studio based and lightweight filed cameras and recorders, sound control and recording rooms, digital video paintbox systems and telecine facilities. The course includes a minimum six week work placement during the Summer Vacation between years one and two.

Film and Television Production Course
Royal College of Art

The aim of the course is to develop the skills of creative producers and to give them the practical opportunity to take total responsibility for film and television productions from the initial concept through to marketing the finished product. Producing students work as production managers on each other's films, acting as producer for at least one student film. By the second year students are expected to take full responsibility for initiating and producing graduation films and sponsored productions. Students cover areas such as law, insurance cover, budgeting and financial control, negotiating contracts together with workshops on scripting and working with actors. One of the aims of the course is to create working relationships with the student directors and designers.

Entrance is by submission of examples of their work on video, plus a portfolio containing budget procedures and final costing of the film as well as a schedule and contracts, if applicable. Applicants should also provide evidence of other production experience in film or television, as well as any related experience in the filed of communication, business and any creative experience.

Television and Film Direction Course
Royal College of Art

This is a practical craft Course, in which a high level of professional skill combined with originality and creativity is expected of all students. One or two students may be able to specialise in camera work, and there may also be places for students wishing to specialise in post-production, sound and scriptwriting. Emphasis is placed on the development of ideas and scripting both for drama and documentary. The first year reinforces the collaborative nature of film and television production, with all students working together on a number of projects and commission. Workshops in scriptwriting and professionally oriented technical/craft skills play a major part of this year. There are also seminars, workshops and lectures on subjects such as cinematography and lighting, sound design, post-production editing and dubbing, directing actors, the development and history of cinema and television, current

aspects in advertising and promotional films. The second year provides opportunities for film and video making, either on their own or as part of a group. For the final examination each student is required to submit a finished film or video.
Entrance is by submission of their work on video, plus at least one additional script of up to 30 pages, together with any other related material.

Short Courses

British Kinematograph Sound and Television Society
The BKSTS run a training programme which mainly consists of one to three day courses such as: Intro to Video technology, Lighting for 16mm drama, Basic Special Effects, Introduction to 35mm cameras, Betacam update, Sound for the cinema and so on.

Black Witch
The Black Women's Media Project aims to enable black women to gain skills in what is a predominantly white, male workplace. 12 week courses run (starting September 1993) which include Video and Radio Production, Photography and Media Skills for Black women under 25 years, Introductory camera techniques, sound recording, lighting, scripting, production and editing. The course also includes work placement, personal, social and vocational skills with Open College accreditation.

There will be a training allowance, plus additional travel expenses. Child-care allowance is provided.

The London Screenwriters Workshop
The LSW was founded by writers to offer a forum for contact, information and tuition. There is a continuous programme of activities, events, courses and seminars, many of which non members may attend. Membership is £18 per annum and gives a bulletin (with reports on industry news, openings competitions etc.), LSW events programme, discount book-

ing, screen writing workshops and a script reading service among other benefits. Recent workshops included: Writing Creatively, Screenwriting and an Outline Workshop.

The National Film and Television School
At the time of writing the NFTS was in a state of flux with entry to the three year course being closed for at least a year. Critics maintained that the school was out of touch and old fashioned; supporters held that the school had an international reputation for excellence. Whichever are right, changes are likely in response to crisis of confidence and funding. At the moment the school aims to offer a short course programme, probably in the following areas: Animation, Art Direction, Camera, Directing, Documentary, Editing, Music Composition, Producing and Sound. Each course will last between 2-3 months.

Ravensbourne College of Design and Communication
As well as their full time courses Ravensbourne run numerous short courses lasting 1-15 days on aspects relating to television and broadcasting. Courses include: Basic television programme operations, Television engineering principles and practice, Data compression techniques, VTR operational technology, basic video tape technical principals, Basic video tape editing, Component VTR technology, single camera production, Digital video recording technology, off-line editing, Basic lighting for television, Creative editing, Digital audio recording systems, Satellite broad casting for engineers, classical musical recording and so on.
Fees range from £107 to £1732.

Video Engineering and Training Ltd

VET offer short courses lasting from 1-5 days in various aspects of video technique. Course fees range from £150 - £600. They can also run tailor-made courses. Shooting kits are available to hire by the day. Courses currently on offer include: Introduction to Video Production; Understanding Video Technology; U-matic maintenance; Sound recording for Video; Camera and Lighting (Beginners and Advanced) ; Camera/ Betacam first line maintenance; Off-line editing for beginners; Editing Technology; and Digital Video among others.

The Television Works Training Packages
Workhouse Ltd

Each package contains a course tape (55 minutes), and Open learning Coursebook and a Workbook of source materials. The Research/Scripting Course also contains a 50 minute worktape. Each course carries a study guideline of 40 hours. As well as the two courses itemised below there is also a 'Two machine Editing' course which needs to be based in a Two Machine Edit suite with a Trainer, or Editor who is prepared to assume a training role in the workplace. Workhouse Ltd is a production company, and the course is sponsored by the IVCA, Hampshire Training Agency and Sony.

Research/Scripting:
"After completing the course participants will be able to: understand the brief for a programme, interpret it and carry out the initial research; understand the development of the programme Outline, identifying the audience and the programme style; Identify source materials: documents, newspapers and statistics, interviews, library material. Identify people suitable for inclusion in programmes; Conduct a recce;

Write the Outline up into a Script; Understand basic camera and editing equipment and the creative use of graphics." £350 + VAT (Total £402.50)

Production Management:
"After completing the course participants will be able to: Demonstrate a working knowledge about all areas of programme making; Identify the skills knowledge and attitude required for successful product management; Put together budgets and schedules; Understand how to book people, facilities and equipment; state how archive footage, stills and music can be secured and used within copyright constraints. " £500 + VAT (Total £575)

Short courses are also held at many centres around the UK. Your regional Arts Board will have details of those which are currently running.

Section III

Production & Administration

Getting into the Film and Television Industries

Introduction

Prior to the 1980's these industries were to a large extent separate. Film and the ITV companies were controlled by the unions who restricted entry. It was virtually essential to have good contacts to get started, often quite literally father to son. Once in a first job the trainee had to stay there for two years before being allowed to move on. Training was on the job, as in an apprenticeship. This continued throughout the business, and usually a person was fully competent to perform a job years before being promoted to that position, thus ensuring that standards were high - indeed British technicians had the reputation of being the best in the world. Jobs were for life, and it was often a good life, with heavy staffing levels insisted on by the unions, and over-time abuses rife.

The BBC, the single largest employer, ran their own training schemes. These too were hard to get into, not through union dominance, but through the sheer numbers of people who wished to go on one of the BBC's training programmes. At the higher levels of programme making - the producers, directors and managers - there was a particular culture which gave preference (and still, to a certain extent, does) to white, middle class, male Oxbridge graduates. Jobs were secure and often for life, although many employees left for less prestigious (and better paid) jobs with the independent companies.

Videos had just begun, but were very much confined to the fringes of broadcasting, areas such as pop promos and corporate information films. Technically the quality of video was poor and looked down on by the rest of the industry, and the production teams were also often untrained. Many of these were unable to get into the industry through the conventional openings and saw video as a way in. More often than not they were young and not hidebound by the traditions of film and television.

During the 1980's three things happened which have effectively changed the industries in the 1990's: The Conservative government's battle with the unions; the technical improvement in the quality of video tape; and the boom in consumerism and the cult of 'the free market'.

The power of television unions, in particular at the ITV companies, was destroyed during the decade. Strikes, most particularly the one at TV AM, showed that with modern equipment many of the jobs that previously needed trained technicians could now be operated by those with little previous knowledge (at TV AM the non-union management, administration and secretarial staff ran the station for many months until the strike was broken).

Technically video tape improved so that it became hard to tell the difference between film, electronic tape (as used in television studios) and video. Video is also cheap and flexible, lending itself to experiments in production and direction. Pop promos provided a good environment for innovation in techniques and many technical staff were attracted to this. Aspiring directors would choose to go into video production in preference to trying any of the more traditional routes.

Thirdly the boom in consumerism meant that there was considerable money to be made in fields such as pop promos and corporate films, and many video makers set up their own companies. Production standards rocketed and the video industry could no longer be reckoned as a poor relation. On the grounds of the free market (and for other, political, reasons) the government imposed the 'twenty five per cent quota on the BBC. This meant that at least 25% of the BBC's out put had to come from the independent sector, which (combined with the impact of Channel 4 as a commissioner of programmes) led to an explosion of small production companies. The free market also led to the changes when the ITV franchises came to auction, with new companies taking over from the established. Many of the new companies bought programmes rather than producing themselves.

These three factors combined to produce a fundamental change in the way the industry had operated: 'Casualisation'.

'Casualisation' means that today most of the workers within the film, television and video industry are self-employed on short term contracts. These may be as short as one day, or may last a year. Some are employed on longer 'fixed' contracts for maybe two or three years; these are usually administrative staff. A very small group are on permanent or open contracts. The would-be entrant into the industry must be aware that their career is more likely to be that of a freelance than that of an employee. Among other things a freelance must be able to:

* Organise their own accounts, National Insurance, Tax, Pension, Sickness insurance and perhaps VAT.
* Find their own work (knocking on doors, making contacts, self presentation etc.).
* Be consistently efficient and good at their job; employers feel no compunction about sacking the unreliable or incompetent freelance.
* Be aware that there may be long periods out of work, or times when work must be done from home.

The advantages of the changes in the 1980's are numerous, such as easier entry for the new comer, greater and more varied programme making, livelier programme making, cheaper productions, few union restrictions on where you can work, over 1000 new production companies and a greater fluidity between film, television and video.

The disadvantages were less expected, for example the recession has meant that advertising budgets have been cut, which means that many of the production companies are struggling and independent television revenues are down, leaving less money for productions - especially after paying the huge sums that some companies bid to secure their franchises. One of the unforeseen disadvantages has been that suddenly there were fewer companies offering training and no rigid union regulations to ensure apprenticeships. In effect much of the training structure has been dismantled.

The replacement for the old method of training is still being developed, and until then the industry is, in effect, open to anyone with the will to enter.

How to get into film and television

1. Get in at any level you can. Be a runner, a receptionist, the tea lady, the dogsbody. Once in start to network. Make sure everybody knows that you want to move on.

2. Get to know people. Most jobs are not advertised and are filled by word of mouth recommendations. Contacts are the name of the game. See if you can shadow someone or act as an unpaid assistant for a few weeks.

3. Get a show reel together. Ideally this is a short film showing what you can do presented in whatever format you can manage. A film or television course should have the facilities and the structure to make sure every student leaves with a showreel, but there is nothing to stop you from making your own with a domestic camcorder.

4. Watch and learn to analyse the sort of programme you would like to make. Too many people think it would be nice to get into television or film without knowing what they would like to do.

5. Act on your own initiative. Most job vacancies are never advertised so you need to put yourself forward. Write off to producers of programmes you like and ask for an interview.

6. If you get an interview do some research. You should have seen something the company or department has done: get in touch with the department secretary who will send you information and a production tape if you ask.

7. Follow up. Write thank-you letters if anyone gives you their time, phone up after you send a CV out, keep in touch anyone you have made contact with.

8. Training courses are an advantage, especially a training scheme like ft2. Make sure that any courses is what you want - a short specialised course may be of more value than a long general one. Wherever possible take courses which have a high percentage of industry input.

Production & Administration

Where there is a clear career path and structure the courses are included immediately after the particular career entry. This includes Theatre Directors, Stage Managers and Arts Administrators. For the rest entry is usually by working your way up from the bottom, often from technical or secretarial jobs. A lucky few may be able to leap-frog this process by attending one of the film courses or training schemes listed in the Film and Television Courses and Training Schemes Section.

Production

Producer

The producer is the person who pulls the whole production together. They will have chosen the idea, chosen the director and the main members of the production team and, perhaps most important of all, found the money. This is why the producer collects the "best picture or best production" award. Almost all producers are freelance, even within television.

Theatre producers

There are no producers in subsidised theatre, only in the commercial sector. The producer calls on a team of backers, known as angels, to raise the money for the production. Often the only reward for the angel is a few tickets to see the production and a chance to meet the actors. Occasionally the returns can be great, for example, an investment in The Mousetrap has repaid itself many times. Sometimes the profits made in the West End are lost on tour, or vice versa. It is a high risk business to be in. Many theatre producers specialise, such as Cameron Mackintosh in musical theatre.

It is possible to start as a producer with no capital, no connections and no experience at all, although they help. Many theatre producers have previous experience within theatre, often as stage managers. Peter Elliott of E & B Productions started while working as a stage manager for another company using a nearby phone box as his 'office'. Some have good connections, such as Pola Jones, which started by mounting productions featuring Oxbridge contemporaries Griff Rhys Jones and Mel Smith.

Television Producer

Within television the job of Producer and Director may be combined. The producer argues for, and then controls the budget for the production. The BBC has recently introduced 'Producers Choice' which means that the producer need not use in-house staff for a production but can go to independent production companies. Producers may work in fields outside drama production such as documentaries, light entertainment, sports and news. All producers have previous experience usually as production manager, director or researcher. Although they are now technically freelances most work consistently for one company.

Film Producer

With the main stream film the film producer is much more the money man than in television and is as likely to have a background in accountancy and business as theatre and film. Films are expensive costing millions of pounds and the producer has to first raise that money and then check that the director does not run over budget. Even low-budget productions are likely to cost £500,000. This money is raised from institutions rather than individuals. The producer also raises money by selling the production to overseas distributors, television, satellite, video and so on. In the UK Channel 4 has played an important part in maintaining a British film industry by commissioning films such as The Crying Game

Independent and Video Producers

Many independent production companies were formed in the wake of the deregulation of television and the entrepreneurial spirit of the '80s. A television programme is as likely to be produced by an independent company as by the broadcaster

- Euston Films for example produced television dramas such as 'Capital City' and 'Minder' for Thames Television. Most production companies are producer/director teams, although a few have been formed by actors, agents or presenters to create work for themselves, for example, agent Michael Whitehall produced 'The Good Guys' from his original idea. The production starred Nigel Havers and Keith Barron, both clients of Michael Whitehall (as well as Mrs Whitehall and the Whitehall children). This is commonplace in Hollywood where agents wield more power than in the UK. Many companies are looking for work such as producing commercials, promotional films and so on. This is an area which has been badly hit by the recession.

Becoming a producer is determined by talent and determination rather than qualifications; there are no courses for would-be producers, although in the past the BBC has offered in-house training.

Directors

The role of the director is to take charge of the production and convert it from ideas into a finished product, whether on stage or screen. Directors normally work in either the theatre or in television and film with relatively little cross-over between the areas. Kenneth Rea's report "A Better Direction" for the Calouste Gulbenkian Foundation showed that most directors have had no training at all, and that over all the profession is dominated by white, middle class males. Since the report was published more directing courses have been established, although the number of television companies offering in-house training has dropped. The report also showed that a large majority of the younger directors were graduates. Degree courses in relevant areas are listed in the 'General Courses' section together with film and television courses and training schemes. Theatre director courses are listed in this section.

Television directors

Most television directors have previous experience, either as a trainee or in some other area of employment such as camera crew, floor manager or researcher. A few may move direct from theatre into television but that is unusual. The television drama director needs to know about the technical demands of television and be able, if necessary, to story board the production shot by shot as well as directing the actors' performance. A director is also needed in areas such as news, documentaries or light entertainment; these are more likely to be staff positions.

Film director

The film director may have worked in television or have come up from a technical position such as camera crew, or assistant director. Many come in from allied areas such as commercials and video production, Alan Parker and Ridley Scott being two famous examples. Films, of course, can be made by anybody and so in some ways is easier to get into film rather than television. The most important element is a showreel. This may be a series of clips or a short film but is essential for any one wanting to start in the industry. One of the advantages of going on a film and television course is the opportunity to make a showreel so it is important to check that a course has the facilities for this. There are also many community projects, collectives and workshops, some of which run short courses or give the opportunity to make a film. The regional Arts Boards and Films Councils have details of what is available in your area, see the Film and Television Courses and Training Schemes section for details.

Theatre Director

Most directors are freelance. The exceptions are:
The **Artistic Director** runs a repertory theatre company and is an employee. The job in some ways is like that of a producer, negotiating the overall budget with funding bodies such as the Arts Council and/or local council, and overseeing all productions. This includes choosing the theatre season of plays and assigning directors and designers to each. The artistic director may direct a majority of plays or hardly any. Being an artistic director is one of the few stable jobs within theatre - so long as the theatre is profitable - and many stay in their positions for decades. Others see it as a creative dead end as few repertory theatre audiences support experimental work. **The Associate Director** is also an employee. Depending on their contract

Associates may only direct for that theatre or may spend time directing elsewhere as a freelance. The advantage of being an associate director is that it brings a certain level of security and status. **The Assistant Director** is a trainee. They may direct productions on their own or be assistants, helping the director. Assisting the director may include taking rehearsals or being confined to making the tea. The assistant director may be a member of staff, an un-paid volunteer looking for experience, or on a bursary scheme such as that run by the Arts Council of Great Britain. At the moment the current scheme is for those who wish to further their careers (i.e. have already done some directing, probably on the fringe). One or two directors are chosen (from several hundred applicants) and receive a placement of about six months at a regional repertory theatre. The scheme (which may change format from year to year) is confirmed in early spring and usually advertised in mid-summer.

Freelance directors find obtaining work almost as hard as actors do and often form their own theatre companies to create work. To supplement income many directors work in drama schools or colleges.

Simon Curtis, 33, Director

At school I was obsessed with the theatre. I was a member of the Royal Court Youth Theatre, and worked at the National Theatre as an usher so I used to see everything there. I used to write to everyone and ask if I could watch things, so I'd be hanging round the set of Upstairs, Downstairs, just watching and learning. I was assiduous in that sense. The day I left school the Riverside Studios opened and I went there to become a dogsbody. I spent two years there and ended up as Peter Gill's assistant which was a great experience. Then I went to Bristol University to read English. While I was there they let me off a term to go to Los Angeles to direct a play with a friend there.

After leaving Bristol I started on the Regional Training Directors Scheme, and went to the Royal Court as an Assistant Director. I was there seven years and ended up as Deputy Director. I was very interested in television and while at the Royal Court went on the BBC directors scheme. It seemed to me that all the interesting new writing was in television drama and I wanted to work on new writing, not old plays. At a Royal Court Benefit dinner I sat next to Alan Yentob and the result was we set up Performance together, which is now on its third season.

Things are always hard in the business, in the 80's there weren't the opportunities that there were in the 70's, and I've moved into television just as the budgets are being cut for the first time. Things like the directors scheme are harder to get now I suppose, but if you have the right attitude and are prepared to do dogsbody work and are very serious about it....it's no good idly wanting to be an actor, a director or a producer. I meet people who say they want to get into television and when you ask them what they've seen they say they don't have time to watch much. If you want to do television drama then you must watch it. Most people shoot themselves in the foot like that. Just be dedicated.

Director Courses

Three Year Courses, Directors, Full Time

BA Hons Theatre - Directors
Rose Bruford

The college is split between two sites. The main base is in a mansion with its own park land and lake in Sidcup on the edges of London, while at the Greenwich site they have workshops, performance, rehearsal and classroom space. The directors study in three different areas: firstly with the actors course, to develop awareness of the actors basic working methods and to give experience of working with a group; secondly with the technical theatre course, to learn the technical possibilities of theatre - this part includes, stage management, wardrobe, properties, stage settings, lighting and sound and there will also be an element of design; and thirdly, the course covers research and interpretation of text, such as the development of dramatic styles, the historical, social, and artistic aspects of a play. Actual directing starts with observation and assisting of directors, either at the school or on a placement, through to working on a production as a full director.

Entrance by a workshop and an interview, part of which will be based on a given play script.

Audition fee: £25 (£5 for the unemployed or those in receipt of income support)   Fees: c£3000 (mandatory grants)   CDS

East 15

East 15 is based on the methods of Joan Littlewood who pioneered ensemble work in this country. Understanding character is at the heart of this approach and involves much research and staying in character for days, even weeks. They are help by the school's secondary site at Sheriff Hutton Hall in Yorkshire, a beautiful Jacobean mansion, where, for example, Miss Julie can be rehearsed (and performed) in an authentic servants hall beside a real 19th century kitchen range. Classical texts are almost exclusively studied, until the last year when modern plays may be performed. Directors basically follow the actors training for the first year then gradually are allowed more opportunities to direct during the second and third years. 18+

Auditions

Workshop based, in groups of up to ten. Expect lots of improvisation.

Audition fee: £20 Fees: c£6000 per annum

Two Year Courses, Directors, Full Time

Court Theatre Training Company

The training company came into existence when the Court Theatre Company, a touring company, started to operate workshops for young and aspiring actors. This developed into a second, training theatre company. Both companies are now based at The Courtyard Theatre, a fringe theatre in central London. The course runs from 9am to 10pm on four days a week, Thursday to Sunday inclusive (about 44 hours), leaving three days free to take a part time job if necessary. The duration of course varies from one year to two, depending on the previous level of experience. Directing starts from the beginning and by the end of the first year will have directed and produced a production. The second year involves more production, and if desired the CTC will enable the director to set up his or her own company using the facilities of Courtyard Theatre. A feature of the CTC is that they are making a conscious effort to avoid traditional text-based theatre (although both classical and modern texts are studied) and are looking to Europe for new ideas - "a physical, visual and total theatre experience". Directors may be accepted, depending on vacancies in the company, at the start of each term i.e. January, April and

September. 18+, but they are looking for "mature members who are seeking post-experience training."
Entrance by interview. A submission in theory of a short scene from a play is required at least one week before the interview.
Audition Fee: £20 Fees: c£4000 per annum

School of the Science of Acting
The course is run in association with GITIS (The Moscow Institute of Theatre Arts) and follows its tradition of teaching inherited from the methods developed by Stanislavski. The principal claims that English translations of Stanislavski's books are "mis-translated, mis-edited and even mis-invented" and secondly, that the transcripts of Stanislavskis rehearsals show that they had not been based on his system as described in his book. The principal has evolved his own method which is called the Science of Acting. Put simply, acting is a technique that can be taught, and this method teaches it (alongside other staples of drama school training such as dance, speech, improvisation and so on). The course follows a structured syllabus and develops directing skills in a coherent fashion, and rehearsals of productions mostly take place outside school hours.
Entrance by interview and audition. A short play will be sent out to applicants which will form the basis of discussion. Applicants must also prepare a Shakespeare speech, a fable, a piece of modern poetry or prose, and a song or dance, none of the pieces lasting more than two minutes.
Interview fee: £20 Fees: c£5000 per annum

One Year Courses, Directing, Full Time

The Academy
The first school to offer a complete part time training. The school has its own theatre (which operates as a fringe venue for other, outside productions), and plenty of rehearsal/classroom space. The company puts on about 9 plays per year at the school's theatre, with morning classes covering the basics and afternoons spent in rehearsal. There is a separate show case, and a three week run at another fringe theatre. Directors are expected to join in with the acting workshops and classes. The directing element comes with one to one tutorials and acting as assistant to all productions, with opportunities to observe, assist or co-direct productions for other courses as well. 30+ hours per week.
Entry requirements: No formal qualifications required, but applicants are expected to have had some previous training or reasonable experience. Each application is judged individually. 18+.
Fees: c£3500 for course

Advanced Residential Theatre and Television Skillcentre International
ARTTS is the only school where students are expected to live on site, about 17 miles south of York. Accommodation is in residential units continuing dining and sitting

rooms, kitchen and utility room and single study/bedrooms. There are three advanced courses available in Acting, Directing and Production/Operations although each contains element of each other as the aim is to produce actors who can also direct or operate a sound boom, directors who can stage manage etc. Facilities are comprehensive and include television and recording studios and a 200 seat theatre. Audiences are almost entirely limited to locals except when productions are staged in York. There are no London based showcase productions. There are two intakes per year. The Directing course is unusual among directing courses in that it can offer experience of directing for film and television from start to finish, including subjects such as developing a camera script or story board, treatments, script writing, production management, budgeting and scheduling among others. Directors are also given training in acting and production operations. Students are required to present a final written presentation.

Entrance requirements: 21+. All applicants are treated in the same way, regardless of which course/option they are applying for. Candidates are selected first on the basis of their application form, and then by interview. Audition fee: None   Fees c£6500 + £2000 for accommodation

Central School of Speech and Drama

Central must be the most dynamic drama school at the moment; it has always been one of the best. Directors start with exercises, whether related to classical texts, new writing, or acting. There is an emphasis on the visual and technical forms of theatre as well as opportunity to develop administrative/marketing/management skills. Productions range from 'showings' with minimal production support to producing a season of new work during the last term. Some students may be offered a placement with a professional company on completion. A school with great opportunities for strong personalities. Post graduate or post experience only.

Entrance by interview and audition in which applicants will take part as actors and also to direct a prescribed scene.

Audition fee: £25   Fees: c£4000 for course

The Drama Studio London

The Drama Studio only offers courses for post-graduate and mature students, and was until recently the only drama school course for directors where the directing students were not just tagged onto the acting course. The two courses do run in parallel however and the directors are expected to attend classes to work with and understand actors. Over the year each directing student should have mounted six projects, some in-house and some at outside venues using outside actors. Exactly what is put on depends on the individual, but the DSL aims that each student leaves with a "property" which can be immediately presented at the Edinburgh Fringe Festival or on the London Fringe.

Entrance is by interview, which may include a number of practical exercises. Preference is given to applicants who can show previous directing experience and she a background in theatre history and dramatic literature.

Application fee: £30   Fees: c£7500 for course

Welsh College

Like Guildhall and RSAMD the drama department is a part of a larger organisation and facilities are good. Musical theatre and singing are very strong here, with several joint productions with the music department. There are strong links with the Sherman Theatre. Welsh speakers receive additional options in Welsh throughout the course. The programme of study varies according to the needs of the students but may include: observation and/or assisting staff or guest directors, participating in the acting programme, directing workshops, projects, directing a production for the Edinburgh Fringe Festival, placement with a professional company, course in technical theatre and backstage work, TV and radio directing. Applicants should be graduates with demonstrable experience in directing or those with extensive theatre experience. 21+.

Entrance by interview, and by directing a practical session with a group of actors.

Interview fee: £15 Fees c£1000 for course

Directing Courses, Part Time

School of the Science of Acting
The course is run in association with GITIS (The Moscow Institute of Theatre Arts) and follows its tradition of teaching inherited from the methods developed by Stanislavski. The principal claims that English translations of Stanislavski's books are "mis-translated, mis-edited and even mis-invented" and secondly, that the transcripts of Stanislavskis rehearsals show that they had not been based on his system as described in his book. The principal has evolved his own method called the Science of Acting. Put simply, acting is a technique that can be taught, and this method teaches it (alongside other staples of drama school training such as dance, speech, improvisation and so on). The three year evening course follows the same structured syllabus as the two year full time directing course (see above) and develops directing skills in a coherent fashion. Classes run from three to five evenings a week, as well as Saturday mornings.
Entrance by interview and audition. A short play will be sent out to applicants which will form the basis of discussion. Applicants must also prepare a Shakespeare speech, a fable, a piece of modern poetry or prose, and a song or dance, none of the pieces lasting more than two minutes.
Interview fee: £20 Fees: c£2500 per annum

The School of the Science of Acting also runs a ten week full time course which basically involves assisting the Head of Directing on one or two productions and operating as an assistant stage manager, plus a 30-40 minute discussion period with the director at the end of each day.
Fees: c£2000

The Production Team

Production Assistant/Continuity

A production assistant provides organisational back-up to the television director and may be staff or, more usually, freelance. At the pre-production stage the production assistant takes notes on all meetings and makes sure that decisions are carried through which may involve work such as hiring catering facilities, accommodation as well as other secretarial services. There may also be changes to the script or other details, which must be typed up and distributed. During production the production assistant times each section of film, and notes down any comments that the director may make. The PA also notes down any changes to detail that will assist with continuity, the smooth transition from one shot to another. For example, if a character eats a meal during a speech they must take each mouthful at the same moment in the speech, throughout the different camera takes and shots. (Most actors quickly learn not to actually eat on screen). Continuity is a separate job in film production.

When recording in the studio the production assistant sits in the control room and tells the camera operators when they will be going on air. They also accurately time each section of the programme.

After the filming the production assistants notes are used to help with editing and any sound tracks that need to be added. A PA is one of the few people who follow a production from the initial stages through to post-production and transmission and it is one of the best jobs for gaining an all-round knowledge. An experienced PA may well be more capable than the producers and directors they are working with.

Production assistants need to be unflappable and have good secretarial skills. Most trainee posts are recruited in-house from secretarial and administrative staff. Would-be PAs may also be able to learn on the job if they can find an experienced PA who is prepared to train an assistant. Entrance as a secretary and then Production Assistant and then to Producer has traditionally been one of the ways that women have been able to move up the ranks of the male dominated television industry.

Sue Stamp, 33, Production Assistant
Basically I did a drama A level course, and I then went to secretarial college. They had talks from people like the Foreign Office about working for them, and some one from the BBC came along. They paid secretaries £2500 and the FO paid £2900 which really mattered then, so no one wanted to go to the BBC except me because I thought I wanted to get into drama and I thought the BBC was the place. They offered me a job, and I was allocated to the editor of Tomorrow's World.
On my first day the editor took me out to lunch and said I expect you want to be a PA, and I didn't even know what one was. I worked there for 9 months, then went to drama and then to LE and then applied for a PA course. There were 10 jobs and 400 applications, just internally from the BBC, and I didn't even get interviewed. I was lucky on the third time. There was a training course, and then I spent a year following a PA around. I ended up on the panel, which is like being a freelance within the BBC, they assigned you to different departments. I bought a flat, and it all got too much, I had to work 7 days a week at the BBC to keep up the payments.
So I applied to Central in Birmingham and almost doubled my pay, and the cost of living was lower. The atmosphere was really great, people knew who you were and said hello, at the BBC it had been really anonymous. Then I got married and we came back to London. By

then it was already heading towards the freelance world, but luckily I had a contact at LWT. It's absolutely contacts. I've sent hundreds of CVs out and I don't think I've ever had a job through them. I rely on word of mouth.

Most people who become PAs stay as PAs. Perhaps its because most are female, or because you come from the secretarial side. Often I've worked with directors and producers and I know I could do their job, but you really need the extra push, to start again with experience and enthusiasm. It's impossible to become a PA without being a secretary first. You can learn by following an experienced PA but some other PAs hate that, I was almost black listed for training some one. The BBC still train within the company and I'd advise any one to go for that, to have the BBC on your CV.

Researchers

A researcher's job is one of the most sought after starting positions in television as it is seen as a means to become a television director or producer. Researchers normally move up to these positions within 3-8 years. Traditionally it has attracted high-calibre graduates and competition for jobs has always been fierce; staff researchers have all but disappeared, but the competition is as great for the freelances. Most work is in documentaries and current affairs, although a drama production may have a researcher attached to check on the historical accuracy and authenticity. The researchers day is spent preparing material and finding suitable people to interview for a programme. They are also expected to come up with new ideas and approaches. Most researchers are graduates. Entry is by interview. One producer who interviews some 300 would-be researchers a year said that those he employed acted like researchers from the start i.e. they had researched the company, the department and its recent output, they were pleasant to talk to and interview, they had a wide range of interests and could produce ideas, they could get on with people, they were persistent, and they always followed up. Of the 300 only about 10% bothered to find out about the department, and only one or two ever followed up their interview. These were the ones who were employed.

Livia Russell, 27, Researcher

I trained to be a ballet dancer and did it professionally for a short time, but realised that the sort of effort you had to put in to get to the top was enormous, and that there had to be more to life than just dancing. I did secretarial work at the Actors Centre in London, and they did television workshops there, and I got interested in that. I then temped at the newsroom at TVS, first as a secretary and then as a copy taker. I worked hard and got them to take me on as a newsdesk researcher for the 1997 election. I then persuaded the documentary department to take me on. When TVS lost the franchise I spent 3-4 months out of work, then the 1992 election came up so I worked for the ITN newsroom on that. Then I heard that Central were looking for a researcher so since then I've been doing lots of documentary research. You have to be quite sharp and get on with lots of people. My news training was invaluable, and a good was to learn about TV production. The trouble is, if you haven't been through film school, or haven't got a degree, it's hard to push up to the next level. I have done some directing and producing. I'm really doing some associate producing now, but it suits them to pay me less as a researcher. If I was starting now I'd try to some attachments to either and independent or a broadcast company. Look at the credits of a programme you really like, get in touch with the producer and see if you could shadow them for a week. Get involved with amateur things like hospital radio, it helps you decide if you really want to do it as well. There are lots of companies who are very happy to have an extra pair of hands who

work for nothing, and once you are in there don't hang around, use your initiative, make yourself needed.
As competition for jobs get stiffer it's useful to have a degree or specialist knowledge such as languages, computer literacy, picture sources. Work out which programmes, which channel you like and then target them. It gets you past personnel, who usually aren't very helpful. Always watch the programmes if you are up for an interview and you've got to have some ideas about what you'd like to make, or subjects that would make a documentary, they want to see people who can come up with new things. You've got to be prepared, and so many people don't bother.

Production Manager, Location Manager, Assistant Directors, Runner (Film)
Floor Manager, Assistant Floor Manager (Television)
Stage Manager, Deputy Stage Manager, Assistant Stage Manager (Theatre)

Film
The **Production Manager** mainly works in film and is responsible for the day-to-day management of the filming, such as equipment hire and the preparation for budgets for shooting and shooting schedules (sometimes called a line producer). They may also take on the role of the location manager. Within a small company these tasks would be taken on by either the director or producer. Production managers are usually very experienced in the television and film industry, often as floor managers.

Location Managers are used on larger film and television productions. Their job falls in two areas, location research and finding and location management. Some location managers specialise in just one of these areas. The location manager finds suitable locations for the production and negotiate the fee for their use. A suitable location is not just a building but also the surrounding area, such as checking on noise levels (for example, is there an railway nearby), where can the production vans can park, and so on. Having done the research the location manager takes photographs and the director makes the final decision. Ideally all the locations chosen are near each other. The second part of the job is to manage the location and making sure there are no hitches on a daily basis. There is no training required to become a location manager, and most have been drawn into the job from another area within the industry such as floor manager.

The **First Assistant Director** takes on the role of the floor manager in television and is the link between the director and the crew and cast. They help production managers draw up shooting schedules, co-ordinate any special effects or stunts, and generally make sure that everything is in the right place at the right time. A major film may divide the responsibilities up between a second and third assistant director.

The **Runner** is also known as a gofer, as in "Go for this" and "Go for that". Runners are poorly paid (if at all) and may find themselves going to get takeaways or collect dry-cleaning more often than actually working on a set. Being a runner is one of the traditional ways of starting in the industry and is open to those who are prepared to knock on doors and ask for the job. Most runners stay for six months to a year in the job and move on when they have found their opportunity.

Marilla Elliott, 30, Location Manager

I'd applied to the BBC to get into production since I'd left school but never got anywhere. I worked for a guy who did location management for about two months. I hadn't known what that job was, and still thought of it in terms of production but I really liked it. I applied for JOBFIT and had a really hard interview and I didn't get on. Then I had a really hard time the second time I applied. I kept saying I'll just apply next year if you don't take me this year, so they took me on. Funnily enough I had an interview with the BBC for the producer scheme at the same time. I didn't know if that was what I wanted, being a producer, because I'm very practical. So I decided to be a production trainee at JOBFIT, although I always had in my mind that I wanted to do locations. I was advised not to make my mind up, it's a very male oriented role, you get a hard time on set - a real hard time. I did the Blackheath Poisonings and was left very much on my own to get on with it, and I loved it.

I do still want to be a production manager, but going the location route. I'd done the management training at M&S so I've got a good business sense and can budget and so on. I left JOBFIT at Christmas, which was a really bad time, and sent out loads of CVs, but in fact all my jobs have not been with people who I've sent CVs to, its all word of mouth. Locations are a huge proportion of the overall budget so it's got to be right, you've got to be able to find the perfect building with the perfect things in, and all from the right angles. You have to be able to interpret the set and get out of the director and the set designer exactly what they want.

There are two sides to location management, first there's research and finding and then there's the management side of things. It takes lots of different skills, like there are some things that I think women are better at, like going into somewhere and persuading some one to let 60 people walk through their house and wreck their furniture, but you also have to have a sense of authority without antagonising the crew. I think an army background would be great, at least you could park a truck. When you're working, it's at least an eighteen hour day, six days a week, quite often you only get two or three hours sleep, and every thing is always your fault so you have to be able to take abuse first thing in the morning. And no one ever says thank you. I think it's one of the hardest jobs. I love it.

Television

When a production is being filmed the director moves into control room where he or she can watch the screens. The **Floor Manager**'s job is to provide the link between the director and the crew and cast on the studio floor. They also manage everything that goes on during the day of filming, such as actors cues, camera marks, and generally make sure that everything and everybody are in the proper place at the right time. Depending on the company the floor manager may also take wider responsibilities such as preparing the shooting order, and the final script (which covers exactly who will be where and doing what during filming).

The job of **Assistant Floor Manager**, who helped the floor manager, is gradually disappearing due to cut-backs. They help the floor manager and may also take on the equivalent work of the runner. Floor managers may come from theatre stage management or be trainees.

Ailish Heneberry, 35, Production Manager
I studied in Ireland and came to England to train as a nurse. I worked in intensive care and then decided to make a career change and go into publishing. I wrote to everybody and got a temporary job as a credit controller with a magazine that had collapsed. I managed to raise £40,000 in two weeks, and was offered a job on another magazine as a manager so I'd doubled my salary, and I didn't even know what I was doing. That magazine also folded so I did a bit of freelance nursing while trying to get a job. I was selling paintings for a friend on Bayswater Road, and the girl on the next stall's boyfriend worked

in a sound studio so I went there and learnt the technical side of audio production, and from then on I just kept on being offered jobs.

I went into facilities management, and then went to work as head of production for a company that had set up to offer news and current affairs to satellite broadcasters. After that I set up a production company with a friend which lasted 2 years. I had a friend at Central who was moving on and she suggested me, now broadcast companies normally want the devil they know, but they didn't know much about satellite so took me on. It was a four month contract and three years on I'm still there.

The key is being good with figures - I was hopeless at maths at school, but you have to be able to budget. The essence is to let the director make the programme they want to make and the producer wants to spend as little as possible and the production manager is the bad guy in the middle. It's making order out of chaos. It is creative because you often have to think of other ways of doing things, how someone can get what they want within the budget. In the broadcast sector we're a new breed, it was all money being no object before.

To get started, I'd say, identify your industry and get in at a junior level and then make your mark. It sounds awful, but try and find patronage, find a mentor, some one who can help you, some one you can shadow and learn from. I look for rounded CVs, for people who've gone to India, who've done something, not just come straight from film school. It used to be so different, but now there's a negative feeling to people who've come the orthodox route. Having a specialist interest or hobby is useful, languages are helpful, but if you're doing a documentary on a country say, and you know someone was brought up there as a child then you use them.

It's really a fun industry to work in, it's a good crack but it's not everything. The industry's been in turmoil the last few years. Having worked in intensive care I have a different attitude, if the programme doesn't go out there's only a black hole, big deal. It's not a matter of life and death.

Theatre

Like the floor manager in television the **Stage Manager** provides the link between the director and the crew and cast. In some ways the job is simpler, because there are fewer technical elements to worry about, but the production is complicated by the fact that each show is live, rather than being recorded. A missed cue in television is a nuisance but not destructive where a missed cue in theatre may literally stop the show. In repertory theatre there is normally a production in rehearsal and a production on stage. The stage manager supervises the **Deputy Stage Manager** and the **Assistant Stage Manager**. Each take responsibility for a particular production or "run the book", from sitting in on rehearsals taking notes on cues and changes to the script through to being in the prompt corner each night giving all the lighting and sound cues etc. Traditionally stage managers moved into television floor management, and there are new careers developing in exhibition and trade show management. Because theatre training is more established there are many courses for stage managers. Here one should look out for the level of equipment, opportunities for a wide variety of work, and work placements.

Stage Management Courses

Three Year Courses, Stage Management, Full Time

BA Hons Technical Theatre
Rose Bruford

The college is split between two sites. The main base is in a mansion with its own park land and lake in Sidcup on the edges of London, while at the Greenwich site they have workshops, performance, rehearsal and classroom space. Rose Bruford was for a long time the only college to offer training that was at degree level, and even now there is only one other technical theatre degree course. The first two years aim to get a thorough grounding in the basic professional departments: Stage management, properties and Scenic Techniques, Costume and Wardrobe, Staging and Scenic Construction, Lighting and Sound. For the final year students may select one of these options to study specialise in. The course also includes Voice and Movement, Score reading, Business Management and Office Skills. The extra year gives this course the chance to cover all the areas of specialisation thoroughly and get the chance to specialise in one of them.

Entrance by interview. Applicants are also asked to write a short paper and take part in a series of 'hands-on' exercises in the workshops.
Audition fee: £25 (£5 for the unemployed or those in receipt of income support)   Fees: c£3000 (mandatory grants) NCDT

BA Hons Theatre Studies (Stage Management) Welsh College

Like Guildhall and RSAMD the drama department is a part of a larger organisation, although it lacks kudos. Facilities are good. The degree course runs concurrently with the three year diploma course and is virtually the same, there being an extra academic element of about four hours a week on the degree. Musical theatre and singing are very strong here, with several joint productions with the music department. There are strong links with the Sherman Theatre. Welsh speakers receive additional options in Welsh throughout the course. The course starts with two foundation terms that cover the basic elements of Stage Management, Technical Studies, and stagecraft. It also includes a course covering basic television and video techniques. Production work gradually increases, and by the end of three years each student will have been in charge of a production department at least once. Productions cover a wide range of theatrical styles, both drama and opera, and small scale venues for Schools tours and Community theatre.
Entrance is by interview.
Interview fee: £15 Fees c1000 per annum. NCDT

Queen Margaret College

The college is a multi-discipline further education college with the advantages of a larger establishment such as a students union, bar, cafeteria, squash and tennis courts, swimming pool and fully equipped television and radio studios, two theatres and the social life that goes with 1500 students. The first year is common to both the acting and the stage management students (although it is not possible to change between the courses). The course covers management skills, Lighting, Sound, Design, craft skills, and with stage projects and productions in the college theatre and on tour. There is also a period of placement. 18+, and they actively encourage mature students to apply.

Entrance by interview. Students should have one A Level and four or more passes at GCSE, although this can be waived at the college's discretion.

Audition fee: NONE Fees: vary from under £1000 to near £5000 (for international students) per annum CDS

Two Year Courses, Stage Management, Full Time

Arden School of Theatre
A new school set up in association with the renowned Royal Exchange Theatre Company of Manchester and using the facilities of the South Manchester College. The course aims to cover all areas of work within theatre except for acting (although movement and voice classes are taken). Areas covered include: scenery and property making; the maintenance and use of stage, sound and lighting equipment; wardrobe; Front of House skills; working with video and television equipment; music and sound recording. Good facilities include: a 250 seat flexible theatre (including a cyclorama screen, computer controlled lighting, sixteen track sound system and intercom controls), a fully equipped 16 track recording studio, Television and Video studios, and workshops and design studios. A welcome addition as so many training facilities are concentrated on London.
Entrance Requirements: minimum of 4 GCSE's (grade C or above) and 1 'A' level or BTEC National Diploma in Performing Arts. Entry may be possible for students with other relevant experience. Entrance by interview.
Fees: c£4000 (If you have been resident in the City of Manchester for at least three years you may apply for a discretionary grant to cover fees from the City of Manchester Education Committee. There are up to five re-

served places fro those who would otherwise be unable to attend any other drama school in. the UK).

Birmingham School of Speech and Drama
The school is run on traditional lines with a strong emphasis on voice. It is very friendly and relaxed, with enthusiastic students and staff. Their theatre is run as a proper theatre which has built up a loyal local audience (about sixteen productions a year). Final performances are also held at a West End theatre. Each term starts with about four weeks of theory, with the rest spent practically. During the second year students are seconded to a professional producing theatre. There is little provision for Radio and television experience. Less pressurised than London, the school provides a thorough training.
Entrance: by interview and a practical aptitude test. 17+
Interview fee: £12 Fees: c£6000 per annum NCDT

Bristol Old Vic
Well established and respected, the course at Bristol Old Vic is known as being a strongly text based course with an emphasis on the classics, especially Shakespeare. Direct links with the Bristol Old Vic Repertory company in Bristol have always existed, and now are being fostered with BBC Radio Bristol and Bristol based HTV. The course aims to provide a foundation in Television and Radio skills as well as those needed to work in theatre. Students cover every aspect of theatre work from carpentry and prop making to Box Office and Administration, only specialising towards the end of the course.
Entrance by interview.
Interview fee: £20 Fees: c£6000 per annum. NCDT.

Central

This is a BTEC course and gives the Higher National Diploma in Stage Management on completion. Central is one of the best known schools, and has a large technical theatre department (there are several one year diplomas in aspects such as prop making and scenic construction). The course aims to provide a grounding in a range of technical skills including Lighting, Sound, Carpentry, Design and Wardrobe. The aim is to enable students to enter the profession as Assistant Stage Managers, and to progress through stage management to the more specialised areas of production management, administration or direction. The use of audio visual equipment is taught. There is a programme of secondments to professional theatres and to technical service companies.

Entrance by interview. Students should have a minimum of 4 GCSE passes at grade C or above and one A Level, although special entry may be considered for students without qualifications is they have relevant experience.

Fees: c£3000 NCDT

Court Theatre Training Company

The training company came into existence when the Court Theatre Company, a touring company, started to operate workshops for young and aspiring actors. This developed into a second, training theatre company. Both companies are now based at The Courtyard Theatre, a fringe theatre in central London. The course runs from 9am to 10pm on four days a week, Thursday to Sunday inclusive (approx. 44 hours), leaving three days free to take a part time job if necessary. The duration of course

varies from one term to seven, depending on the previous level of experience and aptitude. About half the time is spent in classes/workshops learning technical skills and the other is spent actually working on productions. The course is not intended as competition to conventional stage management courses, rather to train for small scale, flexible theatre companies where the stage manager takes on a multitude of roles. Students may be accepted, depending on company vacancies, at the start of each term i.e. January, April and September. 18+.
Entrance by interview, and please bring examples or pictures of any creative work.
Interview Fee: £20 Fees: c£4000 per annum

Cygnet Training Theatre

Cygnet Training theatre operates as a repertory company of sixteen to twenty four performers with classes interspersed with rehearsals and performances. There is no fixed length of time for anyone to be with Cygnet, but stage managers usually stay for two years. In this time they will have toured extensively in the West Country, and taken shows to the Edinburgh Festival and London, all within the context of a theatre company. Addition work experience is provided with secondments to local theatres. There is no television and limited radio equipment. As well as this course there is an option that is acting plus stage management.
Interview fee: £20 Fees: c£3000 per annum

East 15

East 15 is based on the methods of Joan Littlewood who pioneered ensemble work in this country. Understanding character is at the heart of this approach and involves

much research and staying in character for days, even weeks. They are help by the school's secondary site at Sheriff Hutton Hall in Yorkshire, a beautiful Jacobean mansion, where, for example, Miss Julie can be rehearsed (and performed) in an authentic servants hall beside a real 19th century kitchen range. At the Loughton site there is a fully equipped theatre, workshop, and television studio. The school also tours extensively. Practical experience is gained by mounting and stage managing all these productions. As well as the technical subjects students are invited to join the acting students for movement, play analysis, background research, and history of theatre lectures. 18+
Entrance by interview.
Audition fee: £20 Fees: c£6000 per annum

Guildford School of Acting

GSA is a friendly and enthusiastic place to study. As well as the facilities of the school the technical course uses the workshop of the Yvonne Arnaud Theatre in Guildford. The first year is a mixture of technical classes, project work and other classes such as basic acting techniques. The second year continues with specialist classes and more production experience. This includes a period of secondment to a professional theatre. There are also three specialist secondments of four to eight weeks available, one in lighting design with an international lighting designer, one in sound at the National Theatre and one in carpentry at the Yvonne Arnaud.
Entrance is by interview and lasts half a day (including a tour of the facilities and school). Students should have five GCSE's at Grade C or above, BTec or 2 A Level passes

although this may be waived where students show exceptional ability.
Interview fee: £15 Fees: c£5500 per annum NCDT

Guildhall School of Music and Drama

The drama department is a relatively small part of the school as a whole set in a marvellous location within the Barbican Centre (the school backs onto the Royal Shakespeare Company). The school benefits from having modern theatre facilities and workshops of a high standard. There is also a fully professional sixteen track recording studio with closed circuit video, and an electronic studio with a comprehensive range of synthesisers, effects units and computer software. The course starts with lectures and theory but quickly becomes more practical. By the second year the students are fully responsible for the mounting and running of all the school productions - these will include operas and other music based works as well as dramatic pieces. There are visits to other theatres and television studios. 18+.
Entrance by interview. Students should have at lease five GCSE's at grade C or above.
Audition fees: £25 Fees: c£3000 NCDT

London Academy of Music and Dramatic Art

The longest established drama school of all, LAMDA is well known for its examinations in subjects such as Spoken English, taken by over 40,000 school children and students each year. The stage management course has a very good reputation within the business. The training aims for a broad technical base, with the emphasis on stage management. The theatre and workshops are well equipped. All students have at least one second-

ment to a professional theatre or production company. 18+.
Entrance by interview. Ideally the applicant should have had some experience in school, amateur or professional productions and have some basic knowledge of stage management.
Interview fee: £15   Fees: c£6000 per annum   NCDT

Mountview

Mountview is a professional, forward looking school, constantly adding to facilities and fine-tuning the courses it offers. Compared to a school like the Bristol Old Vic it has a large intake, which can lead to some students feeling they have been left on the sidelines. The first year is a foundation year in the basics of stage management technique. Because all the school productions are student designed by second year students there is in the first year additional design classes for those who are intending to specialise in design. In the second year students take production roles on the schools public performances. These include general stage craft, stage management, lighting and sound, and design. Students may also be seconded to a professional theatre, workshop, designer or studios for several weeks depending on their interests.
Entrance is by interview. Students wishing to be considered for the design option should bring a portfolio with them, and will also have a project set by the technical staff.
Interview fee: £20 Fees: £6500 per annum NCDT

Oxford School of Drama

The school is based in a converted farmhouse and buildings on the Bleinheim Palace Estate some 10 miles from Oxford. The school is small and offers individual attention. Facilities on site are limited but the school benefits from a close association with The Old Fire Station Studio Theatre in Oxford where all the practical experience is gained, including theatre administration such as marketing, Front of House, Box office, and business matters such as basic book-keeping and publicity. Practical classes include sound and lighting, set building, wardrobe maintenance and the making and acquiring of props. Lectures cover theatre design and history, ground plans, set models and musical scores. Students can attend lectures and seminars given by the Professor of Contemporary Theatre (currently Alan Ayckbourn). Productions take place at a variety of venues in Oxford, the Edinburgh Festival and London. Placements are either at The Old Fire Station or on secondments to professional companies or touring with the OSD. 17+.
Entrance by interview.
Interview fee: £15 Fees: c£4500

Royal Academy of Dramatic Art

RADA is the most famous drama school in the UK, if not the world. It also has an excellent technical theatre department. During the course students spend about 30-40% of their time in classwork, such as the history of staging, technical drawing, music score reading, stage fighting, movement, make-up techniques, theatre administration, industrial safety and first aid. The remainder of the time is spent working in every production department, including lighting, sound, design and sce-

nic art, stage carpentry, property making, wardrobe, stagecraft and stage management. There are also courses on television production and radio techniques. Each student stage manages at least one production during the second year. Also in the second year is a four to six week attachment to a relevant theatre or organisation. Students may specialise in one area in the second year.
Entrance is by interview.
Interview fee: £20 Fees: c£5000

Royal Scottish Academy of Music and Drama

RSAMD is said to be the best equipped drama school in Europe, and the facilities are extraordinary, with two theatres (comparable to any repertory company theatres), a television studio, sound broadcast studio, and numerous rehearsal rooms (often with their own video equipment). The course covers all the technical aspects of stage management, carpentry, lighting sound etc. for theatrical presentation, and unusually, gives a basic level of instruction for television presentation including camera work, floor management, vision mixing, and so on. Students provide stage management for all the theatre, television and opera presentations on the course and the school rents a hall for the entire three weeks of the Edinburgh Fringe Festival for student productions - another useful source of experience. Probably the best all round for facilities.

Entrance is by interview. Formal qualifications are not required, but students should bring to the interview evidence of their suitability for the course and their ability to work with their hands such as sketches, samples of woodwork, dress or costume designs or prompt books from previous productions.
Audition fee: £30   Fees: c£1000 NCDT

One Year Courses, Stage Management, Full Time

The Academy
The first school to offer a complete part time training. The school has its own theatre which operates as a fringe venue for other, outside productions and plenty of rehearsal/classroom space. The company puts on about nine plays per year at the school's theatre, with morning classes covering the basics and afternoons spent in rehearsal. There is a separate show case, and a three week run at another fringe theatre. Stage Managers are expected to join in with the acting workshops and classes. This course does not lead to a stage management qualification that is accepted by major theatres. 30+ hours per week.
Entry requirements: No formal qualifications required, but applicants are expected to have had some previous training or reasonable experience. Each application is judged individually. 18+.
Fees: c£3500 for course

Advanced Residential Theatre and Television Skillcentre International
ARTTS is the only school where students are expected to live on site, about 17 miles south of York. Accommodation is in residential units continuing dining and sitting rooms, kitchen and utility room and single study/bed-

rooms. There are three advanced courses available in Acting, Directing and Production/Operations although each contains element of each other as the aim is to produce actors who can also direct or operate a sound boom, directors who can stage manage etc. Facilities are comprehensive and include television and recording studios and a 200 seat theatre. Audiences are almost entirely limited to locals except when productions are staged in York. There are no London based showcase productions. There are two intakes per year. Students can study all aspects of media production operations, from theatre to film and television. Particular to this course are the technical elements such as sound mixing and recording, video and film editing, camera operation whether film, studio or mobile units. Students also receive some acting and directing training. Students are required to present a final written presentation.
Entrance requirements: 21+. All applicants are treated in the same way, regardless of which course/option they are applying for. Candidates are selected first on the basis of their application form, and then by interview.
Audition fee: None   Fees c£6500 + £2000 for accommodation

Academy of Live and Recorded Arts

Of the "new" drama schools, ALRA is probably the largest and most established. It was founded to fill the gap in training students for work in television and television work as an integral part of the course. This course is considered to be an apprenticeship and students work on all ALRA's public performances, moving from ASM to DSM responsibilities. Most productions are at ALRA's own studio theatre which is of fringe

standard, and not comparable to most of the theatres used by other stage management courses. Technical Radio and Video are included.
Interview fee: £11.75 Fees: c£5000 for course

Guildford School of Acting

GSA is a friendly and enthusiastic place to study. As well as the facilities of the school the technical course uses the workshop of the Yvonne Arnaud Theatre in Guildford. The course closely follows the two year course (see above) and shares some classes and lectures with them. Productions and rehearsal projects are mainly with the post graduate acting students.

Entrance is by interview and lasts half a day (including a tour of the facilities and school). Students usually have a degree or equivalent experience. Many who have attended this course have been intending to be directors and have used it to prepare themselves and in some cases to set up their own touring companies.
Interview fee: £15 Fees: c£5500 for course

St Catherine's Drama Studio

The course is based in a converted chapel on the outskirts of Guildford. Television plays a large part in the training, and includes pre- and post-production management and techniques. Theatre techniques such as stage craft, lighting, design, sound and management are also covered. Students work on all the drama courses productions. Performances take place either at the school's own studio theatre (fringe standard) or in schools and other small scale venues. Running exhibitions, presentations and conferences are also covered as many stage managers will work in these and related areas. 16+.

Entrance by interview. Applicants are expected to be able to show that they have researched some of the qualities required of stage management.
Audition fee: £15 Fees c £4500 per annum

Welsh College of Music and Drama

Like Guildhall and RSAMD the drama department is a part of a larger organisation and facilities generally are good. Musical theatre and singing are very strong here, with several joint productions with the music department. There are strong links with the Sherman Theatre. Welsh speakers receive additional options in Welsh throughout the course. Areas studied on this intensive course include lighting, sound, prop making, handling scenery, and the work of the touring stage manager and company manager. On the design side, scene painting, prop and model making, working drawings, carpentry, pattern draughting, costume constructing and the work of the wardrobe supervisor. Students opt for either stage management or design at the start of the course but the course content overlaps considerably.
Entrance by interview.
Interview fee: £15 Fees: c£1000 per annum. CDS NCDT

Short/Part Time Courses

Central School of Speech and Drama
One of the best known drama schools, Central has a strong technical department. This two week course gives a basic grounding in stage management and technical theatre, such as blocking, cueing and prompting, making a simple sound tape, scene changing and so on plus management and communication skills. At the end of the course students put into practise what they have learnt with two theatre exercises; there is also the opportunity of continuing for a further week of production experience.
Fees: £500

Court Theatre Training Company
The training company came into existence when the Court Theatre Company, a touring company, started to operate workshops for young and aspiring actors. This developed into a second, training theatre company. Both companies are now based at The Courtyard Theatre, a fringe theatre in central London. The course runs on Saturday for a year and covers production work, stage management, theatre design, lighting and sound. It is expected that most students are aiming to go on to further training.
Audition Fee: £20 Fees: £400

City Lit

The course runs on two evenings per week, plus extra time during productions. This is a practical course covering all aspects of back stage work, with a special module on stage lighting. After the first term of classes students stage manage productions and rehearsals. A good (and cheap) introduction.
Fees: £124 concessions, £248 others.

Morley College

This part time foundation course aims to provide a basic training in stage management, lighting, sound and the general running of a production. It runs on three evenings per week, and there are opportunities to assist on College productions.
Entrance by interview.
Fees: £20 for concessions to £60.

Managerial

Arts Administrator

Within repertory theatres the artistic director used to do the work of the **Arts Administrator**, that is being in charge of the running of the theatre in all non-creative aspects. In many theatres this job has now been split, partly in response to the fact that many theatres are under financial pressure and therefore need careful day to day management. It is becoming more apparent that a director is not necessarily the best person for this job. The arts administrator is not an accountant, although they keep a careful eye on the budgets and daily running costs. They have to be aware of creative sensibilities, while being entirely practical themselves. Arts administrators are also needed to run arts centres, which may involve screening films, staging dance and theatre events, exhibitions, and special events. As a whole the profession of arts administrator is expanding. A prime example might be David Aukin who was the non-directing artistic director at Hampstead and the Leicester Haymarket Theatres, then administrator at the National Theatre. He is currently commissioning editor for Channel 4 Film. Currently arts administration courses are limited, although many drama/theatre studies degrees and stage management courses include the subject as options within their programme.

Arts Administration Courses

BA Joint Hons with Arts Management
Dartington College of Arts

Arts Management at Dartington is a Minor Subject and may only be taken with Theatre, Music or Visual Performance. The approach is characterised as 'arts management for performers', which means that it aims for students to be able to set up their own company, or be a freelance, or to work within a company or to teach. It does not claim to train arts administrators although students may go on take this career path. Subjects covered include management theory, IT and basic business skills, information and debate on current politics and arts support systems. In the second year students plan and carry out projects for arts events. There is a period of placement within an arts organisation during the third year.

BA Arts Management
De Montfort University

"The principal aim of the course is to ensure students are competent at analysing and interpreting information and integrating artistic and management objectives in order that they may be able to manage complex organisations." The course covers topics such as Finance, the Individual and the Organisation, Customers and Computers, Law for Arts Management, Studies in the History and Organisation FO Culture, Arts Information Technology among others. Courses from other subjects may also be taken, or the degree may be Joint or Combined Honours. Single subject students may study with an arts organisation for one day a week in the second year and undertake a seven week placement.

Oxford School of Drama

The school is based in a converted farmhouse and buildings on the Bleinheim Palace Estate some 10 miles from Oxford. The school is small and offers individual attention. Facilities on site are limited but the school benefits from a close association with The Old Fire Station Studio Theatre in Oxford where all the practical experience is gained, including theatre administration such as marketing, Front of House, Box office, and business matters such as basic book-keeping and publicity. Practical classes include sound and lighting, set building, wardrobe maintenance and the making and acquiring of props. Lectures cover theatre design and history, ground plans, set models and musical scores. Students can attend lectures and seminars given by the Professor of Contemporary Theatre (currently Alan Ayckbourn). Productions take place at a variety of venues in Oxford, the Edinburgh Festival and London. Placements are either at The Old Fire Station or on secondments to professional companies or touring with the ODs. 17+.
Entrance by interview.
Interview fee: £15 Fees: c£4500

Casting Director

Most casting directors are now freelances although a few independent television companies and the larger theatre companies retain them as staff. Most will work in any area, although many specialise in say commercials or films. The casting director has to be aware of all the actors available, including all the newcomers. This means that a large part of the casting director's day is spent on going to drama school final shows, theatre productions from fringe to West End, keeping in touch with agents and giving general interviews to actors who they have not met before. This knowledge is their qualification for the job. For a casting session the casting director will have selected a number of actors who seem to meet the directors brief. This is likely to be upwards of 20 actors per part. The final decision is the directors. Casting directors have often been actors or theatrical agents.

Andy Prior, 26, Casting Director

Casting is just one of those things that I ended up doing, I can't say that I set my heart on it from the start. I trained as a stage manager at the Central School of Speech and Drama, worked at various places, did a bit of touring, a bit of fringe. I worked at the Royal Court and then went to work at the Bush. It's a producing venue, and all new writing which I was interested in. Anyway there were a few productions and they were stuck on the casting, so I helped them with a few names, and that worked out well, so then I helped on some other casting. I then became an assistant director there, which was about 30 to 40% casting as well as script development and the like. The assistant director was on a bursary sort of scheme and only lasted for a year, so when that had finished I decided I'd like to carry on with a bit of casting work, and got in touch with Gail Stevens, who had a theatre background like me.

It's a bit like being a freelance within her company, sometimes I assist her, and sometimes I do work for myself. Most casting directors have a theatre or production background, a few come in through the secretarial route. you have to have seen a lot of things, but it's a lot more than keeping some huge list of actors in your head. I don't think you could teach it. You can be paid quite a lot of money - casting directors who just do commercials can really rake it in - but to my mind I do projects I'm interested in, and often they don't pay well. We do mainly TV and film, but there's not a lot of filming in this country so it's mainly TV. We do theatre too sometimes, but they don't have any money so it's usually just helping out or just for expenses. Generally we get between 5 to 10 CVs a day, but it can be more like 30 or 40 when the drama school courses are finishing. People assume we have endless vaults of filing cabinets - its really hard because we know that the photos and CVs cost a lot, but we can't keep them all. We do if there's something unusual, there aren't too many oriental actors around, so we keep a file on them, or Australians, or whatever. We do try and have a good look at them all though. We were doing one job for the BBC, a big drama series, and it was taking 3 hours every day just to open the mail. We had to move offices in the end.

Writers

Journalists, Scriptwriters, Script Editors, Script readers, Playwrights

Journalists
Television journalists work in three main areas; news, current affairs and documentaries. The first job is likely to be as a news writer. News writing involves finding stories and writing them up for the news reader. With more experience they may become reporters, going out with a camera team. Opportunities are greater in local news rooms. Reporters may specialise, and become foreign correspondents or war reporters such as Kate Adie, or become experts on particular areas such as politics or industry. Some move into production while others become presenters. Most news readers are former journalists and may still write their own copy.

Almost all television journalists enter through newspaper or radio journalism. Traditionally the BBC trained news journalists, but their programme has been suspended for the moment although they offer trainee posts in radio journalism. Other ways include Journalism courses and newspaper trainee schemes.

Script Editors, Commissioning Editors and Script readers
Script Editors work almost entirely in drama departments. The script editor works with the writer prepare the script for production. This may be a original work, an adaptation or part of a series. The script must fit certain requirements (such as length, number of locations, size of cast). it is the script editors job to ensure that it does. Script editors also need to be aware

of any new writing talents and will spend time visiting fringe theatres where there may be new writing. A few script editors work within theatre. The Royal Court has always had a reputation of finding new writers thanks to their script department.

The **Commissioning Editor** asks writers to prepare treatments of ideas, or to produce new work. Many commissioning editors work on long running series such as Brookside or Coronation Street and part of their job is to make sure that writers stay within the established storyline and are true to the characters.

The **Script Reader** is employed as a freelance by larger companies through out the industry. Their job is to read through the scripts that are sent to the company and select any worth passing on to the script editor. The work is very poorly paid, but may be a starting point for becoming an editor.

Script writers, Screen writers, Playwrights

How to write plays or scripts is beyond the scope of this book. However over the last ten years numerous courses have sprung up to address this problem. Short courses can be located by subscribing to writers magazines such as Writers News or Writers Monthly. There are a few longer courses including one at degree level.

Writing Courses

BA Hons Theatre (Writer)
Rose Bruford

The Writers Course aims to give the understanding and techniques need to write for the theatre and broadcast media, within the frame work of the other skills that go into creating theatre. Writers therefore work with the actors, learning how they build characters and use text, with the technical theatre course, learning about the potential of the theatre and how to convey technical elements to technicians, and finally work on actual writing, including research, theory and analysis.

Entrance by interview, a devising and writing workshop and the presentation of examples of the students previous work such as scripts.

Audition fee: £25 (£5 for the unemployed or those in receipt of income support) Fees: c£3000 (mandatory grants)

One Year Theatre Writing Course Full Time
Central School of Speech and Drama

Rapidly expanding, Central must be the most dynamic drama school at the moment; it has always been one of the best. The majority of the course is given over to the writing and development of creative work, but classical texts and the demands of differing media (radio/film/

TV) are also studied. Students will work with a professional writer as supervisor throughout the year and at the end are offered an appropriate showcase for a piece of writing. Applications from those interested in writing for musical, physical or puppet theatre are particularly welcomed. A school with great opportunities for strong personalities. Post graduate or post experience only.
Entrance by interview and submission of two pieces of creative writing at least one of which is a substantial dramatic piece ready for performance.
Interview fee: £25   Fees: c£3500 per annum

Administration/Management

There are a number of jobs within theatre, film and television which are non-creative. These are concerned with the administration, sales and general management. Generally the jobs are the same as any outside, for example an accountant will be doing the same work whether in a theatre or in an insurance office. Similarly, most of those involved with sales are salesmen and women first and foremost, the fact that they are selling television airspace is secondary. The routes into these jobs is not covered here for that reason.

Sales and Marketing

Television

Independent television relies on the income from advertising. Television sales involve selling 'slots' to companies for their commercials. Rates for the slots vary according to which channel, the time of day, which programme it is next to, demand and so on. They are not fixed, and it is the salespersons job fill each slot at the highest price. The commercials are monitored by 'traffic' or 'makeup' staff who send out the invoices to the advertising agencies.

There are also those who sell programmes to other companies, such as foreign television stations, satellite or cable companies. The costs of many programmes are 'under written' by these sales. There is also some sponsorship, such as the series 'Poirot' by the electrical manufacturer AEG. This is an increasingly important area.

Marketing covers a wide field, and could include promoting a programme to selling merchandising rights (for example, Thomas the Tank Engine soap, Darling Buds of May cook books, East Enders mugs). Many television programmes have spin-offs in the form of books, games and/or videos. These are usually handled by separate 'Enterprise' companies. Most companies have research departments where the viewing figures are assessed. Viewing analysis is increasingly sophisticated. It is important to the advertisers and programme makers that they know who and how many people are watching their programme. An example is the programme 'The Equaliser' with Edward Woodward. This had low general audience viewing figures, but most of those who did watch were young, fairly affluent men. Because this audience was attractive to high spending advertisers such as beer, lager and car companies, the programme continued to be made and shown.

Film sales

Films rely on sales to recoup costs. These could include sales to distributors at home and abroad, sales to video, sales to television and satellite. Ideally most of the sales will be in place before the film is actually made. The sales agent works for the producer in organising these sales and arranging the contracts. Sales agents often have a legal or financial background.

Distributors handle films going into cinemas. The market is dominated by American distribution companies, who also own many of the UK's cinemas. The independent sector concentrates on non mainstream films, which are often difficult to place in larger cinemas. There are no restrictions on entry, although experience/qualifications in marketing, sales, finance or public relations are helpful. Jobs are advertised in the trade press. It is unusual (though not unknown) for distribution staff to move into production. Generally distributors get one third of the box office while the exhibitor, who owns and runs the cinema, gets two thirds. The exhibitor employs sales staff and ushers, and projectionists. This used to be a technical job but modern systems are increasingly automated.

Marketing a film can cost as much as the film itself. Advertising is important as well as PR and special promotions (free tickets to winners of competitions etc.). Merchandising is well established for important films, although this can back fire, for example the film Dick Tracy which was a flop leaving shops full of related merchandise that no one wanted to buy. In 'Jurassic Park' there were several shots in the film of a shop selling Jurassic Park merchandise, all of which became available to the general public.

Press and Public Relations

Press and public relations work is very similar throughout film, television and theatre work. The main difference is one of scale as film and television are usually looking for a national audience whereas theatre (especially repertory) is more locally based. The press or PR officer arranges interviews with the cast, photo opportunities, competitions and so on. Contacts and knowledge of the business are all important. Qualifications in PR or marketing are helpful, but most important is the right sort of personality.

House Manager

The house manager is the person in charge of the running of a theatre. This includes box office, catering staff, ushers and cleaners. Business or managerial qualifications are helpful.

Technical

Camera Crew

Cinematographer/ Lighting Camera Operator/ Director of Photography
Lighting Director, Camera Operator
Camera Assistants: Grip/focus Puller/Loader/ Clapper Loader

Film
Cinematographer/ Lighting Camera Operator/ Director of Photography
The **Lighting Camera Operator** is in charge of the overall look of a film, determining lighting and camera angles, filters and lens. Together with the director he or she discusses each shot, choosing the position of the camera, the lighting and composition of shots. They then produce a camera script showing all these elements. The Lighting Camera Operator supervises the camera operators, although they do not operate the cameras themselves. However most have come up through the ranks of the camera crew and are former camera operators. The few exceptions enter from television and theatre lighting. **Cinematographer** or **Director of Photography** is a term used mainly on major feature films where the atmosphere of the film is almost as important as the script. Some cinematographers are as famous as the directors they work with, for

example, Sven Nykvist who has worked on many Ingmar Bergman films and has recently become a director himself.

Camera Operator
Most camera operators work in television and video as well as film, although there are a few who specialise. They are the people who actually work the camera on a day to day basis, and have usually come up through the ranks of camera assistants. Film Camera Operators usually have more creative say in how a shot is composed than camera operators working in television studios.

Camera Assistants
Generally all camera assistants are in charge of the cameras, making sure that they are maintained and not damaged and of the actual film that is used. They also keep a record of each 'take'. On a small shoot there may be only one camera assistant who has to do all of the camera jobs, but on a large production there may be several who perform a specific function.

The **Grip** has several duties, including moving the cameras to position, operating 'dollies' and cranes, laying track for tracking shots, and generally being responsible for the camera's safety. On long tracking shots the camera may have to move towards or away from the scene so that it must change focus. The **Focus Puller** operates the focus ring on the camera, while the camera operator moves the camera away. This is a tricky job which must be done smoothly and accurately. The focus puller is also in charge of maintaining and protecting the camera lens and filters. The **Loader** is responsible for loading and unloading film into the camera, and keeping both new and used film safe. The clapper board is numbered for each scene and each take of that scene and is operated at the start and end of the take. Keeping track of the takes and operating the board is the job of the **Clapper Board Operator** or **Clapper Loader**.

Television Lighting Director

The lighting director works with the set designer to create suitable lighting for a production. This may be simple, for example for a news broadcast, or complicated such as for an atmospheric drama production. Within the studio most lights are fixed to a grid in the ceiling. It is the lighting directors job to design a lighting plan which the electricians can follow showing the position of all the lights. Lighting directors start as **Lighting Assistants** and are in charge (under supervision) of programmes such as news broadcasts which have simple backgrounds and presenters who remain seated. Lighting directors have usually had previous experience within television, such as with a camera crew, or as an electrician or engineer.

Television Camera Operator

Within the studio electronic cameras are used which relay images back to the control room, where the director sits selecting shots. There may be as many as six cameras in the studio, each set up to for a different shot. The shots will normally have been rehearsed before the programme is taped and in general there is less chance for creative in-put from the camera operator. However the director normally only specifies the type of shot (close up, mid shot etc.) and the camera operator can choose the composition within that framework. During live shows when there is little opportunity for rehearsal the camera operator may 'suggest' camera shots through the studio monitor for the director to select.

Each camera is operated by one person with **Camera Assistants** taking on extra jobs, such as moving the camera cables around the floor to allow free passage of the cameras as they move position for each shot. This is called cable bashing. An assistant will also help when the camera is on a crane, to allow for 'bird's eye' and 'worm's view' shots. The Camera Operator operates the camera, but an assistant may be needed to drive the crane to position and another may operate the counter balancing arm of the crane.

Outside Broadcast Camera Operator

The 'OB' unit is traditionally a mobile control room, with all the cameras connected to it. These are still used for large public events such as coronations and sporting events and, for the camera operator, work in a very similar way to normal studio productions. Smaller units are being used more and more which have lightweight, hand held camera equipment. These are worked in a similar way to film cameras.

News camera operators have the most independence, working in small teams or even alone. It is not unusual for a news team to consist of just a camera operator and a presenter/journalist. In this case the camera operator is also taking on the functions of director, sound and so on. Much of this work may be done in dangerous places where conditions are hard and unpredictable. News camera operators are normally specialists. There are also freelance news camera operators who cover a certain area and are to hand should a news story break in their area.

Graham Johnston, 36, Director/Cameraman/Producer

It was an accident really. I was halfway through university and most people were going for interviews at merchant banks and I didn't want that. I was a keen canoeist and a bunch of mates decided to go canoeing along the longest river in Canada. We got some funding, including from the BBC who were doing a series on expeditions. They sent us on an intensive training course, and we filmed the expedition ourselves. I'd always been visual; it was a toss up between art school and university, and here was the meeting of the visual and the intellectual. I left university with great hopes of waltzing into the BBC or ITV and of course none of this happened, but someone suggested trying the National Film School. At that time there was a big push to get documentary students into the school rather than drama. Colin Young (principal of the NFS, now retired) was very much in favour of teaching documentary students to do everything, to train up film makers who could initiate, carry out, shoot and if necessary edit their own films.

On coming out it was still difficult to get work. I had a lucky break, I had made two films about the Eskimos in Alaska and people were interested in that, but you still have to persuade them you can do other subjects apart from the Innuit. I did a charity film on the Prince's Trust, and began directing small religious programmes at TVS. Gradually I was able to persuade people I could shoot as well as direct. It took me about six years.

Film school is definitely the best bet. The other training resources have just about dried up now. In terms of technology there's a lot more available, like High 8 and home editing facilities. Effectively one can have a crack at making ones own films. I'm keen to take attachments or secondments and try and explain things as we go along. For fly on the wall documentaries, cinema verite, you want to keep camera crew to a minimum, so it works with more structured productions. The old fashioned film documentary is a bit more of a rarefied thing now. I wouldn't advise people to put all their eggs into one basket, like, just do film. I think there is a big future for video and multi-media.

Vision Mixer
The vision mixer sits in the control room and cuts between the images as presented on the screens as instructed by the director. The images may be coming from cameras in the studio or previously recorded video tape. Mixing six or eight images is not unusual. Split second timing is important and the vision mixer usually develops a feel for the work, with an experienced vision mixer often knowing when to cut better than an inexperienced director. There are various effects that the vision mixer can use, such as fading in and out of an image, or 'wiping' it so that the image slides sideways off the screen with next one sliding on from the other direction. The end result is either transmitted live, or recorded onto another tape for transmission later. Vision mixers are usually recruited from internal applicants from departments such as secretarial, administration, and technical posts.

Theatre
Lighting Director
The lighting director designs a lighting plan for the production after consulting the set designer and director. Lighting can play a very important part, not just in creating atmosphere but also to create effects. For example, actors behind a gauze screen may be invisible, visible or in silhouette depending on the lighting used. Modern theatres have computerised lighting systems which mean that once the lights have been set in place by the electricians and the plan fed into the computer the system will give lighting cues automatically.

Lighting Courses

Central
Central is one of the best known drama schools and has a long established and thriving technical theatre department. This one year full time course explores the role of light and the lighting designer within performance. Areas studied include text analysis, design, communication, technology and the creative team. Students will have both project and performance experience and the opportunity to work alongside profession theatre directors, designers and lighting designers.
Entrance by interview. Students should either have studied Theatre Arts or Design to degree or equivalent level or have had considerable work experience with light or a related field.

Northern Contemporary Dance School
The course lasts for one year and aims to train lighting technicians for the theatre. Trainees are funded through an Adult Training Scheme and are awarded NVQ's as they progress through the course. The course is entirely hands-on and is based at the NSCD's Dome Theatre. The school is committed to an equal opportunities and equal access policy.

Sound crew

Sound operator/Recordist/Technician
Boom operator, Grams operator, Sound dubbing Editor/Mixer

Film and Television
The sound operator is in charge of the recording of the sound track. This may be on tape or film, but the job is similar whichever medium is being used. The main difference is that with film the sound track is seperate from the pictures. This is why the clappeboard comes down with a noise so that sound can be synchronised exactly with the picture. When video tape is used the pictures and sound are combined on the same tape so do not need putting together. In television the sound technician is also responsible for the communications systems within the studio, such as "talk-back" which links the studio with the control room.

During filming the **Sound Technician** concentrates on the sound. The microphone may pick up noise such as aircraft or sirens which no one else notices, and so the take is ruined. A outside broadcast may have other difficulties such as the noise of wind or rain on the microphone. The sound technician will also take "wild" tracks. These will supply background noise. For example, for a party scene there will be two sound tapes, one of the actors speaking their lines, and a wild track of general party talk. The two will be joined together at the editing stage.

Gary Desmond, 32, Sound Recordist

I left school at 17 and went to tech college to do an electronics and communications course. After that I hung out in clubs and round bands and learnt to do multi track recording. I got fed up with that and knew what I wanted to do, but nepotism ruled at that time and I couldn't get in. I heard about JOBFIT (now ft2) and got onto the course. The first year you can do whatever bits and bobs you want to do, and then in the second year I specialised in sound. That was mainly on films. When I left I got a staff job at Mersey TV doing sound mixing for Brookside. The only sound I'm really interested in now is in documentaries. Normally there's a three man sound crew, sound mixer, boom operator and assistant sound mixer who might do boom as well but on documentaries you end up doing it all.

It helps to know what type of sound you want to do, drama, documentary or post-production. Don't be afraid to ring people up and hassle them, well, not hassle them but tell them who you are. It's who you know that counts. Ask if you can come out on shoots; it's no good for fly-on-the-wall, but for drama, why not because unless there's older people encouraging younger people then there's going to be no one left. Knowing the equipment is essential, you could try facilities houses and spend a few weeks there just learning about it. It's good to have a reasonable technology level if equipment breaks down. I'd say punctuality is the single most important thing, even if they all turn up at 8 you should be there at 7 if that's when you were called for. Even a minute or two late is no good.

Sound Editor

Editing brings together different tapes, including music and any effects. They have to create a sound track that is believable to the audience so variations in tone (if perhaps an actor had a cold through part of the filming, or if there were any sudden changes in acoustics) are ironed out. Any distracting back ground noise such as a telephone ringing can be disguised.

The sound track may need to re-record the sound track to make it match with the picture.
The Sound Mixer works from the television sound control room during the taping of a programme. All the different sounds (music, sound effects, speech) are fed into the system and the the mixer adjusts and, where neccessary, alters the sound track. There can be as many as 56 separate sound sources, although it is more usual for 16 or 24 to be used. The **Grams Operator** feeds various sound into the sound mixers control desk such as sound effects and music. These may be on tape or compact disc. The boom is basically a long pole with a microphone at the end of it. In the studio it is usually mounted onto a dolly and so can be moved around by the operator. On location the **Boom Operator** will actually hold it. Ideally the microphone is as close to the person talking as possible. This means that the boom operator tries to place the microphone just out of shot, and where it does not create a shadow across the picture. One of the hall marks of amateurish films is the visible microphone.
There are many developments within the sound crew. Many of the jobs double up, so the sound man also operates the boom. The more experienced sound operators will also be editors. Technical developments mean that more outside broadcasts are on tape not film, so the camera operator may also be the sound operator. In Nick Broomfield's films he is the director and sound operator. Further technical developments include the use of digital audio, which may be standard by the trun of the century. Any one wishing to go into sound should be aware of the new technology.
There is no particular career path for sound operators. Some start as trainees with a company such as the BBC, others go in through video where there may be opportunities for the keen to offer their services to work for little or nothing alongside a

more experiecnced sound operator or mixer and so get in that way. Having got in some sound operators stay in the job for life, while others move on to production or direction. Most sound operators are interested in electronics and music.
Useful qualifications include: BTEC/City & Guilds/ Degree in a subject such as Electronics, Communications, Film and Television, Computer Science.

Theatre

The sound technican designs a sound track of effects that may consist of music, noises (the howl of the Hound of the Baskervilles perhaps) and other cues. This may be from pre-recorded tapes or specially recorded by the sound technician. The sound technician may also have to provide a backing tape should there be no live musicians. Unless the sound tape is very complex the system during production will be operated by a stage manager. Entry is similar to that for film and television, but there is a specific City and Guilds Qualification for Theatre Sound Techinicians:
Sound Engineering Competances 1820   C&G Levels 2 & 3

Ian Campbell, 29, Sound Operator

After doing my degree I was temping, doing a cycle courier job, and basically a friend said do you want a job at the BBC, in film despatch. So I went and saw the guy and he said, start on Monday. That was six or seven years ago - it's not like that now! That was a temporary job, then I got a permanent job, as a programme servicing clerk, it doesn't really exist now as a job, but effectively it meant looking after film crews, making sure everything was OK for them, that they'd got all the right equipment. That taught me about equipment and how the production worked. I then applied for, and got, a job as a trainee film recordist, but that was actually to do with sound. I was multi-

skill trained; it used to be three years doing just one thing, now it's 18 months for multi skills and you could be a film editor, or a VT operator.

Within the area I'm in (post-production sound) people move into dubbing, and then to dubbing mixer, some go into management. You don't need any educational qualifications, just a general basic education, common sense, and be slightly technically minded. It's difficult at the moment. The BBC hasn't done any training for two or three years. The only way to do it now is to teach yourself, unless you're rich and can pay to go on a course, otherwise you can go and be a runner and dogsbody at outside dubbing theatres. They do things differently outside, although a lots of just different words for different things. If you join the BBC you've got to learn their ways. Last year we lost four jobs. There's about 45 in the department and they're rumoured to be losing another six next year. I don't know what I'll do. The thing about the BBC, you just do your job and you have no other worries.

Post Production

Editors, Technical Operators, Electronic Engineers, Special Effects, Animators, Model-Makers

Editors

Editors may work in either film or video tape editing, and increasingly they work in both areas. The two types of recording need different techniques but the creative process is the same. The editor looks at all the recorded film or tape, removes unwanted sections and combines the rest together to make the programme or film. This can be a very creative process as a few seconds can make all the difference to the atmosphere. David Lean was an editor before becoming a director.

Film is actually cut during the editing process and spliced together to make the final version. The editing equipment is hand operated and relatively simple to use, the skill comes in choosing the cuts. Obviously manual dexterity is important. The film editor starts as an **Assistant Editor** and is responsible for supporting the editor. This includes synchronising the rushes which are recorded on different tapes, using the picture and sound of the clapperboard at the beginning and end of each shot. They keep track of all the film in the editing suite, whether discarded (off cuts) or waiting to be used. Off cuts are stored and have led to programmes such as 'It'll be Alright on the Night'.

Video tape differs in that the picture and sound are already on one tape. The equipment used is very complicated and many video tape editors have technical background. Together with the director the editor decides which sections of scenes are to be kept and then the whole is re-recorded onto a separate tape in the correct sequence. The film is never actually handled during the editing process. The assistant's role is to set the controls ready for use as well as general handling and storage of the tapes. Previous experience is essential, such as having been a vision mixer, engineer or camera crew although some may start by being a runner and then persuading an editor to take them on as an assistant.

Technical Operators

Technical operators work in several areas of television production and post production. Most have a background in electronics or engineering. Areas covered include **Vision Control**, where the technician works within the control room making sure that the out put from the video cameras is satisfactory, checking for colour balance, light exposure and consistency, **Video Tape Recording** (VTR, VT) the recording and relaying of programmes, including adding any inserts and operating the Telecine which converts film into a television signal for transmission. The technical operator may be required to maintain the equipment as well. There are opportunities to become an engineer or move into the more creative areas.

Jeremy Whitton, 28, Post Production Resources Section Assistant.

I'd always wanted to work at the BBC and spent two to three years writing to them asking to be considered for any jobs. Finally I was offered a job for two weeks in the picture library - I think there had been a fire or something, anyway it was a foot in the door. Once you are in it's actually very easy, because people prefer to employ someone they know - it also means that they don't have to do the paperwork of interviewing hundreds of people. In my first week of college doing a teaching degree I was offered a full time job at the BBC in the film and tape movement department. I decided to defer my college place, but then having been there I realised that you needed a degree to succeed at the BBC. So I went back and spent four years doing my course, spending each holiday doing relief work. I went back to work full time in the film and tape movement department. It's a clerical job, although you do some lugging of tapes around. I think it was a good all round start because you get to know all the different departments, like production and editing.

I transferred departments because I wanted to train as a cameraman, and I'm now in current operations which means being responsible for all the video tape that go out on transmission. It's very computer based. The BBC have now stopped all trainee cameraman positions; the last were taken on about three years ago, so I applied for a post as a trainee technical operator. There were 7000 applicants for 2 places, and there were people who had already been working as camera assistants applying, so it was quite good that I made it to the last 12. Now there are no more recruits for the next two years. As a result of my application they did agree that I could 'trail'. This means that you follow an experienced cameraman around in your spare time, at weekends and so on. Hopefully you learn the ropes from him. Now I'm not sure what to do. I was always told that once you were in the BBC the training was there, but because of renewing the Charter in 1996 they seem to have dropped all training. I probably would have been better off not going to college because four years ago the training was there. Some people have said that I should get a job outside and them re-apply. I took a "design for TV" course last year because design is good for camera work, but even that is very computer based. A few years ago if anyone had asked my advice about how to get in to camera work I'd have said A levels in Maths and Physics, or a degree in Engineering or Electronics, but now I think a college course is best, somewhere like Ravensbourne, where you can specialise. In the past they didn't like to take on people who had trained elsewhere, *they liked to train them in their own way, but now I think they will just employ freelances.*

Electronic Engineers
The engineers department is involved in two specific areas, firstly the maintenance of equipment and secondly the development of systems. This may involve planning, purchasing and testing a system, and possibly research and development of new systems. Electronic engineers need a degree or equivalent in electronics or telecommunications.

Special Effects
Many departments create their own special effects, such as make-up or vision mixing but for more complicated effects most television and film companies go to outside specialist companies. Special effects can be divided into two areas, those generated by computer and those that are physically made. Those who work in the 'physical' side may have a background in engineering, props, mechanics or electrics or may simply be people who are fascinated by the business, such as inventors. Pyrotechnic specialists need a licence to practice because effects such as blowing a house up can be exceptionally dangerous. These specialists are often ex-army with experience in explosives. Those in computer generated effects may be computer experts or electronic engineers. In both cases although practical skills are valuable it is the ability to think imaginatively and creatively that is most important. There is no set pattern of entry, although many in the computer generated effects companies have degrees in electronics or computing.

Animators

Animation may be done by hand or computer, although the computer generated effects are not as subtle as the hand drawn cartoons. The animation director has the original ideas and designs how the scene will look much in the same way as a conventional director. The animators draw the main characters with assistant animators drawing the minor characters. 'In-betweeners' draw the sequences between the major actions. The completed drawings are copied onto cells (transparent sheets) by the pain and trace department before being photographed.

Animators may also take physical objects and animate them, such as 'Morph', the animated plasticine man. This work involves moving the model a small amount, taking a photograph, then moving it again, taking another and so on.

Animation is labour intensive and good animators are always required. To be a good animator involves having good ideas as well as being able to draw. Most animators have been to art school. There has been a revival of interest in animation recently, in film and in commercials. Both areas can be very well paid. London is considered to be the one of the top centres for animators.

John Craney, 26, Model maker.

I didn't bother with the VIth form, and did a general foundation course in Art and Design at my local art college. I then went to Bristol Poly to do a Ceramics degree. At the end of the course I had an exhibition. I was lucky, Lyons came to my show and liked my work and offered me some work as a sculptor, so I freelanced for a year. In the end I was doing so much work for them I couldn't stay self employed so they offered me a job and I've been here for 5 years.

We are general model makers, but we also do some special effects. It's a team effort, you need to pull together. You need to have a lot of commitment because you never have enough time, you find yourself working at weekends and through the night, and the money's not brilliant. There are perks, like going abroad, and you get to do something new all the time. We do mainly commercials like the Crunchie ads and Cuprinol man and title sequences for the BBC. Bristol's a bit of a centre for animation - it's cheaper than London. If I was starting now, well, they prefer you to have done a degree, usually fine art. In fact, I'm not saying it wasn't helpful and I wouldn't have missed it, but I could have gone in straight after the foundation course. I've learnt a lot more here than on the degree. You need to get a portfolio together and go to somewhere like Shepperton where there's lots of little workshops. You could start doing pack shots, that sort of job, it's really a one man job, you don't need technical support. There is work around, it's been bad last year, but it's picking up now.

Crafts and Trades

Carpenters

Carpenters are used to build sets and furniture. Some sets may be simple, others as elaborate as a space ship interior. As they are normally dismantled at the end of the production the level of carpentry and joinery skills do not need to be high. Theatre sets may be used for a short run, for example in repertory, or over a long period, for example a West End run. Touring productions need sets that can be easily dismantled and reassembled again and again. Carpenters may have to work very fast to create and erect a set. Carpenters work to drawings by the set designer.

Scenic Construction Courses

Central

Central is one of the best known drama schools and has a long established and thriving technical theatre department. The one year **Scenic Technology** course is an advanced training for technical students who wish to enter the field of design, construction and control of scenic and specialist technical effect as used in theatre, television, film and other presentational media. The course examines the practical use of pneumatics, hydraulics and electronics in control, actuation and operation of stage machinery, mechanical effects in scenery, properties and a range of puppetry applications and includes the use of high technology for system analysis and development, design and drafting applications.

Entrance by interview. Students should have a sound engineering or electronics background and ideally some technical or engineering drawing skills.
Fees c£3500

Central
Central is one of the best known drama schools and has a large technical theatre department. The one year **Scenic Construction** course aims to equip the students with the necessary practical training and work experience required for a career in scenic and theatre production workshops. Various areas are covered such as theatre, film, television and trade-shows. The course includes a period of placement in a professional scenic construction or theatre production workshop.
Entrance by interview. Ideally applicants will have had some previous workshop experience and have good practical skills.
Fees: c£3500

Royal Academy of Dramatic Art
The best known of all drama schools, with a strong technical theatre department. The course lasts for 4 terms and covers bench work, handling and maintenance of tools, knowledge of timber, hardware and canvas, building, erecting and maintaining sets, mechanics of scene handling, rigging etc., working drawings and ground plans, budgeting and ordering. There is a period of secondment to a professional organisation in the final term. 18+
Entrance by interview. No formal qualifications necessary but students should have previous practical knowledge.

Interview fee: £20   Fees: c.£6500

Scenic Painters

Scenic painters often work to create effects in paint, such as convincingly antiquing wood. One film production required accurate sets of the Pope's apartments, including wall frescoes. A theatre scenic artist may create views of woods and fields using flats. The main difference between working for theatre and film and television is that the audience never sees the detail in a theatre production, unlike a television or film production.

Scenic Painting Courses

Central

Central has a very strong technical theatre department, with a wide variety of specialised subjects being taught. The one year **Scenic Painting** course aims to equip all students with the necessary practical skills and professional understanding to make a direct entry to a professional career in the field o scenic studies. It is aimed at those who have good basic creative visual and drawing skills. The course is very practical and includes a period of industrial placement.

Entrance by interview. Qualifications are not necessary, but candidates must be able to demonstrate, by a portfolio of previous work the capability to follow and intensive course of study.

Fees c£3500

Royal Academy of Dramatic Art

The best known of all drama schools, with a strong technical theatre department. The one year **Scenic Art** course runs for four terms and aims to equip students for a career as a set painter, scenic artist or design assistant. There is a mixture of practical experience working with professional designers and directors and lectures and tutorial sessions covering aspects such as ground plans, working drawings, perspective, budgeting, painting and texturing among others. There is a period of secondment to a professional organisation in the final term. 18+.

Entrance by interview. No formal qualifications are needed, but a good portfolio helps.

Interview fee: £20 Fees: c£6500 per course.

Upholsterers

Upholsterers are occasionally required to make curtains or furniture padding. These are more likely to be freelance staff or brought in on contract from an upholstery firm.

Armoury

A specialist department to provide guns, swords and so on, found in the largest of theatre production companies. Elsewhere experts and equipment are brought in. Generally members are already experts in their field.

Metal Workshop

On certain productions it may be necessary to have scaffolding, and this will need specialist fitters. Theatre productions in particular may require complicated sets on two levels, perhaps revolving and the fitting will be done by the metal workshop, or by outside metal workers.

Scene Shifters

Scene shifters work in theatre. Their main work comes in the "get out" and "get in" when the old set is taken down or "struck" and the new set is erected. This may involve working flat out from the moment the curtain goes down on the last performance on Saturday night to when the actors come in to start the technical and dress rehearsals on the Monday morning. Sets can be extremely complicated, for example, Alan Ayckbourn's play "Way Upstream" is almost entirely set on a moveable boat in a tank of water set onto a stage.

Electricians

House Electricians run the 'off stage' side of things, such as electricity to offices and front of house. Production or lighting electricians, also known as "sparks", are in charge of the production electrics, whether in the studio or outside. Sometimes one electrical team does both jobs. Their main job is to place the lights under the supervision of the chief lighting electrician, as directed by the lighting cameraman or director (in films the chief electrician is known as the gaffer, and the second in command as the best boy). On location the lights will usually be free standing; in the studio or theatre they are fixed to a grid hung from the ceiling. A good head for heights is essential.

Stage Electrics Courses

Royal Academy of Dramatic Art

The best known of all drama schools, with a strong technical theatre department. The **Stage Electrics** course lasts for 4 terms and covers basic backstage work, includ-

ing scenery handling and flying, continuing with all aspects of theatre lighting and sound, and signing lighting and sound for public shows with professional designers. There is a period of secondment to a professional organisation in the final term. 18+
Entrance by interview. No formal qualifications necessary but students should have previous practical knowledge.
Interview fee: £20   Fees: c.£6500

Properties

The props department may be required to supply almost anything, from authentic watches and glasses to furniture to specials props such as collapsing chairs. Props may be made, bought or borrowed, depending on the type of production and the budget. In smaller theatre companies finding props is often the responsibility of the assistant stage manager and are often borrowed.

Prop Making Courses

Central

Central is one of the best known drama schools and has a large technical theatre department. This course teaches the basic skills of Prop making. Various areas are covered such as modelling, sculpting, casting in fibre glass, latex and plaster, and basic carpentry and scene painting. There will be professional secondments.
Entrance by interview and portfolio of previous work, although formal qualifications are not necessary.
Fees: c£3000

Royal Academy of Dramatic Art
The best known of all drama schools, with a strong technical theatre department. The prop making course lasts for 4 terms and covers general backstage work, use of materials in depth, fibreglass, casting, modelling, upholstery, wood turning, budgeting, and research on finding props. There is a period of secondment to a professional organisation in the final term. 18+
Entrance by interview. No formal qualifications necessary but students should have previous practical knowledge.
Interview fee: £20   Fees: c.£6500

General Courses

Central
Central is one of the best known drama schools and has a large and thriving technical theatre department. This two week course covers practical classes and projects in various areas of theatre crafts such as scenic painting, scenic construction, prop-making, stage design and costume design. Practical experience is given in support of the four week summer acting course performances.

Most stage management courses also cover crafts and trades.

Design

Design Team

Production Designer/Set Designer/Art Director Set Decorator, Design Assistants

The designer needs to have extensive knowledge of what is historically accurate and to be able to research when necessary. Almost all set designers, whether for film, theatre or television have a degree level qualification. This may be in design, art, art history, or architecture. There are several theatre design courses, which are listed below.

Film and Television
Most designers are now freelance with the television staff set designer a rapidly disappearing breed - half of all the designers at the BBC were made redundant last year, with more estimated to follow.

Set Designer/Production Designer
The **Set Designer** or **Production Designer** is involved from the first stages of a production. They interpret the script and produce rough drawings. As well as designing sets which are to be constructed the designer may find locations or alter locations once found, such as disguising modern shop fronts in a period production. The set designer must be aware to allow for the scene to be shot from different angles and for

actors to move as necessary. In a studio based production there must also be allowance for the movement of the cameras. The **Art Director** draws up floor plans, and usually makes a working model, and a storyboard. The storyboard looks rather like a strip cartoon and tells the story scene by scene showing how all the sets are to look. Some storyboards are very elaborate and depict the production virtually shot by shot. To make life confusing on some sets (and especially on commercial shoots) the Art Director may be the head of the creative team, with the second-in-command role being performed by the production designer.

Next simplified architectural drawings are produced by the **Design Assistants**. These used to be done manually but can be produced by computer aided design (CAD) programmes. CAD is more common in television, where sets may be for documentaries, light entertainment programmes and so on. The drawings are then costed. Having been approved the set is constructed and any set dressing bought, hired or made by the **Set Decorator**. Set dressing includes furniture, curtains, tables, lampshades and so on. Anachronisms, such as a character using tea bags before they had been invented, are always noticed. Finally the designer supervises the erection of the sets and the set dressing. Usually the job finishes as the production starts recording.

Alison Riva, 30, Art Director

I want to art school and did graphic design and photography. I then worked as a graphic designer for a bit, but also went to the National Film School and art directed a couple of students films. They didn't have a very good art department then, there wasn't much there. I really liked doing it so I went onto JOBFIT - I just saw an ad in the Guardian and got on, it was only after that I realised how much competition there had been. Contacts wise it was brilliant, you worked with different crews all the time. One of the reasons for going on JOBFIT was that you needed to be part of the union, and going onto it meant you could get a card, but the whole thing was disbanded the year I left.

I started as an assistant art director, which is a bit like being a runner, cataloguing the drawings, a bit of graphics, you take photos, measure things up. Then I became a set dresser, which means you work closely with the buyer and props, choose colours and so on. The art director is second to the designer and is in charge of construction, the draughtsmen, and generally carrying out anything that needs to be done. I want to be a designer, which is why I'm working on a film now for no money, just to get a show reel. Had I gone to film school I'd probably have come out and tried to get work as a designer straight away. If you do that it can get a lot of peoples backs up, there are lots of people who work on the big films who believe that you shouldn't work as an art director until you've done at least ten years on the board. I think it's better to try and get as much experience as possible. I'd hate to be a designer and not know as much as the art director, but perhaps that's not fair, some one can have very good ideas and not be so technically minded. The National Film School and Royal College of Art courses are best for filmwork, and the BBC do a set design evening course and that teaches you the basics of drawing. You need to get those technical skills.

It's pretty impossible to work in films the whole time now, there aren't enough being made. Most people work across the board. TV is mainly shot on location now so there isn't that much construction, and it's pretty difficult to get into commercials. Ring round, send out your CV and follow it up with a phone call so you've not anonymous. It can be hard, because if someone's out of work they don't want to see people, and if you're in work you're too busy. I'm using three people on this film I'm designing at the moment and they're working for nothing, doing it for the experience. It's lucky breaks and who you know and that's it.

Theatre
Set Designers

Theatre design is simpler than television and film design for three reasons. Firstly most theatre productions are designed to be seen from one direction through the proscenium arch, and if in the round, have little actual set beyond props. Secondly there is no need to worry about where the cameras are to go and thirdly because the audience is at a distance the set need not be as detailed as that for a television or film production. On the other hand the constraints of theatre may make for more interesting design projects. A Sherlock Holmes play will need several sets, from Victorian interiors to misty moors to train stations and so on, all of which the designer must recreate within a limited budget and the limitations of making each set change quickly from one to another. The set designer in theatre is normally the costume designer as well and so the opportunity to create one style is available.

Design Courses
Three Year Courses, Design, Full Time

BA Joint Hons Theatre Design Disciplines
Central

Central is one of the best known drama schools and has a long established and thriving technical theatre department. The first year of the course acts as an introduction to four basic areas: set design, costume design, lighting design and sound design. Students thereafter can choose

which area or combination or areas they wish to follow. The course offers a range of practical opportunities supported by a broad base of theatrical work.
Entrance by interview and submission of a portfolio. Normally minimum entrance requirements are two A levels and three GCSE passes at Grade C or above, but applicants who have previous related experience will also be considered.
Fees c£3500 (mandatory grants)

BA Theatre Studies (Design)
Welsh College of Music and Drama
The course is meant to provide a foundation for young designers, although those who wish to become technicians are able to concentrate on their chosen specialisation. Skill classes cover subjects such as prop making, model making, working drawings, costume construction, millinery and decorative fabric techniques. Some classes are held at the Welsh National Opera Company. Projects include Drama, Ballet, Music Hall, Pantomime, Community theatre, Children's theatre, and theatre in Education. In the second year students start to work on public productions mounted by the Drama and Music schools.
Entrance by interview.
Interview fee: £15 Fees: c£3000 (mandatory grants)

DipHE/BA Hons Theatre Design
Wimbledon School of Art
The course is broad based with equal emphasis on Set Design and Costume Design, with attention to lighting. It is intended fro those who wish to enter the theatre as

all round designers. Students are taught a variety of approaches to Text Analysis and Research Techniques, as well as being taught the skills of Modelmaking and Technical Drawing, including ground plans, elevations and other working drawings. In the second and third years there are opportunities for designs to be realised in a variety of projects, working with professional directors and choosing pieces from a wide range of plays, opera and dance from different periods.

Entrance is by interview and submission of a portfolio of work. This should include a variety of personal work as well as evidence of foundation study where applicable. A special project may be set by the department to be presented at interview. The Diploma of Higher Education is a nationally recognised qualification equivalent to, and identical in content to, the first two years of the BA Hons course.

DipHE/BA Hons Technical Arts Design Wimbledon School of Art

The course has been devised fro those who wish to work as set and lighting designers in theatre. The course strives for a balance between the development of practical skills and the student's talent as a set designer, as well as gaining knowledge and experience of current professional practices. On the practical side training is given in the skills of model making, preparation of ground plans, elevations and working drawing, lighting design and practice, prop making, scene painting, and scenic construction. Students also work on research techniques, text analysis and workshops on the text with actors. An introductory course in television design is offered by the Design Department of the BBC, which also offers periods of work experience for those students who are thinking of a design career in television.

Entrance is by interview and submission of a portfolio of work. This should include a variety of personal work as well as evidence of foundation study where applicable. A special project may be set by the department to be presented at interview. The Diploma of Higher Education is a nationally recognised qualification equivalent to, and identical in content to, the first two years of the BA Hons course.

DipHE/BA Hons Technical Arts Interpretation Wimbledon School of Art

The course has been devised for students wishing to develop their creativity and self awareness through an exploration and application of a wide range of materials and skills in a theatrical context. Students are taught in all the major technical areas of theatre practise: modelmaking, prop making, modelling in clay, mould making and casting using fibreglass, silicon, vynamould and plaster, scene painting, technical drawing, scenic construction, metal and wood work, lighting and sound design and practise. The high level of technical skills equips the students for professional work in theatre, film or television. In the second and third years students work on projects and collaborations, often with professional design companies. Work experience can usually be offered in the third year.

Entrance is by interview and submission of a portfolio of work. This should include a variety of personal work as well as evidence of foundation study where applicable. A special project may be set by the department to be presented at interview. The Diploma of Higher Education is a nationally recognised qualification equivalent to, and identical in content to, the first two years of the BA Hons course.

Two Year Courses, Design, Full Time

Mountview
Mountview is a large professionally run school. The first year on the **Stage Management (Design)** is a foundation year in the basics of stage management technique. Because all the school productions are student designed by second year students there is in the first year additional design classes for those who are intending to specialise in design. In the second year students take production roles on the schools public performances. These include general stage craft, stage management, lighting and sound, and Design. Students may also be seconded to a professional theatre, workshop, designer or studios for several weeks depending on their interests.

Entrance is by interview. Students wishing to be considered for the design option should bring a portfolio with them, and will also have a project set by the technical staff.

Interview fee: Fees: NCDT CDS

Royal College of Art
The Design for Film and Television course is based on all aspects of production design for film and television. In the first year students attend a series of seminars and lectures both in-house and from visiting professionals on subjects such as the history, aesthetics and techniques of

theatre, film and television design, design techniques, construction, budgeting, location design, special effects, design for pop-promos and advertising commercials. Workshops include drawing up floor plans and elevations, planning camera angles, model making, storyboard techniques, props and costume design. Students are expected to design and construct the sets for directing/producer student film and television productions. The second year is has two major components; the design for a graduation film and the redesigning of sets for a 'classic' film.

Entrance is by submission of work on video plus a portfolio of related design work, sets, costumes etc., together with, if possible, storyboards and any other supporting material. In general students are expected to have a background in theatre design, graphic design, architectural studies, interior design, film and television production studies. There is a biennial intake i.e. the start of the next course will be academic year 1995/6.

Higher Diploma/MA in Fine Art (Theatre design)
The Slade School of Fine Art

Entrance to the course is restricted, currently to 5 students per year. The detailed content of the course is planned on a term by term basis, in discussion with the students. The aim is to provide a comprehensive and balanced selection of projects. Specialist subjects taught include scene painting, model making, scale drawings, ground plans, elevations, direction, costume history and construction and lighting. Practitioners from relevant disciplines are consulted such as actors, writers, choreographers, anthropologists, translators, mask-, prop- and puppet makers. For the Higher Diploma, students submit work, normally in the form of an exhibition. In addition, for the MA, students submit two reports, one of 5000 words and the other of 10,000 words.

One Year Courses, Design, Full Time

Central
Central is one of the best known drama schools and has a thriving technical department. This **Stage Design** course is aimed at students at a post-graduate level and provides a practical grounding in professional practice in relation to the designer's role in theatre production. The work is a combination of lectures, project work, written study and some practical instruction and experience. Students work in close association with professional directors, as well as a range or other theatre professionals towards completion of the major project work.

Entrance by interview, a portfolio of previous work and a completed interview project. Formal qualifications are not essential but students will probably have creative visual skills in other art-related areas or previous education or experience within a theatre context.
Fees: c£3000

Central
This **part time Computer Aided Design** course provides the necessary skills to operate CAD Technology against a background of current industrial practice and also allows students to explore the many potential future

applications of such systems. The course is run in conjunction with Modelbox Ltd the UK leading industrial practitioners in this field. Students start with acquiring basic CAD skills, and becoming competent at operating all relevant hardware and software. These skill are then used for project work simulating current industrial practise, becoming more experimental towards the end of the course.

Entrance by interview. Applicants may already have experience within the field and look towards enhancing their skills in order to increase employability, where others may be looking at it as a form of re-training where previous knowledge or experience can provide a suitable foundation.

Fees: c£1000

MA Stage Design Full Time
Central

Central is one of the largest and best known drama schools which also contains a thriving technical theatre department. The MA course looks into the designer's role within the process of realising text into performance and also with the relationship between the performance and the audience. The course emphasises the relationship between the physical, spatial and aural work or the director and performer and the visual work of the designer. Through a series of projects and written appraisals students are encouraged to promote their individual theoretical understandings of design as a performance tool. The course lasts three terms with a further twelve week period for completion of the Master's project.

A two year part time version of this course is expected to be offered from October 1993.

Entrance by interview and submission of a portfolio of previous work and a written statement which outlines their creative design aesthetic to date and sets out clear proposals for the further development of their work and understanding of the design process. Applicants are expected to have a good Honours degree in Theatre Design and at least one year's professional experience in the theatre. Occasionally degrees in other subjects and exceptional practical experience may be considered.
Fees c£3000

Welsh College of Music and Drama
Like Guildhall and RSAMD the drama department is a part of a larger organisation and facilities are generally good. Areas studied on this design and Stage Management intensive course include lighting, sound , prop making, handling scenery, and the work of the touring stage manager and company manager and on the design side, scene painting, prop and model making, working drawings, carpentry, pattern draughting, costume constructing and the work of the wardrobe supervisor. Students opt for either stage management or design at the start of the course but the course content overlaps considerably.
Entrance by interview.
Interview fee: £15 Fees: c£1000 per annum. CDS NCDT

MA Theatre Design
Wimbledon School of Art
The course is rooted in the exchange of ideas about central issues of Theatre design. This takes place between design and directing tutors and a peer-group of

experienced designers. Each students programme of work is negotiated with the course team to meet the individual demands of professional practise. The practical elements of the course are based on workshops and projects, with also discussion, individual tutorials, writing exercises and a research piece. Students are expected to be graduates from Theatre Design Courses with at least one year's professional experience or its equivalent.

Graphic Design

The graphic designer works closely with the set designer. Their work is most noticeable in the opening and closing credits, but they may be asked to produce cartoons, charts and props such as maps, letters and so on. Most of the work is now done on computers, using graphic systems such as 'Paintbox'. The various Art and Art and Design courses fall out of the scope of this book.

Costume and Wardrobe

Wardrobe/Costume Designer
Wardrobe assistants
Dressers

Wardrobe or Costume Designer
A costume designer usually has the same background and qualifications whether working in theatre, film, television or video. They need to be knowledgeable about period dress including accessories such as wigs, gloves, shoes, jewellery over a wide span of history. They need to be sensitive to character details, so that a flamboyant character will dress in a flamboyant way, a retiring person would be more likely to be dressed inconspicuously. They do not actually make costumes but must be able to supervise the wardrobe department. Another attribute of the costume designer is to be able to get along with people as for actors the way they look in a production may well affect their performance and the designer must be flexible and amenable to changes.
The designs will have been discussed with the director in pre-production, and also with the set designer and lighting designer in film. The design will be affected by the mood of the production, even for a contemporary production. For example a thriller might have a hard edge, perhaps black leather and sharp city suits, but a rural romance might have soft clothes in autumnal or pastel colours. There may be restrictions on design by what the character has to do in a costume, for example a tight skirt would be unsuitable for someone who had to run.

Period costumes are either made for the production or hired from theatrical costumiers such as Morris Angel. Contemporary productions use clothes bought or hired from ordinary shops and part of the designers job is to go shopping with actors to choose clothes.

Costume designers usually have an appropriate degree in Art, Fashion or Theatre Design. A few come up through the ranks of wardrobe assistants. A small percentage may have no qualifications at all and work on productions such as commercials where most costumes are contemporary and flair is more important. The majority of costume designers are freelance, except in subsidised theatre.

Making clothes, fitting them and maintaining them is the job of the **Wardrobe Supervisor** and **Wardrobe Assistants**. Maintenance involves cleaning, repairs, alterations and so on. For the most part their job is finished by the time the work is in production. Wardrobe supervisors and assistants will have considerable dressmaking skills, from a trainee or apprenticeship post or from a course. Some may go on to become costume designers. Wardrobe departments are maintained in subsidised theatre, and a few large television production companies such as the BBC and Granada.

Dressers help to dress the actors on set or during performances, and check that the clothes are clean and in good repair. They should have basic sewing skills, such as sewing on a button. Most dressers are unqualified and may be retired performers who wish to stay in the industry, students earning extra cash, or young actors who wish to gain experience of being on a production. To become a dresser simply apply and wait for a vacancy.

Theatre
In theatre costume design is usually combined with set design as part of one job. This means that the theatre designer has more control over the look of a production. Theatre design has more opportunities for the designer to make a creative statement. Many productions are set in period, or involve sets other than in modern day dress. Productions may be stylised, with all characters wearing a particular colour scheme, or fantastic clothes to reflect their characters. The costumes of the traditional pantomime dame are one of the highlights of the year and most designers relish the chance to let their imaginations rip. Within theatre the main constraint is budget, a point to be borne in mind when the hiring of a Restoration wig is likely to cost more than the hiring of an actor. Costumes are often made of cheap materials such as lining fabrics and synthetics which will look good at a distance.

Film and Television
In film, television and video costume design is usually a separate job. Productions are more likely to be modern dress although there are exceptions. A production such as the film "Dangerous Liaisons" required exquisite costume design of historical accuracy and elaborate period detail and budgetary constraints were minimal (the designs won an Oscar). The costume designers role may be reduced by the leading actors being dressed by their favourite designers as a contractual perk.

Costume and Wardrobe Design Courses

Three Year Courses, Wardrobe Design, Full Time

DipHE/BA Hons Costume Design
Wimbledon School of Art

The costume design course is for those who wish to enter the theatre solely as costume designers. The first year is spent learning a variety of basic practical skills such as use of equipment, sewing, pattern drafting and some period costume cutting and making as well as working on costume design and research projects, play analysis and collaborative work. More elaborate projects occur in the second year and the students have the opportunity or realising some of their own designs to a given budget. In the third year there are usually four major studio-based design projects in with students work with a professional director and in collaboration with a student set designer.

Entrance is by interview and submission of a portfolio of work. This should include a variety of personal work as well as evidence of foundation study where applicable. This should include evidence of sewing ability. A special project may be set by the department to be presented at interview. The Diploma of Higher Education is a nationally recognised qualification equivalent to, and identical in content to, the first two years of the BA Hons course.

DipHE/BA Hons Costume Interpretation Wimbledon School of Art

The Costume interpretation Course is for those who wish to train as wardrobe supervisors and highly skilled makers in the professional theatre. While the course is concerned with the practical expertise of the student there is great emphasis place on design interpretation as a creative skill. In the first year students learn the basic practical skills in the uses of equipment, sewing, costume cutting and making, pattern drafting, textile dyeing and printing, millinery, wig making and so on. More advanced skills are taught during the second year and opportunities are provided for students who wish to specialise in one or two particular crafts. In the third year students gain experience through work placements, by working on outside, large scale professional productions, and from acting as Wardrobe supervisors on internal productions.

Entrance is by interview and submission of a portfolio of work. This should include a variety of personal work as well as evidence of foundation study where applicable. It should also include evidence of sewing ability. A special project may be set by the department to be presented at interview. The Diploma of Higher Education is a nationally recognised qualification equivalent to, and identical in content to, the first two years of the BA Hons course.

Two Year Course, Wardrobe Design, Full Time

BTEC HND Theatre Studies: Costume Interpretation
London College of Fashion
The central theme of the course is to prepare students for the research and technical skills that are needed in order to achieve the highest standards of costume production. Students will have a thorough training in cutting fro all aspects of costume and will be expected to be able to use both traditional and modern materials as appropriate. Courses include: cutting and making costumes from ancient times to the present day, including underwear and corsets; Dying and Printing, Millinery; Embroidery; Head-dresses and Jewellery; Visual Studies; History of Costume: History of the Theatre; Business and communication Studies.
Entrance by interview and submission of art and design work plus a garment they have made.

One Year Courses, Wardrobe Design, Full Time

Bristol Old Vic
Well established and respected, the course at Bristol Old Vic is known as being a strongly text based course with an emphasis on the classics, especially Shakespeare. Direct links with the Bristol Old Vic Repertory company in Bristol have always existed, and now are being fostered with BBC radio Bristol and Bristol based HTV. This course for four students covers all practical aspects of

Theatre wardrobe work. from pattern cutting and costume making to the history of costume and organisational aspects of the work.

Entrance by interview. Students should have a basic knowledge and practical experience of dress making., bringing samples of their work to interview.

Interview fee: £20 Fees: c£6000 per annum. CDS. NCDT.

Central

Central is one of the best known drama schools and has a long established and thriving technical theatre department. The **Costume Cutting and Construction** course aims to make students familiar with working practises in theatre/film/television. Students learn cutting and making techniques plus an element of design interpretation. There is continual consultation with industrial partners, and on-going involvement should be continued and developed throughout the year.

Entrance by interview. Suitable applicants are either those who have established practical skill in professional wardrobe or clothing industries or for graduate of degree or equivalent Fashion or Theatre Design courses.

Fees: c£3000

Central

Central is one of the best known drama schools and has a long established and thriving technical theatre department. The **Costume Design** course aims to provide a practical grounding in professional practices in relation to the costume designer's role in theatre, as well as to examine the creative aspects of costume design and construction supervision. The course is for those who intend to make their careers as professional costume designers within the performing arts and explores and develop design skills in relation to costume design through close co-operation with a director and a clear understanding of the needs of text.

Entrance by interview and portfolio. Applicants need not have qualifications but will have established practical wardrobe/garment skills, either by being a graduate of a costume, fashion or theatre design course, or by have considerable professional experience in the clothing industry.

City Lit
A practical **part time Design and Costume** course on two evenings a week (plus extra time during productions) on stage and costume design, including wardrobe maintenance. After a first term of classes students work closely with directors and performers in rehearsal and presentations.
Fees: £124 concessions, £248 others

City and Guilds
Wigmaking 3013, level 2
The course is open to non-hairdressers and aimed at those who hope to go into theatre and television work.

BTEC Fashion and Clothing

BTEC National Diploma in Fashion and Clothing

Course content
Visual studies - develops skills in drawing and using colour texture and form.
Manufacture and production - includes pattern cutting, taking designs and making them into clothes, becoming familiar with the range of machinery and equipment used.
Historical and Contextual Studies - the history of fashion and clothing.
Business Studies - costing, business procedures, working with clients, laws and regulations covering the fashion industry
Communication Studies - develops written and spoken communication skills.

BTEC National Diploma Design (fashion)

Greater London
Barnet College of Further Education
Croydon College
Hounslow Borough College
London College of Fashion, The London Institute
Waltham Forest College
Westminster College
Thames & Chilterns
Barnfield College (Luton)
Berkshire College of Art and Design

Central
University of Central England in Birmingham
Gloucestershire College of Arts and Technology
Herefordshire College of Art and Design
Leek College of Further Education and School of Art
North Warwickshire College of Technology and Art
Solihull College of Technology
Stafford College
Stoke on Trent College

Yorkshire & Humberside
Bradford and Ilkley Community College
Dewsbury College
Doncaster College
Parkwood College, Sheffield
Scarborough Technical College
York College of Further and Higher Education

East Anglia
Isle College
Norfolk Institute of Art and Design
Redbridge Technical College
South East Essex College of Arts and Technology
Thurrock Technical College

North West
Mid Cheshire College of Further Education
Oldham College
Southport College of Art and Technology
Tameside College of Technology
Wigan and Leigh College
Wirral Metropolitan College

The North
Cleveland College of Art and Design
Darlington College of Technology

Newcastle College
Wales
North East Wales Institute of Higher Education
East Midlands
Chesterfield College of Technology and Arts
Derbyshire College of Higher Education
Loughborough College of Art and Design
Nene College
Southfields College of Further Education
West Nottinghamshire College of Further Education
West Country
Bournemouth and Poole College of Art and Design
Plymouth College of Art and Design
Somerset College of Arts and Technology
South of England
Epsom School of Art and Design
Hastings College of Arts and Technology
Northbrook College
Northern Ireland
East Tyrone College

BTEC Higher National Diploma in Fashion and Clothing

Course Content
Visual Studies - develops the skills or drawing and illustration in a range of media
Historical and Contextual Studies - the history of art, design and fashion as well as changing social trends and influence.
Business Studies - costing, accounting procedures, laws and regulations affecting the fashion industry, running a small business, working with clients.

Communication Studies - develops written and spoken communication skills, may also include photographic or video work.
Optional areas
Design - develops an awareness or current trends, enabling students to eventually design, cost and produce a collection for a client.
Pattern cutting - cutting, modelling and pattern production
Manufacture and production - budgets, quality control, use of a range of machinery and equipment.

BTEC Higher National Diploma Design (fashion)

Greater London
Croydon College
London College of Fashion, The London Institute
Thames & Chilterns
Berkshire College of Art and Design
Central
Cheltenham and Gloucester College of Higher Education
Gloucestershire College of Arts and Technology
Yorkshire & Humberside
York College of Further and Higher Education
North West
Salford College of Technology
Wigan and Leigh College
Wales
Carmarthenshire College of Technology and Art
East Midlands
Derbyshire College of Higher Education
Nene College

West Country
Bournemouth and Poole College of Art and Design
South of England
Epsom School of Art and Design
Kent Institute of Art and Design
Southampton Institute of Higher Education

Make up

The make-up artist works almost entirely in film and television. Occasionally a theatre production will need an elaborate make-up (for example, Phantom of the Opera), or will need a make up design for a group (for example, Cats) and this will be designed by a freelance makeup artist but usually actors in theatre put on their own make-up. On a large production there will be a team of make-up artists with make-up director supervising. Most are freelance and move between television, film and commercials.

The director decides what the general effect will be and the make up artist has to interpret these ideas. They must also fit in with the style of the production and so liaise with the set and costume designers. They should be sensitive to people's wishes and be aware that most people are nervous before appearing on camera. During filming the make-up artist stays on hand to correct any damage that may have occurred to the make-up.

Most of the work of the make-up artist is in "corrective" make-up; that is, taking the shine off peoples noses, tidying the hair, correcting blemishes and so on. It is used in news broadcasts, chat shows, quiz programmes and any programme where people appear as they are such as contemporary drama productions. A few programmes require more elaborate designs, such as period, fantasy or science fiction drama. Make-up artists also have to be able to create wounds and scars that are realistic (for example in hospital dramas), or have to age an actor, or to be able to convincingly distort a face. Make up designers may have to research effects, such as making fingers appear frost bitten (prunes were the solution of one designer). The work includes hair dressing, and in general make up departments prefer those who have a hairdressing background as the artist must be able to cut and style hair in both modern and contemporary styles, and to be trained in the use and maintenance of wigs.

There are many training courses for make-up and hairdressing including BTECs. Most of these do not cover Film, Television and Theatre Make-up, which is specialised. The specialised courses generally prefer students who have had some prior training. BECTU recognises three courses (listed below) with the BBC course certain to gain accreditation as soon as it begins.

BECTU Accredited Courses

The Make Up Centre
26 Bute Street
London SW7 SEX
071 584 2188

The Compleat Makeup Artist Training programme runs for 12 weeks, in three modules of four weeks each. Students can choose to take the modules in one block, or spread out over a period of time. The course covers all aspects of makeup, and aims to prepare students for work in the television and film industries. Module 1 covers beauty and fashion makeup and hair, Module 2 theatre, television, period makeup and hair and Module 3 film and special effects makeup. Students may also attend for a day or a week with no compulsion to accumulate modules. As the principal is head of the Skillset working party for makeup/hairdressing it can be assumed that the course will qualify for NVQ's when in place.

Cost: c£5500 for 12 week course

BTEC HND Theatre Studies: Specialist Make-Up
London College of Fashion
20 John Prince's Street
London W1M 0BJ
071 629 9401
This specialist make-up course prepares students for a career in the specific industries of Television, Film, Theatre and Commercial Photography. Most of the teaching is workshop based as this is an essentially practical course. Areas studied include: Visual Studies, Hairdressing, Wig Dressing and Making, History and History of theatre, Cosmetic Techniques, Anatomy and Cosmetic Science, Business Studies, Communications and Media Skills, Specialised Make-Up. Placement in the second year. Entrance by interview and submission of a portfolio with Art and Design Studies.

Greasepaint
143 Northfield Avenue
London W13 9QT
081 840 6000
The complete make-up course runs for three months and comprises of three separate courses each of which may be taken on their own. They are:
6 week Make-Up Course, £2000 plus VAT. Subjects covered include Stage make-up and hair - Corrective, Ageing, Oriental, Special Effects, Witch, Hairdressing including period styles - and Television and Film Make-up and Hair - Corrective, Ageing, Period Hair, Mous-

taches, Special Effects, Clowns, Animals and Fantasy, Period Make-up, Research.

3 week Prosthetic and Special Effects Course, £1500 plus VAT. Subjects covered include Modelling, casting, making scars, burns, animal noses etc. in plastic and latex, teeth in acrylic, Tattoos, Bald Caps etc.

3 week Hair Dressing Course, £1500 plus VAT. Subjects include Period Wig Dressing, Theory and Practical of all basic cutting techniques, Long hair work etc.

Included in the fees are the costs of a kit which the student retains after completion of the course.

There are other courses, including a 3 week Fashion Make-Up Course for Television, Video and Photography, £1000 plus VAT.

BBC Make-Up Training School
Room 374, Design Building
BBC Television Centre
Wood Lane
London W12 7RJ

The BBC used to run a world famous 16 month training scheme for make-up artists. Due to the BBC restructuring programme this has been closed, but they are opening a commercial Make-Up Training School in its place. This will run for 16 weeks and covers all aspects of hair and Make-Up. (The first course start in May 1993). Applicants should have had some formal training in hair and make-up.

Cost £7000 + VAT (Total £8225)

BTEC Beauty Therapy

Core subjects
Beauty Therapy - develops the skills and knowledge needed to operate successfully as a professional beauty therapist. It includes modern treatment methods and safety and hygiene procedures
Anatomy, human physiology and first aid - helps students understand how the various parts of the body function. It also explains the reasons for the different methods practised
Exercise, human nutrition, metabolism and diet - covers the scientific knowledge needed when designing health and fitness programmes for members of the public
Marketing, sales and consumer studies - develops essential marketing skills that can be applied to the beauty industry. These include awareness of consumer needs, and techniques for selling and promoting beauty products and services
Finance, legal aspects and organisational behaviour - covers the basics of running a business - managing finances, meeting legal requirements, customer relations and administration.

BTEC National Diploma Beauty Therapy

Greater London
The College of North East London
Erith College
London College of Fashion, The London Institute
Central
Birmingham College of Food, Tourism and Creative Studies
Gloucestershire College of Arts and Technology
North East Worcestershire College
North Warwickshire College of Technology and Art

Stoke on Trent College
Yorkshire & Humberside
Bradford and Ilkley Community College
Craven College
Hull College of Further Education
Scarborough Technical College
Thomas Danby College
Thames & Chilterns
Aylesbury College
East Anglia
Cambridge Regional College
The North West
Accrington and Rossendale College
Blackburn College
South Cheshire College
The South Manchester College
Stockport College of Further and Higher Education
Wigan and Leigh College
Wirral Metropolitan College
The North
Kirby College of Further Education
Newcastle College
North Tyneside College of Further Education
Wales
Llandrillo Technical College
Pontypridd Technical College
East Midlands
Clarendon College of Further Education
Northampton College
Southfields College of Further Education

Tresham College
South of England
Brighton College of Technology
Chichester College of Technology
Crawley College of Technology
Guildford College of Technology
Kingston College of Further Education
Thanet Technical College
The West Country
Somerset College of Arts and Technology

BTEC Higher National Diploma Beauty Therapy

Greater London
London College of Fashion, The London Institute
Central
Stoke on Trent College
The North West
The South Manchester College
East Midlands
Chesterfield College of Technology and Arts
South of England
Chichester College of Technology

Section IV

General Information

Types of course

The choice for the entrant is from: N/SVQ's, City and Guilds, BTEC, Degrees, Diplomas and trainee positions. A prospective student should consider several points before signing up on a course:

* Who teaches on the course? Have they worked within the industry, and how recently? Are current working professionals frequently invited as guest/visiting lecturers? The more contacts you can make the better.

* What is the equipment like? How modern is it? How often can you use it - for example, is there free access or is it only for class based work?

* What percentage of the course is practical rather than theoretical? The more 'hands on' a course is the better.

* Does the course provide you with the opportunity to leave with a show reel of what you have done? This is very important because a show reel can be your calling card, and may well lead to a job.

N/SVQ's

The NVQ (National Vocation Qualification) and SVQ (Scottish Vocational Qualification) have been set up in response to the realisation that an academic education at 16 + (i.e. A Levels) are irrelevant to most people. The aim is for a simple national framework of vocational qualifications to be established. They set standards of competence for jobs performed and are either assessed in the work place or in a realistic working environment. This means that those who are actually doing a job can gain a qualification at a range of levels. Level 1 shows basic competence, Level 2 is comparable to 5 GCSE's at grade C or above, Level 3 is equivalent to a BTec National Diploma or 2 A levels plus 5 GCSE's at grade C or above, Level 4 is equivalent to a BTec Higher National Diploma or a Diploma in Higher Education, and Level 5 is equivalent to a BA/BSc honours degree.

In an industry such as film where much of the training has been on the job they are well suited. Even in television where academic requirements have traditionally been higher they will become more suitable as the companies bring in so much from the independent sector. Skillset is the body responsible for setting the standards for the industry. It is not clear, at time of writing, exactly which courses will be operating N/SVQ's.

City and Guilds

City and Guilds courses run at approved centres mostly on a part-time day release basis, although some run full-time or at evenings. The awards are at several levels; pre-vocational, occupational and career extension. Several City and Guilds courses are already accepted for NVQ's. Relevant C& G courses are:

Television and Video Production (2790), C&G level 3
Audio Visual Techniques (7340), C&G levels 1 & 2

Professional Photography Competences (7470), C&G levels 1 & 2
Certificate in Media Techniques: Television and Video Competances (7700),C&G level 2
Certificate in Media Techniques: Journalism and Radio (7790), C&G level 2
Advanced Hairdressing (3000), C&G level 3
NVQ in Hairdressing Level 2, C&G level 2
NVQ in Hairdressing including Afro-type Hair Level 2 (3010), C&G level 2
NVQ in Hairdressing Level 3 (3010)
Wigmaking (3013), C&G level 2

BTEC

BTEC courses offer an alternative to A levels and Further Education Diplomas. Their content is based around a number of core subjects and further options which allow colleges to vary the course offered. They come in three levels: the First diploma, the National Diploma and the Higher National Diploma. The National Diploma is an A level equivalent. College funding is now dependent on student numbers. This has meant that courses that students want are being offered (rather than courses which academics think should be offered). Media studies is one of the courses which are being dictated by customer demand and are springing up everywhere, with more coming. Not all of these are of equally high standard, nor will they carry equal weight when it comes to gaining work.

Degrees
University and colleges offering degrees are also subject to the same pressures as the BTec colleges. Students are attracted to drama, media or film courses and so the universities are offering them. However many would maintain that these should be academic and not vocational courses so it is exceptionally important to check the percentage of practical work involved. An academic degree in any subject is not important in the film and video industry, and is becoming less so in television. Degrees in a relevant subject with a proportion of practical experience are increasingly essential even for television. Most of those at director or designer level (lighting, costume etc.) have a degree level qualification. A job such as television researcher (often the first step to becoming a director or producer) often goes to graduates. The same questions should be asked of degree courses as for BTec courses.

Diplomas
Diploma courses vary from the excellent to the poor. In general most of the post graduate diplomas listed here are extremely good. Look for union accreditation.

Trainee schemes
Without doubt the best introduction to film and television is through ft2 (formerly JOBFIT). Funded by the industry is gives the opportunity to work on real productions as well as

having a training programme of lectures and workshops. Vacancies are determined by industry demand and funding. In house training programmes, such as at the BBC, have been severely curtailed in recent years. Vacancies are usually advertised in the Monday Guardian's Media pages.

Accredited Courses

Accredited Courses - Film and Television

British Kinematograph Sound and Television Society
M6 14 Victoria House
Vernon Place
London WC1B 4DF
071 242 8400

BKSTS Accredited Courses

Bournemouth and Poole College of Art and Design
    HND in Film and TV
    Advanced Diploma in Media Production
    BTEC National Diploma in Audio Visual Design
Bradford University
    BSc Electronic Imaging and Data
Newport Film School
    HND in Film and Television
Plymouth College of Art and Design
    HND in Film and Television

Salisbury College of Art and Design
    HND in Film and TV
    Post Qualifying Examination (PQE)
Sheffield City Polytechnic
    MA/PG Diploma in Film Production
West Surrey College of Art and Design
    BA Hons Degree in Film and Video
    BA Hons in Animation
West Herts College
    HND Media Production
South Thames College
    BTEC HNC in TV Production
    BTEC HNC in Audio Visual Design
Bournemouth University
    BA Media Production

Broadcasting, Entertainment, Cinematograph and Theatre Union
111 Wardour Street
London W1N 3TD
071 636 6367

BECTU is the amalgamation of the ACTT and BETA

BECTU Accredited Courses

National Film and Television School
Polytechnic of Central London
Bristol University
Bournemouth and Poole College of Art and Design
West Surrey College of Art and Design
London International Film School
London College of Printing

Accredited Courses - Dance and Drama

Council for Dance Education and Training
5 Tavistock Place
London WC1H 9SS
071 388 5770

CDET Accredited courses

Arts Educational London School
    Dance Course 3 Years
    Musical Theatre Course 3 Years
Benesh Institute
    Dance Notation Course 3 years
Central School of Ballet
    Professional Dancers Diploma Course 3 Years
Doreen Bird College of Theatre Dance
    Dance-based Performers Diploma Course 3 Years
Elmhurst Ballet School
    Senior Dance Course 3 years
English National Ballet
    Classical Ballet Course 2 years
Hammond School
    Dance Course 3 years
Italia Conti Academy of Theatre Arts
    Performing Arts Course 3 years

Laban Centre for Music and Dance
    Diploma in Dance Theatre 3 years
    BA Hons Dance Theatre 3 years
    Professional Diploma in Community Dance 1-2 years
    Advanced Performance Course (Diploma) 1 year
    Professional Diploma 1 Year

Laine Theatre Arts
    Theatre Training Course 3 years
    Musical Theatre Course 3 years
    Teachers Course 3 years

London College of Dance
    Diploma for Teachers of Dance Course 3 years
    BA Hons Degree in Dance 3 years

London Contemporary Dance School
    BA Hons Contemporary Dance 3 years
    4th Year Diploma Course in Contemporary Dance and Choreography 1 year
    Certificate Course 1 year

London Studio Centre
    Dance Performers Course 3 years

Merseyside Dance and Drama Centre
    Professional Dance Course 3 years

Northern Ballet School
    Professional Dancers Course 3 years
    Dance Teachers Course 3 years

Northern School of Contemporary Dance
    Dancers Course 3 years

Performers Dance College
    Students Course 3 years

Rambert School
    Dance Course 3 years

Royal Academy of Dancing
   Teacher Training Course 3 years
Royal Ballet School
   Dancers Course 2 years
   Teacher Training Course 3 years
Stella Mann School of Dancing
   Dance Course 3 years
The Urdang Academy
   Performers Course 3 years
   Teacher Training Course 3 years

National Council for Drama Training
5 Tavistock Place
London WC1H 9SS
071 387 3650

NCDT Accredited Courses

Academy of Live and Recorded Arts
   Drama course 3 years
Arts Educational Schools
   Drama course 3 years
Birmingham School of Speech Training and Dramatic Art
   Drama course 3 years
Bristol Old Vic Theatre School
   Drama course 3 years
   Drama course 2 years
   Stage Management 2 years

Central School of Speech and Drama
    Drama course 3 years
    Stage Management 2 years
Drama Centre London
    Drama course 3 years
Drama Studio London
    Drama course 1 year (21+)
Guildford School of Acting
    Drama course 3 years
    Drama course 1 year (21+)
    Musical Theatre course 3 years
    Stage Management 2 years
Guildhall School of Music and Drama
    Drama course 3 years
    Stage Management 2 years
London Academy of Music and Dramatic Art
    Drama course 3 years
    Stage Management 2 years
Manchester Metropolitan University
    Drama course 3 years
Mountview Theatre School
    Drama course 3 years
    Drama course 1 year (21+)
    Stage Management 2 years
Rose Bruford College of Speech and Drama
    Drama course 3 years
    Stage Management 3 years
Royal Academy of Dramatic Art
    Drama course 3 years
    Stage Management 2 years

Royal Scottish Academy of Music and Drama
    Drama course 3 years
    Stage Management 2 years
Webber Douglas Academy of Dramatic Art
    Drama course 3 years
    Drama course 2 years
    Drama course 1 year (21+)
Welsh College of Music and Drama
    Drama course 3 years
    Drama course 1 year (21+)
    Stage Management 3 years
    Stage Management 1 year (21+)

Grants

Grant Authorities Policies: Discretionary Grants

General eligibility
Usually the students must have been resident in the UK for 3 years before the academic year in which the course is to begin, and at least a year in the county/borough to which you are applying.
Students who have already received a grant for any post-18 course are not eligible unless the second courses can be seen as a logical progression or the students has previously started but not completed the first course.
There may be other restrictions such as students must attend the course nearest to them.

Below are the stated policies of those grant authorities who responded to our questionnaire. It has been reported that in certain circumstances grant authorities may be amenable to deviate from the stated policy.

Barnet
No discretionary awards for 1993/4
Berkshire
18 grants available to students with places on CDET/NCDT accredited courses chosen by drama, dance and

music panel (normally 6 in dance, 6 in drama and 6 in music).

Birmingham
No discretionary awards for 1993/4

Bolton
Grants awarded to all students with places at CDS/CDET/NCDT schools. Tuition fees limited to maximum £710pa. Grant rates paid at 70% of mandatory rates, but steeper parental contribution scales.

Borders
Assistance may be available to students with places on CDET accredited courses after audition with CDET panel.

Bradford
Grants available for students up to £2500 for tuition fees. Students chosen from all applications on 'highest points' basis eg course leading to recognised vocational qualifications = 8 points, student has not previously taken a post-school course = 15 points etc.

Cambridgeshire
c.14 grants available to students chosen after audition with independent panel.

Cheshire
19 partial grants available to students with places at CDET and NCDT accredited schools, chosen after audition/interview with drama and dance panel.

Cleveland
5 grants available to students chosen after audition and interview with independent assessors. £5000 ceiling for fees.

Cornwall
6 grants available to students chosen after audition/interview with our own panel.

Cumbria
Grants awarded to all students with places on NCDT/CDET accredited courses (and CDS member schools for drama courses), tuition fees to a maximum of £2770 per annum.

Derby
No discretionary awards for 1993/4

Devon
10 awards available to students with places on CDET/NCDT courses or at the Cygnet Training Theatre, chosen by audition/interview with own panel.

Dorset
Grants for all students with places on CDET and NCDT accredited courses, tuition fees to a maximum of £1855.

Dudley
No discretionary awards for 1993/4

Durham
No discretionary awards for 1993/4

Dyfed
Grants available up to £240 per annum. No post graduate courses are eligible.

East Sussex
Grants available for exceptional students under 22 with places on CDET/NCDT courses chosen after audition/intervewi with panel.

Enfield
No discretionary awards for 1993/4

Fife
12 grants paid to students with places at CDET accredited schools, chosen after audition with own drama/dance panel

Gateshead
Grants to all students with places on NCDT/CDET accredited courses, subject to individual approval by the Bursary Sub-Committee.

Gloucestershire
8 grants available to students with a place at a CDET accredited school, 8 for a NCDT accredited school. Students selected through audition/interview with drama panel.

Grampian
Grants considered for all students with a place on a NCDT/CDET/CDS course (means tested).

Greenwich
1 grant available to a student aged 16-18 with a place at a school accredited with the CDET, chosen after audition/interview with dance panel.

Guernsey
Grants to students with places on CDET/NCDT courses selected after CDET assessment or LEA interview.

Gwent
Grant aid considered up to a maximum of £3100 towards tuition fees (means tested).

Hammersmith and Fulham
Grants available for students with places on CDET/NCDT courses chosen after interview/audition with panel, numbers limited by available finance (two awards made last year).

Hampshire
10 grants available for students with places on CDET accredited courses, 10 for those with places on NCDT courses, following auditions with county inspector.

Haringay
No discretionary awards for 1993/4

Harrow
3 grants available to students chosen after audition/ interview with own drama panel.

Hertfordshire
30 grants available to students chosen after audition/ interview with own drama panel

Highland
A small number of grants available, awarded on a first come, first served basis.

Hillingdon
Means-tested grants available to all students with places at CDET/NCDT accredited courses, 50% of tuition fees (75% on course leading to a teaching qualification), and 50% of the maintenance grant.

Humberside
6 grants available to students chosen after audition/ interview with own drama panel

Isle of Wight
No discretionary awards for 1993/4

Jersey
Grants to all students with places on CDET/NCDT courses

Kingston
No discretionary awards for 1993/4

Kirklees
No discretionary awards for 1993/4

Leeds
A number of grants available to students chosen after interview with own drama panel (limited funds).

Liverpool
Means-tested grants (tuition fees only) to all students with a place at a CDET/NCDT accredited school.

Lothian
Grants to students with places on the following courses: Dean Academy of Dancing, Northern School of Contemporary Dance, Royal Academy of Dancing (Teacher Training), Royal Ballet School (Teacher Training or Dancers), Theatre School of Dance and Drama.

Norfolk
6 grants available to students chosen after interview/audition with drama, dance and stage management panels, up to £5547 per annum tuition fees.

Northhamptonshire
Grants to all students with places on CDET/NCDT accredited courses, up to £2000 per annum

Northumberland
Grants awarded to all students with places at CDS/CDET/NCDT schools. Tuition fees limited to maximum £792pa.

North Yorkshire
3 grants available to students chosen after audition/interview with our own drama panel.

Oldham
Grants awarded to all students with places at CDET/NCDT courses, tuition fees only up to Mandatory Regualtion rates.

Oxfordshire
Each application considered on its own merits with no limits on the number of awards available, but normally students should have places on NCDT or CDET courses and tuition fees are restricted to 50% of the full cost.

Redbridge
Grants to all students under 21 with a place at one of the following dance/drama schools: Arts Education (dance & musical theatre only), Central School of Ballet, Italia Conti, Laban School, London College of Dance (Bedford)*, London Contemporary Dance School, London Studio Centre, Rambert School of Ballet, Royal Academy of Dancing*, Royal Ballet School*, Urdang Academy*, Bristol Old Vic**, Drama Centre, Guildhall**, LAMDA**, Mountview**, RADA**, Webber Douglas. * = teacher courses as well as dance, ** = stage management courses as well as acting.

Richmond
3 bursaries of up to £5000 for students with places at CDET/NCDT accredited courses, chosen after audition with own drama panel.

S Glamorgan
No discretionary awards for 1993/4

S Tyneside
1 or 2 grants available to students chosen after audition/interview with our own drama panel.

Salford
Grants awarded to all students with places at CDET/NCDT schools. Grants (including tuition fees) limited to maximum £594pa.

Sandwell
No discretionary awards for 1993/4

Shetland Islands
Grants available to students with places on CDET accredited courses.

Shropshire
Limited grants available to students (up to 50% of tuition fees only)

Solihull
Grants available to selected students with places on CDET/NCDT accredited courses after audition by independent assessor.

Southern Region (NI)
Students selected after audition with drama panel (most students receive grants)

Southwark
No discretionary awards for students with places at private colleges for 1993/4

Stockport
No discretionary awards for 1993/4

Suffolk
60 grants available at any one time (i.e. number of new awards per year varies) to students chosen after audition/interview with own drama, music and dance panels.

Sunderland
Contribution towards fees to all students with a place on an NCDT accredited course. Level of contribution decided each year by a committee and is variable.

Tayside
Grants to all students with a place on a NCDT course.

Warwickshire
No discretionary awards for 1993/4

Wirral
Grants to students with places on NCDT/CDET courses of tuition fees and possibly maintenance.

Wolverhampton
>No discretionary awards for 1993/4

Worcester
>No discretionary awards for 1993/4

Bibliography

Books
Allen, J. Careers in TV and Radio, Kogan Page, 1990
- Contacts, Spotlight, 1993
Duncan, S. How to Become a Working Actor, The Cheverell Press, 1989
Langham, J. Lights CamerasAction, BFI Publications 1993
Rea, K. A Better Direction, Calouste Gulbenkain Foundation, 1989
Richardson, J. Careers in the Theatre, Kogan Page, 1990
- The Official ITV Careers Handbook, Headway, Hodder & Stoughton, 1992

Magazines and Newspapers
Audiovisual
Broadcast
Guardian (Monday)
Independent (Wednesday)
Media Week
Plays and Players
Producer
Professional Casting Report
Screen International
Sight and Sound
Stage and Television Today
Studio News
Television Week
Televisual

Times (Wednesday)
TV Production International

Addreses

Degree Colleges & Universities

University College of Wales
Aberystwyth
The Old College
King Street
Aberystwyth
Dyfed SY23 1DB
0970 623111

The Queen's University of Belfast
Belfast BT7 1NN
Northern Ireland
0232 245133

Birkbeck College
Malet Street
London WC1E 7HX
071 631 6307

University of Birmingham
Edgbaston
Birmingham
B15 2TT
021 414 5487

University of Brighton
Mithras House
Lewes Road
Brighton BN2 4AT
0273 600900

University of Bristol
Senate House
Tyndall Avenue
Bristol BS8 1TH
0272-303030

Brunel University
Uxbridge
Middx UB8 3PH
0895 274000

University of Wales, Cardiff
Cardiff CF1 3XA
0222 874412

University of Central Lancashire
Preston
PR1 2TQ
0772 201201

Chester College
Cheyney Road
Chester CH1 4BJ
0244 375444

City University
Northampton Square
London EC1V 0HB
071 477 8000

City of London Poly see London Guildhall University

Coventry University
Priory Street
Coventry CV1 5FB
0203 631313

Crewe and Alsager College of Higher Education
Crewe Green Road
Crewe Cheshire CW1 1DU
0270 500661

Dartington College of Arts
Totnes
Devon TQ9 6EJ
0803 862224

De Montfort University
The Gateway
Leicester LE1 9BH
0533 551551

University of Derby
Kedleston Road
Derby DE3 1GB
0332 47181

University of East Anglia
Norwich NR4 7TJ
0603 56161

University of Exeter
Northcote house
The Queen's Drive
Exeter
EX4 4QJ
0392 263263

University of Glamorgan
Pontypridd
Mid Glamorgan CF37 1DL
0443 480480

Glasgow University
Glasgow
G12 8QQ
041 339 8855

Goldsmiths College
University of London
New Cross London SE14 6NW
 081 692 7171

University of Greenwich
Wellington Street
Woolwich
London SE18 6PF
081 316 8590

Gwent College of Higher Education
Newport School of Art and Design
Allt-yr-yn Avenue
Newport
Gwent NP9 5XA
0633 432432

University of Hertfordshire
St Albans Campus
7 Hatfield Road
St Albans
Herts AL1 3RS
0727 45544

University of Huddersfield
Queensgate
Huddersfield
W Yorks HD1 3DH
0484 422288

University of Hull
Hull
HU6 7RX
0482 46311

University of Kent
Canterbury
Kent CT2 7NZ
0227 764000

King Alfred's College
Sparkford Road
Winchester SO22 4NR
0962 84151

Lancashire Polytechnic see University of Central Lancashire

Lancaster University
University House
Lancaster LA1 4YW
0524 65201

University of Leeds
Bretton Hall
West Bretton
Wakefield
W Yorkshire WF4 4LG
0924 830261

Leicester University
University Road
Leicester LE1 7RH
0533 522522

Liverpool John Moores University
Trueman Building
15-21 Webster Street
Liverpool L3 2ET
051 231 2121

London College of Fashion
20 John Princes Street
London W1M 0BJ
071 629 9401

London Guildhall University
India House
London EC3N 1NL
071 320 1000

Loughborough University of Technology
Loughborough
Leics LE11 3TU
0509 263171

Universioty of Manchester
Oxford Road
Manchester M13 9PL
061 275 2000

Manchester Metropolitan University
School of Television & Theatre
Capitol Building
School Lane
Didsbury
Manchester M20 0HT
061 247 2000

Middlesex University
White Hart Lane
London N17 8HR
081 362 5000

Napier University
219 Colinton Road
Edinburgh
EH14 1DJ
031 444 2266

Nene College
Park Campus
Boughton Green Road
Northampton NN2 7AL
0604 735500

Newport School of Art and Design see Gwent College of Higher Education

University of Northumbria
Squires Building
Newcastle upon Tyne NE1 8ST
091 235 8935

University of Nottingham
University Park
Nottingham NG7 2RD
0602 484848

Nottingham Polytechnic
Burton Street
Nottingham
NG1 4BU
0602 418418

University of Plymouth
Drake Circus
Plymouth PL4 8AA
0752 600600

University of Portsmouth
University House
Winston Churchill Avenue
Portsmouth PO1 2UP
0705 827681

Queen Margaret College
Clerwood Terrace
Edinburgh EH12 8TS
031 317 3000

Queen Mary and Westfield College
Mile End Road
London E1 4NS
071 975 5555

Ravensbourne College of Design and Communication
Walden Road
Elmstead Woods
Chislehurst
Kent BR7 5SN
081 295 0324

University of Reading
Whiteknights
Reading RG6 2AH
0734 875123

University College of Ripon and York St John
Lord Mayor's Walk
York YO3 7EX
0904 656771

Roehampton Institute
Senate House
Roehampton Lane
London SW15 5PU
081 878 8117

Royal College of Art
Kensington Gore
London SW7 2EU
071 584 5020

Royal Holloway and Bedford New College
University of London
Egham Hill
Egham
Surrey TW20 0EX
0784 434455

St Mary's College
Waldegrave Road
Twickenham
Middx TW1 4SX
081 892 0051

University College Salford
Frederick Road
Salford M6 6PU
061 736 6541

Sheffield City Polytechnic
Pond Street
Sheffield
S1 1WB
0742 720911

The Slade School of Fine Art
University College of London
Gower Street
London WC1E 6BT
071 387 7050

University of Southampton
Southampton
SO9 5NH
0703 595000

Staffordshire University
College Road
Stoke on Trent
Staffs ST4 2DE
0782 744531

University of Stirling
Stirling
FK9 4LA
0786 467046

University of Strathclyde
Glasgow G1 1XQ
041 552 4400

University of Sunderland
Langham Tower
Ryhope Road
Sunderland SR2 7EE
091 515 2000

University of Sussex
Falmer
Brighton BN1 9RH
0273 606755

Thames Polytechnic see University of Greenwich

University of Ulster
Cromore Road
Coleraine
Co Londonderry BT52 1SA
0265 44141

University of Warwick
Coventry CV4 7AL
0203 523523

Welsh College of Music and Drama
Castle Grounds
Cathays Park
Cardiff CF1 3ER
0222 342854

West London Institute
300 St Margarets Road
Twickenham TW1 1PT
081 891 0121

West Surrey College of Art and Design
Falkner Road
Farnham
Surrey GU9 7DS
0252 722441

University of Westminster
309 Regent Street
London W1R 8AL
071 911 5000

Wimbledon School of Art
Merton Hall Road
London SW19 3QA
081 540 0231

University of Wolverhampton
Wolverhampton WV1 1SB
0902 321000

Worcester College
Henwick Grove
Worcester WR2 6AJ
0905 748080

University of York
Heslington
York YO1 5DD
0904 430000

Drama and Dance Schools

The Academy of Live and Recorded Arts
Royal Victoria Building
Trinity Road
London SW18 3SX
081 870 6475

The Academy of Musical Theatre
Askew Church Studios
Askew Road
London W12 9RN
081 749 9437

The Academy of Performing Arts
Mardo House
York Road
Acomb
York YO2 4LW
0904 785158/798618

The Actors Centre
4 Chenies Street
London WC1E 7EP
071 631 3599

The Actors Centre Manchester
The Old School
Little John Street
Manchester M3 4PQ
061 832 3430

The Actors Institute
137 Goswell Road
London EC1V 7ET
071 251 8178

Advanced Residential Theatre and Television Skillcentre
International
Highfield Grange
Bubwith
N Yorks YO8 7DP
0757 288088

The Alternative Drama School
20 Waldegrave Road
London SE19 2AJ
081 653 7854

Anna Scher Theatre
70-72 Barnsbury Road
London N1 0ES

The Arden School of Theatre
Arden Centre
Sale Road
Northendon
Manchester M23 0DD
061-957 1715

The Armstrong Arts Academy
9 Grevville Hall
Greville Place
London NW6 5JS
071 372 7110

The Arts Educational Schools
Cone Ripman House
14 Bath Road
Chiswick
London W4 1LY
081 994 9366

The Arts Educational School
Tring Park
Tring
Herts HP23 5LX
044282 4255

The Benesh Institute
12 Lisson Grove
London NW1 6TS
071 258 3041

Blair Theatre School
6 Oldfield Mews
Highgate
London N6 5XA
081 348 2975

The Bloomsbury Alexander Centre
Bristol House
80a Southampton Row
London WC1
071 404 5348

Boden Studio
13 Esswx Road
Enfield
Middx EN2 6TZ
081 367 2692

Bodywise
119 Roman Road
London E2 0QN
081 981 6938

Brighton School of Music and Drama
12 Buxton Road
Brighton
Sussex BN1 5DE
Brighton 553187

Bristol Old Vic Theatre School
1&2 Downside Road
Clifton
Bristol BS8 2XF
0272 733535

British American Drama Academy
Cecil Sharp House
2 Regents Park Road
London NW1 7AY
071 267 4428

The Central School of Ballet
10 Herbal Hill
Clerkenwell Road
London EC1R 5EJ
071 837 6332

Central School of Speech and Drama
Embassy Theatre
Eton Avenue
London NW3 3HY
071 722 8183/4/5/6

The City Lit
16 Stukeley Street
London WC2B 5JL
071 242 9872

The College of the Royal Academy of Dancing
36 Battersea Square
London SW11 3RA
071 223 0091

Court Theatre Training Company
The Courtyard
10 York Way
King's Cross
London N1 9AA
071 833 0870

Cygnet Training Theatre
Friars Gate
Exeter EX2 4AZ
0392 77189

Danceworks
16 Balderton Street
London W1Y 1TF
071 629 6183

The Desmond Jones School of Mime
20 Thornton Avenue
London W4 1QG
081 747 3537

Doreen Bird College of Performing Arts
Birkbeck Centre
Birkbeck Road
Sidcup
Kent DA14 4DE
081 300 6004/3031

Drama Centre London
176 Prince of Wales Road
Chalk Farm
London NW5 3PT
071 267 1177

Drama Studio London
Grange Court
1 Grange Road
Ealing
London W5 5QN
081 579 3897

East 15 Acting School
Hatfields
Rectory Lane
Loughton
Essex IG10 3RU
081 508 5983

Elmhurst Ballet School
Heathcote Road
Camberley
Surrey GU15 2EU
0276 65301

Elliott Clarke College of Dance and Drama
63 Rodney Street
Liverpool L1 9ER
051 709 3323

English National Ballet School
Markova House
39 Jay Mews
London SW7 2ES
071 581 1245

Fool Time
Britannia Road
Kingswood
Bristol BS15 2DA
0272 478788

Guildford School of Acting
Millmead Terrace
Guildford
Surrey GU2 5AT
0483 60701

Guildhall School of Music and Drama
Silk Street
Barbican
London EC2Y 8DT
071 628 2571

Harlequin Theatre School
34 Fernhall Drive
Redbridge
Essex IG4 5BW
081 551 3984/0471

Islington Arts Factory
2 Parkhurst Road
London N7 0SF
071 607 0561

The Italia Conti Academy of Theatre Arts
Italia Cinti House
23 Goswell Road
London EC1M 7BB
071 608 0047/8

The Hammond
Hoole Bank House
Mannings Lane
Chester CH2 2PB
0244 328542

Hertfordshire Theatre School
40 Queen Street
Hitchin
Herts SG4 9TS
0462 421416

Jeannine Greville Dance Academy
Melody House
Gillot's Corner
Henley on Thames
Oxon RG9 1QU
0491 572000

Laban Centre
Laurie Grove
New Cross
London SE14 6NH
081 692 4070

Laine Theatre Arts
The Studios
East Street
Epsom
Surrey KT17 1HH
0372 724648

The Lee Strasberg Studio
Conway Hall
25 Red Lion Square
London WC1R 4RL
071 831 7335

The London Academy of Music and Dramatic Art
Tower House
226 Cromwell Road
London SW5 0SR
071 373 9883

The London Academy of Performing Arts
2 Effie Road
Fulham Broadway
London SW6 1TB
071 736 0121

The London Contemporary Dance School
17 Duke's road
London WC1H 9AB
071 387 0152

The London Institute of Performing Arts
5 Brook Place
Barnet
Herts EN5 2DL
081 441 5010

The London and International School of Acting
138 Westbourne Grove
London W11 2RR
071 727 2342

London Studio Centre
42-50 York Way
London N1 9AB
071 837 7741

The London Theatre School
Askew Church Studios
Askew Road
London W12 9RN
081 749 9437

Merseyside Dance and Drama Centre
The Studios
13-17 Camden Street
Liverpool L3 8JR
051 207 6197

The Midlands Academy of Dance and Drama
50 Cornhill Road
Carlton
Nottingham NG4 1GE
0602 8714360

Morley College
61 Westminster Bridge Road
London SE1 7HT
071 928 8501

Mountview Theatre School
104 Crouch Hill
London N8 9EA
081 340 5885

NW5 Theatre School
14 Fortress Road
London NW5
081 340 1498

The Northern Ballet School
The Dance House
10 Oxford Road
Manchester M1 5QA
061 237 1406

The Northern School of Contemporary Dance
98 Chapeltown Road
Leeds LS7 4BH
0532 625359

The Oxford School of Drama
Sansomes Farm Studio
Woodstock
Oxford OX20 1ER
0993 812883

Queen Margaret College
Clerwood Terace
Edinburgh EH12 8TS
031 317 3000

Questors Theatre
Mattock Lane
Ealing
London W5 5BQ
081 567 0011

Pattison's Dancing Acadmey and College
Cressage
86-90 Binley Road
Coventry CV3 1FQ
0203 455031

Performers Dance College
2-4 Chase Road
Corringham
Essex SS17 7QH
0375 672053

The Poor School
242 Pentonville Road
London N1 9UP
071 837 6030

Pozitiv Productions
5 Strettons,
Southend Bradfield
Berks RG7 6ES
0734 744079/874

The Radio School of Drama
Studio 17, The Promenade
Peacehaven
Sussex BN10 8PU
0273 580250

The Rambert School
West London Institute
Gordon House Campus
300 St Margarets Road
Twickenham
Middx TW1 1PT
081 891 0121

Ravenscourt Theatre School
London House
271-273 King Street
London W6 9LZ
081 741 0707

Redroofs Theatre School
Littlewick Green
Maidenhead
Berks
0628 822982

Richmond Drama School
Richmond ASdult and Community College
Parkshot
Richmond
Surrey TW9 2RE
081 940 0170/5278

Rose Bruford College
Lamorbey Park
Sidcup
Kent DA15 9DF
091 300 3024

The Royal Academy of Dramatic Art
62-64 Gower Street
London WC1E 6ED
071 636 7076

The Royal Ballet School
155 Talgarth Road
London W14 9DE
071 748 6335

The Royal Scottish Academy of Music and Drama
100 Renfrew Street
Glasgow G2 3DB
041 332 4101

St Catherine's Drama Studio
26a Portsmouth Road
Guildford
Surrey GU2 5DH
0483 68788

The School of the Science of Acting
67-83 Seven Sisters Road
Holloway
London N7 6BU
071 272 0027

The Shandy Stage School
57 Livingstone Road
Hove
Sussex BN3 3WN
0273 822244

The Society of Teachers of the Alexander Technique
10 London House
266 Fulham Road
London SW10 9EL
071 351 0828

Stagecoach Traingin Centres
28 Pool Road
West Molesey
Surry KT8 2HE
081 783 0778

Stardust Children's Theatre Workshop
43 Marlands Road
Clyhall
Redbridge
Essex IG5 0JL
081 550 7224

Stella Mann College
343a Finchley Road
Hampstead
London NW3 6ET
071 435 9317

The Sylvia Young Theatre School
Rossmore Road
Marylebone
London NW1 6NJ
071 402 0673

The Urdang Academy
20-22 Shelton Street
Covent Garden
London WC2H 9JJ
071 836 5709/7010/0870

The Van Dyke Academy of Theatre Arts
The Studios
Fairmead
Tolworth
081 399 9429

Voice-Wise
3 Wedgwood Mews
Greek Street
London W1V 5LW
071 437 3935

Voiceworks
8 Great Guildford House
30 Great Guildford Street
London SE1 0HS
071 620 1492

Webber Douglas Academy
Chanticleer Theatre
30 Clareville Street
London SW7 5AP
071 370 4154

The Welsh College of Music and Drama
Castle Grounds
Cathays Park
Cardiff CF1 3ER
0222 342854

White Rose Studio of Speech and Drama
Castlehill House
21 Otley Road
Headingly
Leeds LS6 3AA
0532 757514

BTEC Colleges

Aberdeen College of Further Education
Ruthrieston Centre
Holburn Street
Aberdeen
AB9 2YT
0224 640366

Abingdon College
Northcourt Road
Abingdon
Oxon OX14 1NN
0235 555585

Accrington & Rossendale College
Sandy Lane
Accrington
BB5 2AW
0254 393521

Afan College
Margam
Port Talbot
West Glamorgan
SA13 2AL
0639 882107

Amersham & Wycombe College
Stanley Hill
Amersham
Bucks
HP7 9HN
0494 721121

Anniesland College
Hatfield Drive
Glasgow G12 0YE
041 357 3969

Aylesbury College
Oxford Road
Aylesbury HP21 8PD
0296 434111

Banbridge College of Further Education
Castlewellan Road
Banbridge BT32 4AY
08206 62289

Banff and Buchan College of Further Education
Henderson Road
Fraserburgh AB43 5GA
0346 515777

Barking College
Dagenham Road
Romford
Essex RM7 0XU
0708 766841

Barnet College
Wood Street
Barnet
Herts EN5 4AZ
081 440 6321

Barnfield College
New Bedford Road
Luton LU2 7BF
0582 507531

Barnsley College
Church Street
Barnsley
S Yorks S70 2BR
0226 730191

Basingstoke College of Technology
Worting Road
Basingstoke
RG21 1TN
0256 54141

Belfast Institute of Further and Higher Education
Park House
87-91 Great Victoria Street
Belfast
BT2 7AG
0232 325312

Bell College of Technology
Almada Street
Hamilton
ML3 0JB
0698 283100

Berkshire College of Art and Design
Kings Road
Reading RG1 4HJ
0734 583501

Bilston Community College
Wellington Road
Bilston
Wolverhampton
WV14 6EW
0902 353929

Birmingham College of Food, Tourism and Creative Studies
Summer Row
Birmingham B3 1JB
021 604 1000

Blackburn College
Feilden Street
Blackburn
Lancs BB2 1LH
0254 55144

Blackpool and the Fylde College
Palatine Road
Blackpool
Lancs FY1 4DW
0253 52352

Bolton College
Manchester Road
Bolton BL2 1ER
0204 31411

Borders College
Herderson Building
Cinnercuak Road
Hawick TD9 7AW
0450 74191

Boston College
Rowley Road
Boston
Lincs PE21 6JF
0205 365701

Bournemouth and Poole College of Art and Design
Wallisdown
Poole
Dorset
BH12 5HH
0202 533011

Bradford and Ilkley Community College
Great Horton Road
Bradford BD7 1AY
0274 753026

Bridgwater College
Bath Road
Bridgwater
Somerset TA6 4PZ
0278 455464

Brighton College of Technology
Pelham Street
Brighton
East Sussex BN1 4FA
0273 667788

Brooklands Technical College
Heath Road
Weybridge
Surrey KT13 8TT
0932 853300

Brunel College of Technology
Ashley Down
Bristol BS7 9BU
0272 241241

Burnley College
Shorey Bank
Ormerod Road
Burnley BB11 2RX
0282 36111

Burton upon Trent College
Lichfield Street
Burton upon Trent
DE14 3RL
0283 45401

Bury College
Market Street
Bury
BL9 0BG
061 763 1505

Calderdale College
Francis Street
Halifax HX1 3UZ
0422 358221

Cambridge Regional College
Cambridge
CB5 8BR
0223 357545

Cambuslang College
85 Hamilton Road
Cambuslang G72 7NY
041 641 6600

Cardonald Colege
690 Mosspark Draive
Glasgow G52 3AY
041 883 6151

Carmarthenshire College of Technology and Arts
Alban Road
Llanelli
Dyfed SA15 1NG
0554 759165

Central College of Commerce
300 Cathedral Street
Glasgow G1 2TA
041 552 3941

Central St Martins College of Art and Design
Southampton Row
London WC1B 4AP
071 753 9090

Charles Keene College
Painter Street
Leicester LE1 3WA
0533 516037

Chesterfield College
Infirmary Road
Chesterfield S41 7NG
0246 231212

Chichester College of Arts Science and Technology
Westgate Fields
Chichester
W Sussex PO19 1SB
0243 786321

City of Bath College
Avon Street
Bath BA1 1UP
0225 312191

City of Liverpool Community College
Riversdale Road
Liverpool L19 3QR
051 252 1515

City Technology College
Cooks Lane
Kingshurst
Birmingham B37 6NZ
021 770 8923

City of Westminster College
Paddington Green
London W2 1NB
071 723 8826

Cheltenham and Gloucester College of Higher Education
The Park
Cheltenham
Glos GL50 2QF
0242 532700

Chippenham College
Cocklebury Road
Chippenham
Wilts SN15 3QD
0249 444501

Clarendon College
Pelham Avenue
Mansfield Road
Nottingham NG5 1AL
0602 607201

Cleveland College
Corporation Road
Redcar
Cleveland TS10 1EZ
0642 473132

Cleveland College of Art and Design
Green Lane
Linthorpe
Middlesborough
Cleveland TS5 7RJ
0642 829973

Coatbridge College
Kildonan Street
Coatbridge ML5 3LS
0236 422316

Coleg Glan Hafren
Trowbridge Road
Rumney
Cardiff CF3 8XZ
0222 794226

The College of North East London
High Road
London N15 4RU
081 802 3111

Cornwall College
Pool
Redruth
Cornwall TR15 3RD
0209 712911

Crawley College
College Road
Crawley
W Sussex RH10 1NR
0293 612686

Cricklade College
Charlton Road
Andover
Hants SP10 1EJ
0264 363311

Crosskeys College
Crosskeys
Gwent NP1 7ZA
0495 272138

Croydon College
The Crescent
Croydon CR9 2LY
081 684 9266

Cumbernauld College
Tryst Road
Town Centre
Cumbernauld G67 1HU
0236 731811

Cumbria College of Art and Design
Brampton Road
Carlisle
Cumbria CA3 9AY
0228 25333

Darlington College of Technology
Cleveland Avenue
Darlington
Co. Durham DL3 7BB
0325 467651

Daventry Tertiary College
Badby Road West
Daventry
Northants NN11 4HJ
0372 300232

Derby Tertiary College
London Road
Wilmorton
Derby DE24 8UG
0332 757570

Dewsbury College
Halifax Road
Dewsbury
W Yorks WF13 2AS
0924 465916

Dudley College
The Broadway
Dudley
W Midlands DY1 4AS
0384 455433

Dumfries and Galloway College of Technology
Heathall
Dumfries DG1 3QZ
0387 61261

Duncan of Jordanstone College of Art
13 Perth Road
Dundee DD1 4HT
0382 23261

Dundee College
30 Constitution Road
Dundee DD3 6TB
0382 29151

Dundee Institute of Technology
Bell Street
Dundee DD1 1HG
0382 308000

Ealing Tertiary College
Ealing Green
Ealing
London W5 5EW
081 231 6008

East Berkshire College
Station Road
Langley SL3 8BY
0753 549222

East Surrey College
Claremont Road
Gatton Point
Redhill
Surrey RH1 2JX
0737 772611

East Warwickshire College
Lower Hillmorton Road
Rugby CV21 3QS
0788 541666

Eastbourne College of Arts and Technology
St Anne's Road
Eastbourne
E Sussex BN21 2HS
0323 644711

Eastleigh College
Chestnut Avenue
Eastleigh SO5 5HT
0703 644011

Edinburgh College of Art
Lauriston Place
Edinburgh EH3 9DF
031 229 9311

Elm Park College
Elm Park
Stanmore
Middx HA7 4BR
081 954 9481

Elmwood College
Cupar
Fife KY15 4JB
0334 52781

Epping Forest College
Borders Lane
Loughton
Essex IG10 3SA
081 508 8311

Epsom School of Art and Design
Ashley Road
Epsom
Surrey KT18 5BE
0372 728811

Farnborough College of Technology
Boundary Road
Farnborough
Hants GU1 6SB
0252 515511

Falkirk College
Grangemouth Road
Falkirk FK2 9AD
0324 24981

Falmouth School of Art and Design
Woodlane
Falmouth
Cornwall TR11 4RA
0326 211205

Fareham College
Bishopsfield Road
Fareham
Hants PO14 1NH
0329 220844

Fife College of Technology
St Brycedale Avenue
Kirkaldy KY1 1EX
0592 268591

Filton College
Filton Avenue
Bristol BS12 7AT
0272 694217

Gateshead College
Durham Road
Gateshead
Tyne & Wear NE9 5BN
091 477 0521

Glasgow College of Building and Printing
60 North Hanover Street
Glasgow G1 2BP
041 332 9969

Glenrothes College
Stenton Road
Glenrothes
Fife KY6 2RA
0592 772233

Gloucesterhire College of Arts and Technology
Brunswick Road
Gloucester GL1 1HS
0452 426602

Greenhill College
Lowlands Road
Harrow
Middx HA1 3AQ
081 422 2388

Grimsby College of Technology
Eleanor Street
Grimsby DN32 9DU
0472 279231

Guildford College of Further and Higher Education
Stoke Park
Guildford
Surrey GU1 1EZ
0483 312251

Guthlaxton College
Station Road
Wigston Magna
Leicester LE18 2DS
0533 881611

Gwent College of Higher Education
Newport
Gwent NP6 1YH
0633 432432

Gwynedd Technical College
Ffordd Ffriddoedd
Bangor
Gwynedd LL57 2TP
0284 370125

Hackney Community College
Keltan House
89-115 Mare Street
London E8 4RG
081 533 5922

Halesowen College
Whittingham Road
Halesowen
W Midlands B63 3NA
021 550 1451

Halton College
Kingsway
Widnes
Cheshire WA8 7QQ
051 423 1391

Hammersmith & West London College
Gliddon Road
Barons Court
London W14 9BL
081 563 0063

Harlow College
College Square
The High
Harlow
Essex Cm20 1LT
0279 441288

Harrogate College of Arts and Technology
Hornbeam Park
Harrogate HG2 8QT
0423 879466

Hastings College of Arts and Technology
Archery Road
St Leonards on Sea
E Sussex TN38 0HX
0424 442222

Havant College
New Road
Havant
Hants PO9 1QL
0705 483856

Havering College of Further and Higher Education
Ardleigh Green Road
Hornchurch
Essex RM11 2LL
0708 455011

The Henley College
Deanfield Avenue
Henley on Thames
Oxon RG9 1UH
0491 579988

Henley College Coventry
Henley Road
Bell Green
Coventry CV2 1ED
0203 611021

Herefordshire College of Art and Design
Folly Lane
Hereford HR1 1LT
0432 273359

Highbury College
Portsmouth
Hants PO6 2SA
0705 283237

Hinckley College
London Road
Hinckley
Leics LE10 1HQ
0455 251222

Hopwood Hall College
St Mary's Gate
Rochdale OL12 6RY
0706 345346

Hounslow Borough College see West Thames College

Hull College
Queen's Gardens Centre
Queen's Gardens
Hull HU1 3DG
0482 29943

James Watt College
Finnart Street
Greenock PA16 8HF
0475 24433

Jewel and Esk Valley College
Eskbank Centre
Newbattle Road
Dalkeith EH22 3AE
031 663 1951

Kent Institute of Art and Design
Oakwood Park
Maidstone
Kent ME16 8AG
0622 757286

Kidderminster College
Hoo Road
Kidderminster
Worcs DY10 1LX
0562 820811

Kilmarnock College
Holehouse Road
Kilmarnock KA3 7AT
0563 23501

Kingston College of Further Education
Kingston Hall Road
Kingston Upon Thames
Surrey KT1 2AQ
081 546 2151

Kingsway College
Grays Inn Centres
Sidmouth Street
London WC1H 8JB
071 278 0541

Kirby College
Roman Road
Linthorpe
Middlesborough, Cleveland TS5 5PJ
0642 813706

Kitson College Leeds now Leeds College of Technology

Knowsley Community College
Rupert Road
Roby
Merseyside L36 9TD
051 443 2600

Langside College Glasgow
50 Prospecthill Road
Glasgow G42 9LB
041 636 6066

Leeds College of Technology
Cookridge Street
Leeds LS2 8BL
0532 430381

Leek College
Stockwell Street
Leek
Staffs ST13 6BR
0538 398866

Lews Castle College
Stornaway
Isle of Lewis
0851 703311

Llandrillo College
Llandudno Road
Colwyn Bay
Clwyd
 LL28 4HZ
0492 546666

London College of Printing and Distributive Trades
Elephant and Castle
London SE1 6SB
071 735 8484

The London Institute
The London College of Fashion
20 John Princes Street
London W1M 0BJ
071 629 9401

Longlands College
Douglas Street
Middlesborough
Cleveland TS4 2JW
0642 248351

Loughborough College of Art and Design
Radmoor
Loughborough
Leics LE11 3BT
0509 261515

Lowestoft College
St Peters Street
Lowestoft
Suffolk NR32 2NB
0502 583521

Ludlow College
Ludlow
Shropshire SY8 1BE
0584 872846

Lutterworth Community College
Bitteswell Road
Lutterworth
Leics LE17 4EW
0455 554101

Manchester College of Arts and Technology
Lower Hardman Street
Manchester M3 3ER
061 953 2263

Melton Mowbray College of Further Education
Asfordby Road
Melton Mowbray
Leics LE13 0HJ
0664 67431

Mid Cheshire College of Further Education
Chester Road
Northwich CW8 1LJ
0606 75281

Mid Kent College Of Higher and Further Education
Maidstone Road
Chatham
Kent ME5 9UQ
0634 830633

Mid Warwickshire College of Further Education
Warwick New Road
Leamington Spa CV32 5JE
0926 311711

Milton Keynes College
Stratford Road
Wolverton
Milton Keynes MK12 5NU
0908 668998

Monkwearmouth College
Swan Street Centre
Sunderland SR5 1EB
091 516 2000

Motherwell College
Dalzell Drive
Motherwell ML1 2DD
0698 259641

Mulberry School for Girls
Richard Street
Commercial Road
Stepney
London E1 2JP
071 790 6327

Neath College
Dwr-y-Felin Road
Neath
W Glamorgan SA10 7RF
0639 634271

Nelson and Colne College
Scotland Road
Nelson
Lancs BB9 7YT
0282 603151

Newark and Sherwood College
Friary Road
Newark Nottingham NG24 1PB
0636 705921

Newbury College
Oxgord Road
Newbury
Berks RG13 1PQ
0635 37000

Newcastle College
Donard Street
Newcastle
Co Down
N Ireland
03967 22451

Newcastle College
Maple Terrace
Newcastle upon Tyne
NE4 7SA
091 273 8866

Newcastle under Lyme College
Liverpool Road
Newcastle under Lyme
Staffs ST5 2DF
0782 715111

New College
Helston Road
Park North
Swindon SN3 2LA
0793 611470

Newham Community College
High Street South
London E6 4ER
081 471 6688

Newry College of Further Education
Patrick Street
Newry
Co Down BT35 8DN
0693 61071

Newtownabbey College of Further Education
400 Shore Road
Newtownabbey BT37 9RS
0232 864331

New College Durham
Framwellgate Moor Centre
Durham DH1 5
Coleraine Road
Ballymoney
Co Antrim BT53 6BP
02656 62258

Norfolk College of Arts and Technology
Tennyson Avenue
King's Lynn
Norfolk PE30 2QW
0553 761144

Norfolk Institute of Art and Design
St George Street
Norwich
Norfolk NR3 1BB
0603 610561

North Antrim College
Coleraine Road
Ballymoney
Co Antrim BT53 6BP
02656 62258/9

North Derbyshire Tertiary College
Clowne
ChesterfieldS43 3BQ
0246 810332

North Devon College
Old Sticklepath Hill
Barnstaple
Devon EX31 2BQ
0271 45291

North Down and Ards College
Newtownards Centre
Victoria Avenue
Newtownards BT23 3ED
0247 812116

North East Surrey College of Technology
Reigate Road
Ewell
Epsom
Surrey KT17 3DS
081 394 1731

North East Wales Institute
Cartrefle
Cefn Road
Wrexham LL13 9LN
0978 290390

North Hertfordshire College
Cambridge Road
Hitchin
Herts SG4 0JD
0462 422882

North Glasgow College
110 Flemington Street
Springburn
Glasgow G21 4BX
041 558 9001

North Lindsay College
Kingsway
Scunthorpe
South Humberside
DN17 1AJ
0724 281111

North London College
444 Camden Road
London N7 0SP
071 609 9981

North Nottinghamshire College
Carlton Road
Worksop
Nottinghamshire S81 7HP
0909 473561

North Oxfordshire College and School of Art
Broughton Road
Banbury
Oxon OX16 9QA
0295 252221

North Tyneside College
Embleton Avenue
Wallsend NE28 9NJ
091 262 4081

North Warwickshire College
Hinckley Road
Nuneaton CV11 6BH
0203 349321

North West Institute of Further and Higher Education
Strand Road
Londonderry BT48 7BY
0504 266711

North West Kent College of Technology
Miskin Road
Dartford
Kent DA1 2BR
0322 225471

Northbrook College of Further and Higher Education
Union Place
Worthing
0903 210301

Northumberland College of Arts Technology
College Road
Ashington
Northumberland NE63 9RG
0670813248

Norton College see Sheffield Coollege

Norwich City College of Further and Higher Education
Ipswich Road
Norwich NR2 2LJ
0603 660011

Oaklands College
St Peters Road
St Albans
Herts AL1 3RX
0727 47070

Oldham College
Rochdale Road
Oldham OL9 6AA
061 624 5214

Omagh College of Further Education
Mountjoy Road
Omagh
Co Tyrone BT79 7AH
0662 245433

Oxford College of Further Education
Oxpens Road
Oxford OX1 1SA
0865 245871

Park Lane College
Park Lane
Leeds LS3 1AA
0532 443011

Parkwood College Sheffield
Shirecliffe Road
Sheffield S5 8XZ
768301

Penwith College St Clare Street
Penzance
Cornwall TR18 2SA
0736 62604

Performing Arts and Technology School
60 The Crescent
Croydon CR0 2HN
081 665 5242

Perth College
Crieff Road
Perth PH1 2NX
0738 21171

Plymouth College of Art and Design
Tavistock Place
Plymouth
Devon PL4 8AT
0752 385959

Pontypool and Usk College
Blaendare Road
Pontypool
Gwent NP4 5YE
0495 755141

Portsmouth College of Art and Design
Winston Churchill Avenue
Portsmouth
Hants PO1 2DJ
0705 826435

Preston College
St Vincents Road
Fulwood
Preston PR2 4UR
0772 716511

Ravensbourne College of Design and Communication
Walden Road
Elmstead Woods
Chislehurst
Kent BR7 5SN
081 468 7071

Redbridge College of Further Education
Little Heath
Romford
Essex RM6 4XT
081 599 5231

Reid Kerr College
Renfrew Road
Paisley PA3 4DR
041 889 4225

Richmond upon Thames College
Egerton Road
Twickenham
Middx TW2 7SJ
081 892 6656

Rotherham College of Arts and Technology
Eastwood Lane
Rotherham S65 1EG
0709 362111

Rycotewood College
Priest End
Thame
Oxon OX9 2AF
084421 2501

Sabhal Mor Ostaig
Colaisde Foghlam Ard Ire
An Teanga
An t-Eilean Sgitheanach IV4 8RQ
04714 373

St Austell College
Trevarthian Road
St Austell PL25 4BU
0726 67911

St Helens Community College
Brook Street
St Helens
Merseyside WA10 1PZ
0744 33766

St Wilfrids Catholic High School
Cutsyke Road
North Featherstone
Pontefract
W Yorks WF7 6BD
0977 792228

Salford College
Walkden Road
Worsley
M28 4QD
061 702 8272

Salisbury College
Southampton Road
Salisbury
Wilts SP1 2LW
0722 323711

Sandwell College of Further and Higher Education
Woden Road South
Wednesbury
W Midlands WS10 0PE
021 556 6000

Sheffield College
Norton Centre
Dyche Lane
Sheffield S8 8BR
0742 372741

Shena Simon College
Whitworth Street
Manchester M1 3HB
061 236 3418

Shetland College of Further Education
Gressy Loan
Lewick
Shetland ZE1 0BB
0595 5514

Shrewsbury College of Arts and Technology
London Road
Shrewsbury SY2 6PR
0743 231544

Skelmersdale College
Northway
Skelmersdale
Lancs WN8 6LU
0695 28744

Solihull College of Technology
Blossomfield Road
Solihull
West Midlands B91 1SB
021 711 2111

Somerset College of Arts and Technology
Wellington Road
Taunton TA1 5AX
0823 283403

Southfields College
Aylestone Road
Leicester LE2 7LW
0533 541818

South Bristol College
The Marksbury Centre
Marksbury Road
Bedminster
Bristol BS3 5JL
0272 639033

South Cheshire College
Dane Bank Avenue
Crewe
Cheshire CW2 8AB
0270 69133

South Devon College
Newton Road
Torquay
Devon TQ2 5BY
0803 217551

South Downs College
College Road
Havant
Hants PO7 8AA
0705 257011

South East Derbyshire College
Field Road
Ilkeston
Derbys DE7 5RS
0602 324212

South East Essex College of Arts and Technology
Carnarvon Road
Southend on Sea SS2 5BR
0702 220400

The South Manchester College
Arden Centre
Sale Road
Nothenden
Manchester M23 0DD
061 957 1721

South Nottinghamshire College of Further Education
Greythorn Drive
West Bridgford
Nottingham NG2 7GA
0602 812125

South Thames College
Wandsworth High Street
London SW18 2PP
081 870 2241

South Trafford College
Manchester Road
West Timperley
Altrincham WA14 5PQ
061 973 7064

South Tyneside College
St Georges Avenue
South Sheilds
Tyne & Wear NE34 6ET
091 456 0403

Southampton Institute
East Park Terrace
Southampton SO9 4WW
0703 229381

Southampton Technical College
St Mary Street
Southampton SO9 4WX
0703 635222

Southgate College
High Street
London N14 6BS
081 886 6521

Southport College
Mornington Road
Southport PR9 0TT
0704 500606

Southwark College
Surrey Docks Centre
Drummond Road
London SE16 4EE
071 815 1526

Stafford College
Earl Street
Stafford
ST16 2QR
0785 223800

Stantonbury Campus
Milton Keynes
MK14 6BN
0908 220066

Stevenson College
Bankhead Avenue
Sighthill
Edinburgh EH11 4DE
031 453 2761

Stockport College of Further and Higher Education
Wellington Road South
Stockport SK1 3UQ
061 480 7331

Stoke on Trent College
Stoke Road
Shelton
Stoke on Trent ST4 2DG
0782 208208

Stow College
43 Shamrock Street
Glasgow G4 9LD
041 332 1786

Strode College
Church Road
Street
Somerset BA16 0AB
0458 42277

Stroud College
Stratford Road
Stroud
Glos GL5 4BR
763424

Suffolk College
Rope Walk
Ipswich
Suffolk IP4 1LT
0473 255885

Sutton Coldfield College of Further Education
Lichfield Road
Sutton Coldfield
W Midlands B74 2NW
021 355 5671

Swansea College
Tycoch Road
Swansea SA2 9EB
0792 206871

Swansea Institute of Higher Education
Townhill Road
Swansea SA2 0UT
0792 203482

Tameside College of Technology
Beaufort Road
Ashton under Lyne
Tameside
Gtr Manchester OL6 6NX
061 330 6911

Telford College
Crewe Toll
Edinburgh EH4 2NZ
031 332 2491

Thanet College
Ramsgate Road
Broadstairs
Kent CT10 1PN
0843 865111

Thomas Danby College
Roundhay Road
Leeds LS7 3BG
494912

Thurrock College
Woodview
Grays
Essex RM16 4YR
0375 391199

Thurso College
Ormlie Road
Thurso
Caithness KW14 7EE
0847 66161

Tile Hill College
Tile Hill Lane
Coventry CV4 9SU
0203 694200

Tresham Institute of Further and Higher Education
Rockingham Road
Kettering
Northants NN16 8JY
0536 410933

Ulverston Victoria High School
Springfield Road
Ulverston
Cumbria LA12 0EB
0229 53005

University of Central England in Birmingham
Perry Barr
Birmingham B42 2SU
021 331 5000

Wakefield College
Margaret Street
Wakefield
W Yorks WF1 2DH
0924 370501

Walsall College of Arts and Technology
St Pauls Street
Walsall WS1 1XN
0922 720824

Waltham Forest College
Forest Road
London E17 4JB
081 527 2311

West Cheshire College
Handbridge Centre
Eaton Road
Handbridge
Chester CH4 7ER
0244 677677

West Herts College
Dacorum Campus
Marloes
Hemel HempsteadHP1 1HD
0442 63771

West Kent College
Brook Street
Tonbridge
Kent TN9 2PW
0732 358 101

West Lothian College
Marjoribanks Street
Bathgate EH48 1QJ
0506 634300

West Nottinghamshire College
Derby Road
Mansfield
Notts NG18 5BH
0623 27191

West Surrey College of Art and Design
Falkner Road
Farnham
Surrey GU9 7DS
0252 722441

West Thames College
London Road
Isleworth TW7 4HS
081 568 0244

Weston super Mare College
Knightstone Road
Weston super Mare
Avon BS23 2AL
0934 621301

Westminster College
Battersea Park Road
London SW11 4JR
071 720 2121

Weymouth College
Cranford Avenue
Weymouth
Dorset DT4 7LQ
0305 208752

Wigan and Leigh College
Marshall Street
Leigh
WNY 4HX
0942 608811

Wulfrun College
Paget Road
Wolverhampton WV6 0DU
0902 312062

Yeovil College
Ilchester Road
Yeovil
Somerset BA21 3BA
0935 23921

Yorkshire Coast College
Lady Edith's Drive
Scarborough
N Yorks YO12 5RN
0723 372105

Ystrad Mynach College
Twyn Road
Ystrad Mynach
Hengoed
Mid Glamarogan CF8 7XR
0443 816888

Film and Television Courses and Training Schemes

Black Witch
Women's Independent Cinema House
Trading Places
Holmes Building
46 Wood Street
Liverpool L1 4AH
051-707 0539

British Kinematography Sound and Television Society
M6 14 Victoria House
Vernon Place
London WC1B 4DF
071 242 8400

Film and Television Freelance Training (ft2)
Fourth Floor
5 Dean Street
London W1V 5RN
071 734 5141

London International Film School
24 Shelton Street
London WC2H 9HP
071 836 9642

The London Screenwriters Workshop
84 Wardour Street
London W1V 3LF
071 434 0942

The National Film and Television School
Beaconsfield Studios
Station Road
Beaconsfield
Bucks HP9 1LG
0494 677903

The North East Media Training Centre
Stonewhills Studios
Sheilds Road
Pelaw
Gateshead
Tyne and Wear NE10 0HW
091 438 4044

Video Engineering and Training Ltd
Northburgh House
10 Northburgh
London EC1V 0AH
071 490 4001

Workhouse Ltd
Granville House
St Peter Street
Winchester
Hants SO23 9AF
0962 863449

Make Up Course Addresses

BBC Make-Up Training School
Room 374, Design Building
BBC Television Centre
Wood Lane
London W12 7RJ
081 743 8000

Greasepaint
143 Northfield Avenue
London W13 9QT
081 840 6000

London College of Fashion
20 John Prince's Street
London W1M 0BJ
071 629 9401

The Make Up Centre
26 Bute Street
London SW7 5EX
071 584 2188

Regional Arts Boards

Eastern Arts Board
Cherry Hinton Hall
Cherry Hinton Road
Cambridge CB1 4DW
0223 215355

East Midlands Arts Board
Mountfields House
Forest Road
Loughborough
Leics LE11 3HU
0509 218292

London Arts Board
Elme House
133 Long Acre
London WC2E 9AF
071 240 1313

London Film and Video Development Agency
25 Gosfield Street
London W1P 7HB
071 637 3577

Northern Arts Board
10 Osborne Terrace
Jesmond
Newcastle upon Tyne NE2 1NZ
091 281 6334

North West Arts Board
12 Harter Street
Manchester M1 6HY
061 228 3062

Southern Arts Board
13 St Clement Street
Winchester
Hants SO23 9DQ
0962 855099

South East Arts Board
10 Mount Ephraim
Tunbridge WellsTN4 8As
0892 515210

South West Arts Board
Bradninch Place
Gandy Street
Exeter EX4 3LS
0392 218188

West Midlands Arts Board
82 Granvill Street
Birmingham B1 2LH
021 631 3121

Yorkshire and Humberside Arts Board
21 Bond Street
Dewsbury WF13 1AX
0924 455555

Arts Council of Great Britain
14 Great Peter Street
London SW1P 3NQ
071 333 0100

Northern Ireland Film Council
7 Lower Crescent
Belfast BT7 1NR
0232 232444

Scottish Film Council
Dowanhill
74 Victoria Crescent Road
Glasgow G12 9JN
041 334 4445

Wales Film Council
Canolfan Sgrin Centre
Llandaf
Cardiff CF5 2PU
0222 578633

Index

A

Aberystwyth, University College of
 Wales   166, 202, 203, 204, 206, 207, 208, 209, 211, 212
The Academy   26, 67, 72, 76, 85, 97, 102, 341, 369
Academy of Live and Recorded Arts   35, 46, 53, 120, 370, 457
Acadmey of Musical Theatre   06, 117, 119, 123
Academy of Performing Arts (York)   81
Accrington and Rossendale College   285, 300, 443
Acton College   283
Actors Centre   87
Actors Centre, Manchester 87
Actors Institute   25, 26, 70, 86, 87, 92
Advanced Residential Theatre and Television Skillcentre
 International 54, 67, 93, 97, 341, 369
Afan College   285
Alexander Technique   153
ALRA see Academy of Live and Recorded Arts
The Alternative Drama School 76
Amersham and Wycombe College   284, 300
Anna Scher Theatre   88
Announcers   159, 160
Arden School of Theatre   21, 29, 360
Armstrong Arts Academy   77
Arts Educational Schools
 35, 54, 72, 103, 108, 126, 135, 455, 457
Arts Educational School at Tring 126
ARTTS see Advanced Residential Theatre and Television
 Skillcentre International
Aylesbury College   443

B

BADA see British American Drama Academy
Banbridge College of Further Education 302
Barking College 283, 291, 299, 303
Barnet College 283, 433
Barnfield College 303, 433
Barnsley College 280, 284, 299
Basingstoke College of Technology 301
BECTU see Broadcasting Entertainment, Cinematograph and Theatre Union
Belfast Institute of Further and Higher Education 280, 284
Benesh Institute 147, 151, 455
Berkshire College of Art and Technolog 300, 303, 305, 433, 436
Bilston Community College 286
Birkbeck College 234
Birmingham College of Food, Tourism and Creative Studies 442
Birmingham School of Speech Training and Dramatic Art 17, 36, 54, 361, 457
Birmingham, University of 167, 203, 204, 206-211, 238, 262-267
BKSTS see British Kinematograph Sound and Television Society
Black Witch 317
Blackburn College 300, 304, 443
Blackpool and the Fylde 306
Blair Theatre School 68, 81
The Blake High School 281
Boden Studio 88
Bolton Metropolitan College 285
Boston College 281
Bournemouth and Poole College of Art and Design 290, 291, 294, 304, 306, 435, 437, 452, 454
Bournemouth University 453
Bradford and Ilkley Community College 434, 443
Bradford University 452
Bretton Hall 179
Bridgwater College 280, 283

Brighton College of Technology 301, 304, 444
Brighton School of Music and Drama   88
Brighton, University of 191, 269
Bristol Old Vic Theatre School 17, 23, 24, 37, 41, 46, 47, 55, 62, 114, 121, 287, 361, 366, 430, 457, 466
Bristol, University of   168, 204, 206-208, 211, 454
British American Drama Academy 93
British Film Institute   234
British Kinematograph Sound and Television Society   317, 452
Broadcasting Entertainment, Cinematograph and Theatre Union 453 , 454
Brooklands Technical College   287
Brunel College of Technology   294
Brunel University   239, 267
Burnley College   300
Burton upon Trent Technical   281
Bury Metropolitan College   285

C

Calderdale College   285
Cambridge Regional College   286, 443
Cardiff Institute   293
Carmarthenshire College   436
Central England in Birmingham, University of   224, 303, 434
Central School of Ballet   135, 455, 466
Central School of Speech and Drama 7, 21, 27, 29, 56, 83, 94, 100, 123, 153, 156, 157, 197, 206, 310, 330, 342, 362, 373, 382, 393, 405-407, 410-411, 415, 421-422, 431, 458.
Charles Keene College   281, 286
Cheltenham and Gloucester College of Higher Education   436
Chester College   192, 202, 203, 204, 206, 207, 209, 210, 211
Chesterfield College   286, 435, 444
Chichester College of Art, Science and Technology 281, 287, 301, 444
Chippenham Technical College   299
City and East London College 283

City Lit   26, 73, 78, 88, 154, 155, 157, 374, 432
City of Bath College   283
City of Liverpool Community College   292, 300, 304
City of London Polytechnic see London Guildhall University
City of Westminster College   303, 305
City University   260, 267
Clarendon College   286, 443
Cleveland College   285, 290, 291, 300, 306, 434
Coleg Glan Hafren   285, 301
Coleg Powys   285, 301
College of North East London   442
Cornwall College   283, 299
Court Theatre Training Company   73, 74, 86, 92, 100, 124, 339, 362, 373
Coventry Centre of the Performing Arts   286
Coventry Polytechnic   287, 288
Craven College   443
Crawley College   444
Crewe and Alsager   192
Crosskeys College   281, 285, 301, 304
Croydon College   283, 292, 433, 436
CTC see Court Theatre Training Company
Cumbria College of Art and Design   281, 285, 301
Cygnet Training Theatre   74, 363

D

Dagenham Priory Comprehensive School   280
Darlington College of Technology   301, 434
Dartington College of Arts   169, 203, 209, 212, 376
De Montfort University   169, 202-204, 207, 210, 239, 262-266
Derby Tertiary College   286
Derby, University of   213, 224, 234, 269, 275
Derbyshire College   435, 436
Desmond Jones School of Mime   155
Dewsbury College   284, 294, 304, 434
Doncaster College   284, 434

Doreen Bird College of the Performing Arts 109, 455
Drama Centre London 17, 27, 30, 458
Drama Studio London 57, 94, 343, 458
Dunstable College 294

E

Ealing Tertiary College 299
East 15 Acting School 17, 37, 58, 100, 338, 363
East Anglia, University of 170, 202, 205, 207, 225, 230-232
East Berkshire College 300
East Surrey College 287, 301, 304
East Tyrone College 435
East Warwickshire College 286
Eastbourne College of Art and Technology 301
Eastleigh College 281, 301
Elliott-Clarke College of Dance and Drama 109
Elm Park College 283
Elmhurst Ballet School 127, 136, 455
English National Ballet School 126, 145, 455
Epping Forest College 286
Epsom School of Art 294, 435, 437
Erith College 442
Exeter, University of 171, 205, 207, 211

F

Falmouth School 304
Fareham College 287
Farnborough College 287, 291
Film and Television Production Training see ft2
Filton College 283
Fool Time 154
ft2 310, 311

G

Gateshead College 285, 301
Glamorgan, University of 172, 202, 205-207, 209-212, 240, 263-267

Glasgow University 72, 203, 205-211, 226, 231, 232, 233, 235
Gloucestershire College of Art and Technology 297, 300, 434, 436, 442
Goldsmith's College 173, 241, 267
Gorseinon College 286
Greenhill College of Technology 299
Grimsby College 284, 299
GSA see Guildford School of Acting
Guildford College of Further and Higher Education 304, 444
Guildford School of Acting 17, 21, 38, 58, 95, 98, 110, 57, 364, 371, 438
Guildhall School of Music and Drama 17, 31, 33, 44, 45, 51, 65, 365, 458
Gwent College of Higher Education 216, 291, 306 (Also see Newport School of Art and Design)
Gwynedd Technical College 286

H

Hackney Community College 283
Hammersmith and West London College 283, 299
Hammond School 127, 137, 455
Harlequin Theatre School 89
Harlow College 281, 286
Harrogate College of Art and Technology 280, 284, 298, 304
Hastings College of Art and Technology 435
Havering College of Further and Higher Education 299
Henley College Coventry 300
Herefordshire College of Art and Design 297, 303, 434
Hertford Regional College 303
Hertfordshire College 284, 291
Hertfordshire Theatre School 59, 110
Highbury College 297
Hinckley College 301
Hopwood Hall College 280, 284, 299
Hounslow Borough College 299, 433
Huddersfield, University of 193

Hull College   284, 299, 443
Hull, University of   174, 202, 205-210

I

Isle College   434
Islington Arts Factory   89
Italia Conti Academy of Theatre Arts   39, 69, 101, 103, 111, 455, 466

J

Jeannine Greville Dance Academies   89
JOBFIT   310
John Logie Baird Centre   235
John Moores University   175, 202-22, 226, 230, 232, 242, 262-267

K

Kent Institute of art and Design   291, 306, 437
Kent, University of   65, 176, 194, 202, 203, 205-208, 210, 227, 230-233
Kidderminster College   294
King Alfred's College   177, 202-210, 260, 262-266
Kingston College of Further Education   301, 444
Kingsway College   283, 297, 303
Kirby College   301, 443
Kitson College   299, 304
Knowsley Community College   285

L

Laban Centre   130, 138, 148, 149, 456
Laine Theatre Arts   112, 456
LAMDA   see London Academy of Music and Dramatic Art
Lancaster University   178, 204, 205, 206, 207, 208, 211, 243
Langley College   284
LAPA   see London Academy of Performing Arts
Lee Strasberg Theatre Institute   89
Leeds, University of   179 (Also see Bretton Hall)

Leek College 434
Leicester University 244
Lewisham College 283
Leyton Sixth Form College 280
LIFS see London International Film School
Llandrillo Technical College 286, 443
London Academy of Music and Dramatic Art 40, 60, 95, 365, 458
London Academy of Performing Arts 47, 61, 117
London and International Theatre School 40
London College of Dance 456, 466
London College of Fashion 292, 430, 433, 436, 440, 442, 444
London College of Printing 454
London Contemporary Dance School 131, 132, 146, 151, 456, 466
London Guildhall University 245, 262, 264, 266, 267
London Institute 292, 433, 436, 442, 444
London Institute of Performing Arts 48
London International Film School 311, 454
London Screenwriters Workshop 317
London Studio Centre 48, 106, 113, 456, 466
London Theatre School 49, 62, 69, 91
Longlands College 294, 301, 304
Loughborough College of Art and Design 435
Loughborough University of Technology 181, 205
Lowestoft College 286, 297
Lutterworth Community College 286

M

Manchester College of Arts 294
Manchester Metropolitan University 21, 32, 458
Manchester University of 182, 205-208
Melton Mowbray College of Further Education 286
Merseyside Dance and Drama Centre 456
Mid Cheshire College of Further Education 304, 434
Mid Cornwall College 283

Mid Kent College of Higher and Further Education   281
Mid Warwickshire College of Further Education   281
Middlesex University   183, 204, 235
Midlands Academy of Dance and Drama   90, 114
Milton Keynes College   300
Mime   155
Monkwearmouth College   285, 301
Morley College   83, 89, 374
Morton Comprehensive School   281
Mountview Theatre School
    17, 27, 41, 62, 83, 84, 90, 95, 114, 121, 123, 366, 419, 458, 466
Mulberry School for Girls   280

N

Napier University   215, 270
National Film and Television School   311, 312, 318, 454
Neath College   286
Nelson and Colne College   285
NEMTC   see North East Media Training Centre
Nene College   195, 202, 205, 209, 210, 212, 435, 436
New College   283, 285, 299
Newark and Sherwood College   301
Newbury College   284
Newcastle College   281, 285, 287, 288, 302, 304, 306, 434, 443
Newcastle under Lyme College   286
Newham Sixth Form College   280
Newport   452
Newport School of Art   216, 245, 271, 452 (Also See Gwent
    College of Higher Education)
Newtownabbey College of Further Education   284, 302
NFTS   see Natioanl Film and Television School
Norfolk College of Arts and Technology   286, 305
Norfolk Institute   434
North Antrim College   284, 302
North Derbyshire Tertiary College   286
North Devon College   283

North Down and Ards   284
North East Media Training Centre   312
North East Surrey College of Technology   287, 304
North East Wales Institute   286, 294, 435
North East Worcestershire College   442
North Hertfordshire College   284
North Lindsay College   280, 299
North London College   280, 297
North Nottinghamshire College   286
North Oxfordshire College and School of Art   284, 300
North Tyneside College   443
North Warwickshire College   294, 434, 442
North West College   284
North West Institute of Further and Higher Education   302
Northampton College   286, 301, 443
Northbrook College of Further and Higher Education   287, 292, 295, 301, 435
Northern Ballet School   139, 140, 456
Northern School of Contemporary Dance   133, 140, 147, 456, 465
Northumbria, University of   183
Norton College   284, 299
Norwich City College of Further and Higher Education   302
Nottingham Polytechnic   196, 246, 247, 272
NW5 Theatre School   78

O

Oaklands College   300
Oldham College   284, 292, 300, 434
Omagh College   280, 302
OSD   see Oxford School of Drama
Oulder Hill Community School   284, 299
Oxford College   284, 300
Oxford School of Drama   49, 63, 96, 98, 367, 377

P

Park Lane College   284

Parkwood College   434
Pattison's Dancing Academy and College 104
Penwith College   283
Performers Dance College   115, 456
Performing Arts and Technology School   283, 301
Plymouth College of Art and Design   304, 435, 452
Plymouth, University of 197, 203-205, 208, 209, 261-265, 306
Polytechnic of Central London   454
Pontypool and Usk College   301
Pontypridd Technical College   443
The Poor School 26, 79
Portsmouth College of Art and Design   293, 297
Portsmouth, University of 248, 263
Pozitiv Productions   160
reston College   281, 300

Q

Queen Margaret College   42, 248, 359
Queen Mary and Westfield College   197, 204, 206, 207, 211
Questors Theatre   78, 84

R

RADA   see Royal Academy of Dramatic Art
Radio   155
Rambert School   141, 456, 466
Ravensbourne College of Design and Communication   313, 314, 318
Ravenscourt Theatre School   104
Reading, University of   216, 231-233
Redbridge Technical College   283, 302, 434
Redroofs Theatre School   118, 121
The Regional Centre   287
Richmond Drama School   25, 70
Richmond upon Thames College   297, 303, 305
The Ridge College
Ripon and York St John   198, 202, 205, 212, 217, 230, 231, 233

Roehampton Institute   184, 202-206, 208-212
Rose Bruford College   17, 33, 337, 357, 382, 458
Rotherham College of Art and Technology   285, 300
Royal Academy of Dancing   130, 143, 146, 457, 465, 466
Royal Academy of Dramatic Art   17, 21, 42,
    367, 406, 408, 409, 411, 458
Royal Ballet School   128, 142, 152, 457, 465, 466
Royal College of Art   275, 314, 315, 414, 419
Royal Holloway and Bedford New College   186, 249
Royal Scottish Academy of Music and Drama   17, 33, 43, 45, 65,
    344, 358, 368, 372, 459
RSAMD   see Royal Scottish Academy of Music and Drama
Rycotewood College   291

S

Salford College   287, 293, 298, 436
Salford, University of   218, 236, 250, 251
Salisbury College of Technology   283, 306, 453
Sandwell College of Further and Higher Education 294, 303, 305
Scarborough Technical College   434, 443
School of the Science of Acting   50, 64, 80, 99, 10, 340. 345, 346
Shandy Stage School   105
Sheffield City Polytechnic   218, 237, 252, 453
Shena Simon College   300
Shrewsbury College of Art and Technology   297
Skelmersdale College   300
The Slade School of Fine Art   253, 268, 420
Solihull College of Technology   297, 303, 434
Somerset College of Art and technology   435, 444
South Bristol College   280, 299
South Cheshire College   443
South Devon College   280, 283, 291
South Downs College   281, 287, 301
South East Derbyshire College   281, 286, 301
South East Essex College of Arts and Technology
   281, 286, 297, 302, 434

South Manchester College   281, 285, 294, 443, 444
South Nottinghamshire College of Further Education   298, 304
South Thames College   294, 295, 299, 453
South Trafford College   298
South Tyneside College   281, 285
South Warwickshire College   286, 300
Southampton Institute   437
Southfields College   301, 304, 435, 443
Southgate College   299
Southlands School   281
Southport College of Art and Technology   285, 300, 304, 434
Southwark College   283, 294
St Catherine's Drama Studio   71, 371
St Helens Community College   285
St Mary's College   187, 203, 205, 206, 208, 209, 211, 212
St Wilfrids School   280
Stafford College   286, 434
Staffordshire University   219, 228, 273
Stagecoach Training Centres   90
Stantonbury Campus   284
Stardust Children's Theatre Workshop   90
Stella Mann School of Dancing   143, 457
Stirling, University of   220
Stockport College of Further and Higher Education   292, 304, 443
Stockton and Billingham College   285
Stoke on Trent College   281, 286, 300, 303, 434, 443, 444
Strathclyde, University of   235
Strode College   283
Stroud College   300
Suffolk College   287, 302
Sunderland, University of 254
Sussex, University of 199, 255, 264, 265, 267
Sutton Coldfield College of Further Education   300
Swansea College   286, 301, 304
Swansea Institute of Higher Education   304, 306
Sylvia Young Theatre School   105

T

Tameside College   281, 285, 434
The Television Works   319
Thanet Technical College   444
Thomas Danby College   284, 299, 443
Thurrock Technical College   434
Tile Hill College   300
Tower Hamlets College   284
Tresham Institute of Further and Higher Education   301, 444

U

Ulster, University of   188, 203, 205-210, 254, 262-266, 293
Ulverston Victoria High School   285
Urdang Academy   116, 129, 143, 457, 466

V

Van Dyke Academy   105
VET   see Video Engineering and Training
Video Engineering and Training   319
Voice   156
Voice Overs   158

W

Wakefield District College   284, 299
Walsall College of Art and Technology   281, 285, 300
Waltham Forest College   284, 433
Warwick, University   188, 221
Webber Douglas Academy   40, 44, 51, 60, 65, 96, 459, 466
Welsh College of Music and Drama
     17, 33, 45, 65, 344, 358, 372, 416, 423, 459
West Cheshire College   285, 300
West Herts College   280, 284, 297, 303, 453
West Kent College   287, 297
West London Institute   199, 202-209, 211, 228, 230, 231
West Nottinghamshire College   435
West Surrey College of Art and Design   220, 223, 258, 274, 453,

Westminster College   433
Westminster, University of 222, 256, 257, 263, 273
Weston Super   283
Weymouth College   283, 299
White Rose Studio of Speech and Drama   90
Wigan and Leigh College   281, 285, 300, 304, 434, 436, 443,
Wimbledon School of Art   416, 417, 418, 423, 428, 429
Wirral Metropolitan College   304, 434, 443
Wolverhampton, University of   189, 202-211, 258, 262-267
Worcester College   200, 203, 204, 205, 206, 208, 209, 210, 211
Workhouse Ltd   319
Wulfrun College   300

Y

Yeovil College   283
York College   434, 436
Ysgol Emrys Ap Iwan   301
Ystrad Mynach College   301

From the same author .....
How to become a Working Actor

Everything you ever wanted to know about the "business" side of an acting career, from the beginnings of Equity membership and finding an agent to details of being your own accountant and registering for VAT. All aspects of the acting profession are covered from musical theatre and repertory theatre companies to commercials, voice-overs and radio.

Includes sections on:

* Audition Technique   * Letter Writing
* Interviews   * Film & TV work
* Agents   * Self Presentation
* Equity membership   * Commercial Castings
* Musical Theatre   * CVs & Photographs
* and much much more ....

"In Duncan's handy book there is plenty to keep any young hopeful occupied. Arranged clearly and concisely this well-researched and easily readable book has advice on writing letters, audition techniques, choosing photographs and agents. Mercifully jargon free, this book is a good introduction to the world of the actor. Her advice could put you at least six months ahead of rivals at auditions" *Stage and Television Today.*

"Good value" .. *Birmingham Post.*

A paperback that should be on every actor's bookshelf" .. *Lancashire Evening Post.*

"Essential reading for all actors, whether newcomers to the profession or already established." *Richmond and Twickenham Times.*

ISBN: 1-872390-10-2   £8.95 pbk
Available from bookshops or direct from publishers (please add £1.00 for P&P)

Pocket sized books from The Cheverell Press

The Guide to Equity Membership

All you need to know about getting round the Catch 22 of "no card no job; no job no card"'

"I can recommend a recent book called "The Guide to Equity Membership". It is first hand information to help those who want to act but are restricted by lack of Equity membership." The Birmingham Evening Mail

ISBN: 1872390-05-6   £4.95

The Actor's Address Book

All the names and addresses that an actor should have are in this book, from agents and casting directors to producers and repertory theatre companies.

ISBN: 1-872390-00-5   £4.50
Available direct from the publishers (please add 70p P&P)

The Cheverell Press
Manor Studios
Manningford Abbots
Pewsey, Wilts, SN9 6HS